PRACTICAL GUIDES

ART

TEACHING WITHIN THE NATIONAL CURRICULUM

JANET GRAHAM AND HEATHER JEFFS

Published by Scholastic Publications Ltd
Villiers House, Clarendon Avenue,
Leamington Spa, Warwickshire CV32 5PR

© 1993 Scholastic Publications Ltd

Written by Janet Graham and Heather Jeffs
Edited by Philippa Hudson and Christine Lee
Designed by Micky Pledge
Illustrated by Jane Bottomley
Front cover design by Keith Martin
Front cover illustrated by Andrew Kingham
Photographs by Gordon Marr (pages 5 and 115),
Sally and Richard Greenhill (page 11), John
Twinning (page 27), Bob Bray (pages 37, 101 and
157), Garry Clarke (page 51), Chris Kelly (page
83), Francis Fashesin (page 161)

Every attempt has been made to trace and acknowledge
the photographers whose pictures appear in this book.
The publisher apologises for any omissions.

Designed using Aldus Pagemaker
Processed by Typesetters, Birmingham
Artwork by David Harban Design, Warwick
Printed in Great Britain by Ebenezer Baylis &
Son, Worcester

British Library Cataloguing in Publication Data
A catalogue record for this book is available from the
British Library

ISBN 0-590-53036-4

Contents

Introduction

What is art?

People tend to think of art as painting, sculpture and drawing; we think it is worth drawing attention to the way in which art is an integral part of everyone's lives. Our homes contain clothes, magazines, cups, plates, cutlery and curtains – all of which are art in the broader sense. They have all been designed; the colours, shapes, lines and textures have been carefully chosen as desirable or as saleable. In the same way, pictures are designed and composed.

Teachers should develop children's knowledge of the elements of art and its various forms, so that, when adult, children are able to judge the visual effect of their environment. This will help develop an appreciation of our cities and countryside and an understanding of the importance of caring for them, as well as improving the children's ability to recognise quality and worth in everyday objects.

Art takes many forms – the barge painters on the canals in the nineteenth century, the farmer's wife weaving a corn dolly, the African tribesman creating a fetish figure and the Afghan weaving a carpet were all creating works of art, as much as Michelangelo or Botticelli. Indeed, it can be argued that their contribution to human aesthetic pleasure was greater, as their work had meaning and use for a greater number of people – in the Renaissance only the powerful and rich saw the paintings of Leonardo, Raphael or Botticelli.

Children have their own way of seeing the world. To understand their approach, the teacher needs to be aware of the following aspects.

Children's development in art

To enable children to express themselves fully in art, the teacher has to know about their cognitive development in this area. This has been well investigated and documented for many years, and provides useful guidelines for teachers' expectations of the children's work. The teacher who lacks confidence or is inexperienced in art may judge the children's work by adult standards, with the result that the children sense disappointment at their efforts, and the teacher feels that lack of skilled teaching has led to poor results. This can be overcome by a knowledge of what can be expected from children at particular stages in their development.

Children can be helped through these natural stages by being encouraged to build up a store of visual knowledge through observation and personal experience. The activities in this book should encourage them to see a variety of approaches to subject matter. This can be further enhanced through the provision of examples of good-quality work on similar themes to their own. As *Art for ages 5 to 14* says: 'There are two common teaching difficulties to overcome in pupils' imaginative work. The first arises when pupils are encouraged to work imaginatively without adequate sources, in terms either of their own experience of comparable situations or of good quality information. In such a situation, many pupils tend to use stereotypical symbols which communicate only at a superficial level; for example, the persistent use of "lollipop" trees. The second difficulty arises when pupils are allowed to rely too heavily on the use of ready-made imagery, such as that of illustrators or cartoonists, rather than exercising their own powers of imagination.'(3.15)

Children's use of imagery differs from that of adults, and the teacher needs to be aware of this difference to offer appropriate advice and help. The numerous art educators, such as Goodnow or Lowenfeld, generally agree on the stages that children go through in art on their road to maturity, although the names of the stages can vary from educator to educator.

The scribble stage

Very young children use marks and scribbles as a means of exploring their world, in the same way as they explore through taste, smell and sound. They enjoy the physical activity involved in making marks, but are not in any way recording the appearance of reality. These early experiments should be encouraged, as they lead not only to drawing, but also to writing, and help to develop motor control.

These early scribbles, comparable to the undifferentiated gurgling produced by babies before they master the forms of language, change as the child develops more control of movement and begins to be aware of the connection between the marks that appear on the paper and the movements of the arm. At this point, children will draw the same repetitive scribble over and over again. They begin to experiment with the scribbles until a shape is formed, usually a circle or an oval. Children begin to see meaning in their scribbles, a meaning that often changes as their drawing progresses; for example, a mark can change from a person into a train into an anger shape. They talk to the scribbles, giving them names, which can be as remote from adult concepts of drawing as 'go to sleep lines' or 'running lines' (Lowenfeld and Brittain, 1988). Shapes begin to sprout lines and additions such as hair, ears and feet; small circles and oblongs become buses or cars; texture in the form of dots and scribbles appears in the drawings and tonal differentiations are formed by the lighter and darker areas of scribble.

Searching for symbols

As children's scribbles develop, they seek a schematic way of depicting what they know of the world. Their schema, or symbol, usually starts with the depiction of the human figure. Colour is not related to reality, but chosen for enjoyment, paint texture or arbitrarily. The subjects are those of which children have personal knowledge, such as their houses, families or pets, although pictures are also made of favourite stories and characters.

Symbolic representation

In the symbolic or schema stage, children will repeatedly use the same way of drawing an object, adapting it for different situations, and using size to indicate the importance of objects or people within the picture. The ground is indicated by a base line on which things are firmly placed. As the symbolic stage becomes established, children draw several base lines, with trees, houses and people growing off them at right angles. Colour tends to be used symbolically too – the grass is always green, the sky is always blue and nothing overlaps. The sky is at the top of the picture and the space in between is thought of as air – a logical assumption, as this is what the child experiences, with the ground beneath the feet, the sky overhead and air all around.

Dawning naturalism

Children usually move from the symbolic stage to a stage of dawning naturalism as they reach Y3 or Y4, although stages and ages do not always follow the same format. This is the time when the enjoyment and confidence of making art can be severely damaged or disappear entirely.

At this stage, children are moving away from uncritical self-expression towards the application of adult criteria. They become aware of the varying standards of their peer group. ('She can draw, Miss.' 'He is a real good drawer.' 'I can't draw.') At this stage, teacher intervention, help and encouragement are essential, otherwise the joy and fulfilment of art are lost, often for ever or at least for many years. Most adults do not progress beyond this stage. This is often the result of a lack of simple constructive help to ensure that children can make an adequate representation of the more sophisticated images that are now in their minds.

The role of the teacher

In the earliest years, the teacher can encourage children by providing the right materials and environment, by talking to them about their work and by discussing textures, colours and shapes in the environment.

As the children move towards the naturalistic mode of representation, the teacher can encourage them to notice the range and variations of tones in the environment, and expect a greater awareness of subtleties in their response to colour, shape and texture. The children should become familiar with a wider range of techniques and materials, as well as gaining greater skills with the ones they already use. They benefit from being shown the work of other artists using the same media as themselves.

The teacher needs to provide structured and detailed drawing exercises to help the children realise that their means of representation is only one way of creating art and that they can express themselves in many other ways. This should help the children to progress confidently and easily into the naturalistic stage.

At the naturalistic stage, the teacher needs to reassure the children that all serious attempts at expression are acceptable. This is the time when the work of artists is of enormous value. If children visit galleries and see that the range of ways in which artists' work differs greatly, and if the teacher conveys a real interest in their way of working, encouraging each child to develop their own visual language, the problems of a failure of confidence in their own creative powers can be avoided.

This approach needs to be combined with constructive suggestions for improvement, and a knowledge of each child's capabilities, so that there is no uncritical acceptance of unthinking or lazy work. There also needs to be a positive stimulus towards the development of a capacity to imagine scenes and events that require a leap over the boundaries of the children's own experiences. At this stage children can visualise events beyond themselves to an extent that they were unable to do in earlier years. For example, it is possible for them to become deeply involved in causes like famine, scientific exploration or plant hunting in New Guinea, although they themselves have not had these experiences.

At this age children begin to be interested in hobbies, and these can be a source of material for art subjects, as well as a basis for cross-curricular work. Group activities are also appreciated at this age, usually in the upper classes in the junior school, as the children are moving towards forming gang-type groups, often of a single sex character. Group work can bring the sexes together, and help develop their ability to co-operate, counteracting the early adolescent aggression that is beginning to emerge. The teamwork involved helps create pride and involvement in the class as a unity, important for the children's future in society. Properly guided, children at this age can achieve outstanding levels of quality in their work.

The National Curriculum for Art

The National Curriculum for Art signals a new approach to art teaching in the primary school. It requires a more structured approach to the children's practical work, and wider consideration of art and culture in the curriculum. It is no longer enough for the children to paint and model, or observe and draw from an object or an environment. The document, *Art for ages 5 to 14* (DES, 1991), states that the relationship of past and present cultures to the children's work and thinking, the use of technical and descriptive language applied to art, and the knowledge of skills, tools and materials should all be part of the primary art curriculum.

Paragraph 4.1 of the document outlines eight aims for art education. These can be summarised as follows:
• To help children communicate confidently in their art work and develop aesthetic judgement applied to their own work, to the work of others and to the environment;
• To teach children to look carefully at images and artefacts from past and present times, and from various cultures;
• To develop skills and knowledge of materials so that ideas can be planned, developed and completed successfully and with imagination, using their own personal language of art;
• To increase language skills and the ability to express opinions in relation to children's own and others' art work.

To promote these aims, two Attainment Targets are suggested: AT1 Investigating and Making and AT2 Knowledge and Understanding. Both of these attainment targets are closely linked, and one cannot be taught without the other. It would be difficult to understand art at the primary age without some knowledge of making, and without some investigation. Nevertheless, the knowledge and understanding required in the Art National Curriculum suggest a more thinking and analytical approach than has hitherto been used in many primary schools. This book aims to help teachers deliver the curriculum in the way the Art Working Group clearly intended.

About this book

Looking at the End of Key Stage Statements, the primary school teacher may feel that the skills and knowledge of an art specialist are needed to fulfil the requirements. This is not true, although a certain amount of research study in art books and galleries may be necessary. Teachers would also be well advised to try new materials and techniques themselves before trying them with the children. Given that many primary school teachers already engage in these activities, there should be no problems with the attainment targets; there should be a large element of satisfaction for the teacher in discovering the range of art expressions that children are capable of achieving – their capacity in this area has been underestimated for years. In this book we aim to suggest ways of teaching art that can be carried out by any primary teacher – all that is needed are the usual teaching skills of discussion, questioning and organisation.

Since the primary school timetable is already packed full, all the art activities and projects suggested in this book have cross-curricular applications. We have suggested suitable artists and art/craft/graphic works to support the practical activities. Activities are sequenced, so that the work progresses from recording reality to children using their growing knowledge of shape, colour, texture and line to work from their imaginations.

The new proposals in the Art National Curriculum should enable children to see and understand art in their everyday lives, and to approach the making of art with thought and an understanding of its application to functional objects, as well as an appreciation of its universal language.

Chapter 1
Using two-dimensional materials (Key Stage 1)

Young children enjoy spontaneously using art tools and materials to express their joy in newly acquired knowledge and manipulative skills, as any nursery or reception teacher knows. To keep their happy and uninhibited approach to art, children need to learn the use of basic art tools and materials through a progressive programme of investigation. As *Art for ages 5 to 14*: states, 'in art there is a visual language, a system of marks, symbols and conventions with a syntax of its own, which must be learned systematically if skill, knowledge and understanding are to grow and mature in a coherent way.'(3.2)

The document goes on to point out that art needs to be taught in the same way as reading and writing. It spells out the formal elements of art making up the visual vocabulary that children need to learn to be fluent in the language of art. Part of this process of learning includes discovering the way the tools of art work with different types of materials.

At Key Stage 1, the elements of art that would be appropriate for the children to explore are line, colour, texture, shape and, from Y2, tone. They also need experience of

form through three-dimensional work, using basic materials such as card, clay, Plasticine and dough. Children's knowledge of the vocabulary of art grows as a result of practice, using a limited range of materials. Introducing a wide range of new materials will not help the children, as they need to understand the correct use of basic tools and materials for a particular task, and this understanding takes time and reinforcement. This need not involve sophisticated theoretical knowledge; it takes little theory, but a lot of practical experiment for a child to learn that a soft pencil is usually a more rewarding drawing tool than a hard one.

In the following projects, we suggest an investigative approach towards art, art tools and materials which is methodologically similar to investigations in science or technology. Their suitability to age groups is indicated in the text, but this is only a rough guide; much depends on the children's stage and previous experience. Children who have attended a nursery school or class are usually more skilled in the handling of tools and materials in reception. This advantage does not last long, however, and others soon catch up.

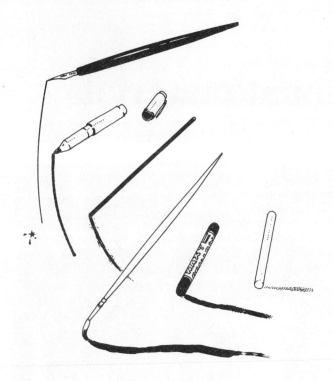

Exploring line

The type of mark produced by a drawing tool depends to a surprising degree on the material to which it is applied. The study of this effect can be worthwhile with Y1 and Y2 infants, and can be closely allied to science. If the children were each given squares of brown wrapping paper, blotting paper, white drawing paper and greaseproof paper, and then told to cover them with scribble, using firstly a 2B pencil and secondly a wax crayon, they would find the scribbles were different in each case. These differences could then be recorded. A similar experiment could be tried with paints, ink, charcoal, felt-tipped pens or chalk. In this way the children could be introduced to exploring the qualities of different materials.

The scribbles could be discussed, and the children asked if they remind them of anything (for example, brambles, the fur of a teddy bear, tangled hair, rain). There is a lot of potential for language development to be gained from this (the feel of the tool on the material, is it smooth, scratchy?). As a progression, the children could try matching textures of furry toys, hair or grass, using a variety of drawing tools.

As a further exploration of line, the children could then be asked to draw a portrait.

My favourite person

This portrait could form part of a project on the family, ourselves or a historical theme and could be connected to a museum or gallery visit. Many art galleries have an excellent education service, and if the theme is explained beforehand, the works that the children see on their visit could be chosen to fit the theme.

Alternatively, the children could bring in photographs of their families and the teacher could provide pictures of family groups and portraits from past and present times, and their composition and costume could be discussed. Drawings by artists showing various approaches to line could also be shown to the children, and the methods pointed out. For example, Picasso's *Sergei Diaghilev and Alfred Seligsburg* (1919) is a drawing in a clear single line, showing full-length figures; this could be compared with Max Beckmann's etching of *Peter with a Pointed Cap* (1920), which is built up from many lines.

What you need

Ruler, A4 drawing paper, pencils (2B to 6B), pencil sharpener.

What to do

Ask the children to look closely at one another and observe the appearance of the eyes, how the size of the forehead compares to the rest of the face and the position of the ears in relation to the corners of the eyes and the sides of the nose. Let the children measure and compare the proportions (Figure 1). Such observation should eventually reduce the number of flat-headed and pop-eyed people in their drawings.

Ask the children to think of a favourite person. Encourage them to think about how they would like to draw their favourite person. Ask them questions such as:
• What is the person going to be doing?
• Is there going to be a background?
• When they think about their favourite person, what do they imagine they look like?

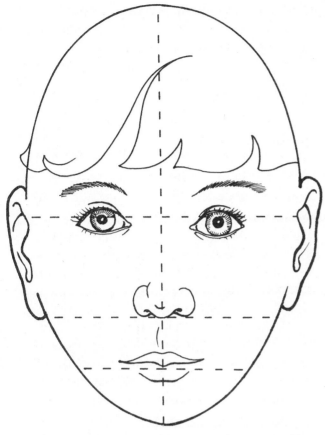

Figure 1

Are they usually laughing, or do they look a bit sad?

• Has the person got a pet? If so, should they be shown with their pet?

Ask the children to draw their favourite person, and go round the group as they work, pointing out the good aspects of their work, but also suggesting where they need to look again at a face or to put in more detail. Children of this age are not going to produce accurate drawings, but they can draw and capture the personality of a subject. Through looking, they can find out a lot about the way our faces are structured, noticing details like the eyes, mouth and ears that they drew in symbolic mode before the observation.
Art: AT1, AT2; History: AT1, AT3

Follow-up

After drawing each other, let the children cut out the figures and assemble them and stick them in place on a sheet of mural paper. Ask them to include a drawing of you. The mural could then be displayed in the corridor, and the other classes could try to identify the

subject. It could be labelled 'Guess who?'

The children could follow this with a visit to look at portraits which can often be found locally. For example, Gawthorpe Hall, Padiham, Lincolnshire, and Bodelwyddan Castle, Clwyd, have a selection of portraits from the National Portrait Gallery, London.
Art: AT1; History: AT1, AT3

Drawing with ink

There are other ways of making line, and a useful medium is ink. The colours of ink are transparent, and can be mixed and diluted (with the exception of black ink, which always overpowers any other colour). Let the children use soft, fine brushes and draw with diluted ink, then drawing over the top with a pen.

Drops of ink blown around white or coloured paper with a straw will show the children how colour mixes. Suggest that they blow from various angles to see if it creates a different effect. The spectacle of the colours mixing together is an experience children find exciting, as is the way the ink can be controlled with the straw.

Star pattern

What you need

A4 coloured paper, ink, ink droppers, straws.

What to do

Ask the children to drop blobs of ink on to the paper. Explain that the blobs should each be of a different colour and not too far apart. Give the children each a straw and show them how the ink blobs can be blown around the paper, so that they spray out, or blown from above to make star patterns; some of the blobs can be mingled, and new colours added. This could be used as an effective background to a silhouette picture in black.

The same technique can be used with runny paint on black sugar paper to make a Bonfire Night picture.
Art: AT1; Science: AT1; English: AT1

Study of a stormy day

This is a suitable project for Y2 and it allows children to work on a bigger scale, combining individual efforts to construct a large group picture. This gives the children practice in planning and assembling work and makes them aware of the need to 'modify their work as they recognise the need for change' (Art for ages 5 to 14).

The work could be based on a study of the local area and changing conditions of the sky or it could be part of a larger project on weather or the seasons. It should be preceded by discussion about cloud formation and the changing colours of the sky. The children could be asked to match the sky colours and to make tonal strips each day to show the relative light or dark of the sky, using a soft pencil such as a 6B.

As a back-up to the children's work, and to make them aware of the ways other people have painted storms, collect and display photographs, books, drawings and paintings that illustrate the effects of stormy skies. Nigel Peake's The Great Storm, which shows the impact of the storm of 1987 on South-East England, is a good reference. If your area was affected by the storm, parents could be asked to recount their memory of that night to the class.

The Great Day of His Wrath (1852) by John Martin is a dramatic scene of a the Last Judgement, with lightning and storm clouds. It is painted on a huge scale. Not for nothing was he known as 'Mad Martin'. The picture is full of detail, and children love it, being an early horror story in the grand Romantic tradition. A less exciting, but artistically sounder work is Leonardo da Vinci's drawing of The Deluge (C.1515) which is in Windsor Castle. These works could both be used to draw attention to the swirling shapes that are used to suggest movement. Display reproductions of the pictures and use them as a starting point for discussion.

What you need

Black felt-tipped pens, paper, an umbrella, cocktail umbrellas, grey frieze paper, charcoal, white chalk, a range of pencils, drawing paper, pencil sharpener, rags, PVA adhesive and spreaders, scissors.

What to do

As a preliminary activity, ask the children to sketch the local houses and trees, using black felt-tipped pens.

Let them look at and draw an umbrella, and examine the construction to find out how it works. Perhaps a discarded, broken umbrella could be compared with one in working order. Ask the children to imagine the force of wind that was needed to blow the umbrella inside out, then let them try blowing hard enough to break a paper cocktail umbrella.

Ask the children to talk and write about storms they remember. Encourage them to think about the rain and the noise of the wind, the way people lean into the wind or huddle themselves up in doorways, how birds fly to their nests and how umbrellas blow away. This will provide a good opportunity for language development.

Divide the class into groups, and let them discuss what they are going to draw. Some children will enjoy drawing and shading clouds to cut out and stick to the sky background, others will want to draw people running home.

Give the children making the background charcoal and chalk to work with. They will also need plenty of space. Outside in the corridor might be a convenient spot, but failing that let them use the floor or a large table.

When the children have finished their drawings and have cut out their contributions, the whole class can decide how to arrange them on the background. After the picture has been assembled and the components stuck in place, hold a class discussion and ask the children if more parts need to be added to the picture. Ask for suggestions as to content and scale. The children could add to the picture over a period of two or three weeks, and the additions discussed.

Art: AT1; Science: AT3, AT4; English: AT3; History: AT1, AT2; Technology: AT1

Exploring paint lines

This project for Y1 and Y2 children will help increase their knowledge of using paint and is connected with a recent work of art. Although not generally used as a teaching aid, modern works of art that can be baffling to adults are often easily accepted by young children. This may be because children's attitudes to art are less fixed and stereotyped than adults', or that art influences media images and the younger generations no longer find the images new or disturbing.

Before starting the activity, arrange a display of pictures by the American abstract expressionist, Jackson Pollock (1912-56). Reproductions of his work are easily available from the Tate Gallery in London or in art books. Talk about his work and explain that he painted like this because he thought it looked pretty, and so that people could see the way he moved the brush over the canvas. Ask the children questions such as:
• How many lines can you see?
• How many colours are there?
• Which line did he put on last?
• How many layers can you find?
• Does the painting remind you of anything?
• Do you like it?

Explain that they are going to find out how many different lines they can make with paint (thick, thin, broken, wavy, etc). To do this, they are going to use a variety of brushes and other things that make marks in paint.

This project gives the children the opportunity to discover a wide range of lines and marks, using a selection of tools; it helps them to understand that colours mingle and mix when thick and thin paint is used. It makes them aware that there are different ways of making a painting.

What you need

Large stiff brushes, small sponges, 5cm house decorators' brushes, old credit cards or pieces of stiff plastic, combs, mural paper, large pots of ready-mixed paint (two primary colours and black and white), plastic sheeting (or other protection for the work surface), a hair-drier.

What to do

Give the children each a selection of brushes and ask them to see how many different lines they can make. When they have finished the first layers, dry their work for them with the hair-drier. Ask them to apply another layer, telling them that they can scrape into the paint with the plastic cards or draw patterns in it with the combs. Suggest they trickle watery paint on to the work from the sponges. Ask the children questions such as:
• What happens if you raise the paper at one end?
• What colour changes can you see?
• How many ways can you make the paint go?

Urge the children to cover the whole sheet of paper, making sure they form several layers, but allowing the layers to dry properly before starting another. There is a general reluctance to overlap shapes at this age, but as this activity is not pictorial, it releases this inhibition, and gives the children the opportunity to find out about depth on a flat surface.

Compare the marks made in this work with those made by the drawing tools, and talk about scale, relating the marks made by tools to the size of image they engender. Compare their work with that of Jackson Pollock. Now they have tried painting the lines, ask the children if they like his picture more. Do they think he was clever? Explain that Jackson Pollock used to pour paint on the work and flick it across the surfaces. Do they think this would be fun? If it is a calm day, the children could add to their picture by flicking paint across it in the playground.

The work of Jackson Pollock could also be compared to a more conventional work, and the children asked which they preferred.
Art: AT1, AT2; English: AT1, AT2

Exploring colour

The exploration of colour can be introduced in any of the following ways.
• Sort fabrics or papers of different colours into sets.
• Sort fabrics or papers into winter, spring, summer and autumn colours.
• Drop ink, using a dropper, on to wet and dry paper, and compare the ways in which it spreads.
• Fold paper in half, unfold it, and put blobs of contrasting coloured paint down the crease. Fold it and press it together. When it unfolds, a symmetrical pattern will emerge, and the colours will have mixed together.
• Cover the windows of the classroom with tissue-paper all of one colour; try red, pink, blue and grey at various times. The light will come through the paper, but it will be changed. Let the children compare the effects of the different light, both on the objects in the classroom, and on their feelings.

Make a magic carpet

Children love discovering new colours and mixes, and they can do this by making a 'magic carpet'. This activity is enjoyed by every age group – including adults!

What you need

A2 white paper, rulers, wax crayons, large brushes, primary colours, black and white paint, painting equipment.

What to do

Ask the children to guess how many colours they can mix from two primary colours. Tell them to divide the paper into squares, roughly 6cm in size, using a wax crayon. Next ask them to choose two colours to fill in the squares. Any two primary colours can be used, but, for the sake of clarity, assume that a child is painting with ultramarine (brilliant) blue and lemon yellow, with black and white. Tell the child to paint the first square yellow, then the next square add a small amount of blue to the yellow paint, and so on.

When the children have found as many colours as they can, suggest they try adding a little black or white to the original colour, and paint the squares, adding more black or white as they go. Many of the children will be surprised to find that yellow and black make green, and blue and black make navy.
Art: AT1; Science: AT3

Seeing a coloured world

As a development from their experiments with colour, the children could make simple spectacles from acetate, and observe the apparent changes that looking through them makes to their surroundings.

What you need

Scissors, ruler, pencil, double- and single-sided adhesive tape, strips of cardboard 60cm × 8cm, strips of pink acetate 30cm × 8cm, strips of a different coloured acetate 30cm × 8cm, felt-tipped pens, paper.

What to do

Give the children each a piece of acetate, and ask them to look through it. What colours can they see? Does the colour change when they look towards the window? Why?

Next ask the children to work in pairs to make acetate spectacles. Using Figure 2 for reference, help them to cut out pink acetate for the lenses. Show them how to attach it to the cardboard strip using double-sided adhesive tape. Make sure that the acetate spectacles are stuck down with their centre line matching the centre line of the cardboard strip. Help the children to fit their spectacles and fasten them together with pieces of adhesive tape.

Let the children wear the spectacles for a time, and encourage them to look at various objects in the room. Ask them to draw, using felt-tipped pens, to discover the apparent effect the acetate has on the colours in the drawing.

Let them repeat the experiment with different coloured acetate.
Art: AT1; Science: AT1; Technology AT3

Paint a pink world

This activity could be done using any colour, but here pink is taken as an example. In 'Make a magic carpet' on page 16, the children will have seen the effect of adding black and white to colour to change the tones. In this project, they use shades of scarlet, crimson and purple, adding white to create as many shades of pink as they can. This activity can be used to build on their experience of looking through the acetate and having coloured light in the classroom. Such an activity should allow the children to fantasise and, in the words of the Art Working Group, 'envisage an end-product'. They should be 'free to use their imagination to combine ideas rationally or irrationally, constructing whatever they like from the remembered and perceived elements at their disposal.' (3.13).

What you need

Red and red-related paints, white paint, large and small soft and hard brushes, white paper, paint charts, reference books.

What to do

Discuss the children's previous experience with the coloured acetate. Ask them to imagine what it would be like to wake up and find that everything in their bedroom had turned to shades of pink, including themselves! What would it be like if it had become a pink world – pink dogs, bicycles, sun, people, even pink oranges?

Ask the children to mix as many pinks as they can, and to paint a scene from the pink world. This could be, for example, someone seeing themselves in the mirror for the first time or swimming in a pink sea. Would people be happy or afraid? What would it be like at night under a pink moon?

As the children paint, go round the class and ask them to tell you what they are going to put in their pictures. Direct them to suitable reference books to remind them of shapes and to the paint charts to see a range of pinks.
Art AT1; Science AT1

Follow-up

The paintings could be the basis for a class drama about the pink world for performance at assembly. This could be supported by masks and stick puppet scenery.

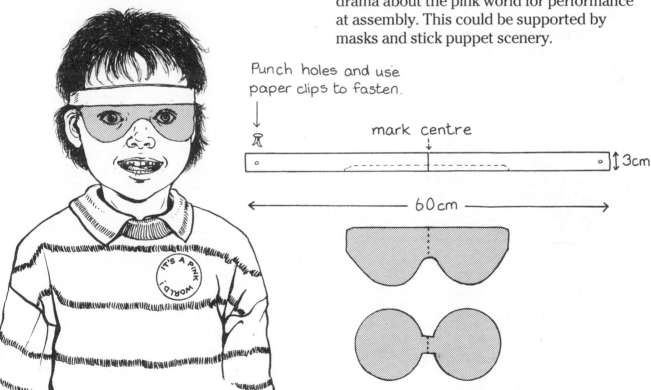

Punch holes and use paper clips to fasten.

mark centre

3cm

60 cm

Figure 2

If feasible, a visit to the Colour Museum, Bradford would help the children build on their discoveries. The exhibits involve the visitor and show the effects of colour.
Art AT1; Technology AT3

Discover orange

This activity is suitable for reception and Y1 children.

Children need to associate colour with the content as well as the surface of objects, and in this activity art and science are closely connected, as the children approach colour-matching through the investigation of a natural form.

What you need

Two similarly sized oranges, knife, pencils, paper, kitchen roll, transparent jug, orange squeezer, yellow and scarlet paint, painting equipment.

What to do

Make sure the children have washed their hands before the start (a good opportunity to reinforce the importance of personal hygiene).

Show the children an orange and ask them if they know what it is. Ask them to describe its shape. What other orange things can they think of? Pass the orange round to be felt, and ask for words that describe its texture.

Peel the orange, and pass the peel round so that the children can feel the weight. Compare this to the weight of the unpeeled orange. The peeled orange can be divided into segments, and the pips counted and drawn, together with the patterns in the orange flesh and the shape of the divisions.

Squeeze the second orange and let the children sip the unsweetened juice. Let the children dip paper into the juice, and examine the colour. What happens when it dries? Does the colour change?

Next ask the children to colour-mix with the paints, and discover how many shades of orange they can find. They will soon discover for themselves that there are many shades of orange, and will realise that some colours can only be found in natural objects.
Art: AT1; Science: AT3

Autumn leaves

This colour project explores autumn colours, and extends the children's knowledge of seasonal change. Although autumn colours are used here, a similar approach could be used for spring, summer or winter.

Ask the children to contribute to a display of autumn leaves, berries and fruit, taking care that no-one brings in any poisonous items. The children can be asked to help to arrange the collection, and can examine the items and try to think of words to describe the colours, textures and shapes. These activities would support work in science and help the acquisition of language skills.

What you need

A display of autumnal objects, knife, magnifying glass, primary colour paints, black and white paint, A4 white paper, wax crayons (in autumn colours), hard and soft brushes.

What to do

Ask the children to select one object from the collection and examine it for colour and shape. Cut some specimens in half and use magnifying glasses to demonstrate the details of texture and form, such as the seeds in the rose-hips. Let the children count the calyces on the rose-hips, and the veins in the leaves. Compare the gloss and colour of a conker newly removed from its shell with one that has dried. After a thorough examination of the display, let the children draw and paint the objects, matching the colours as closely as they can.

Tell the children first of all to draw larger than life, using the wax crayons. Explain that they are going to paint their drawings, so they need to use large shapes, so that they have room to paint with the bold, strong colours that are found in autumn. Ask them to start by putting in the main colours, using big brush strokes; details can be added later, using the soft brushes, once the main shapes and the background are painted in. Tell the children to cover the whole paper, and to include a background. For example, it could be raining, or the leaves might be falling against a windswept sky.

Remind them to try to match the colours. Ask them which colours make russet (vermilion and a small amount of black and scarlet) and which make brown. Suggest they test their colours on a spare sheet of paper before using them in their paintings.

The children could be shown a reproduction of *Autumn Leaves* by John Everett Millais which is in the City Art Galleries, Manchester.
Art AT1; Science: AT1, AT2; English: AT1

Follow-up

• This activity could lead to making a picture of a favourite autumn activity, such as walking in leaves, building a garden bonfire or playing conkers, for example.
• As a progression, the children could paint a picture using tones of one autumn colour, based on a poem such as 'Autumn' by John Clare.

I love the fitful gust that shakes
The casement all the day,
And from the mossy elm tree takes
The faded leaves away,
Twirling them by the window pane
With thousand others down the lane.

After discussing the images and movement in the poem, ask the children to paint a picture, using an autumn colour, mixing it with black or white to make the colour darker or lighter.
• To reinforce the children's knowledge of tone, turn their paintings into a collage, using a range of papers in one colour, but a variety of tones. The same image in a different medium underlines the effect of materials and tools on the work.
Art: AT1; English: AT1

Making a tone collage

What you need

Children's pictures on the theme of autumn, a selection of coloured papers, grouped into colour ranges (for example blues, greys, reds) and with different surfaces (such as tissue, foil, sugar and gloss), scissors, Pritt Sticks.

What to do

Explain to the children that they are going to make new versions of their pictures from torn or cut paper, using only one colour. Ask them:
• Will it still remind people of autumn?
• Will using paper alter the shapes in the picture?
• Will the paper look different to the paint, and if so, why?

Demonstrate the difference between cut and torn edges, and the effect of folding, crumpling and overlaying colours.

Encourage the children to simplify their shapes, and not to worry if they cannot include any detail. Ask them to think which parts of the picture would suit the soft edge of the torn paper, and which the hard edge of the cut paper. Ask them to look out of the window to remind themselves which colours look deepest, those close to, or those far away. Let the children use Pritt Stick to stick their paper shapes in place

When the pictures are finished, put the collages next to the original paintings, and discuss the differences with the children. Ask them:
• How has the picture altered?

• Does it still remind them of autumn?
• Which did they enjoy doing the most?
Art: AT1; Science: AT1; Technology: AT3

Follow-up

Another season that could be approached in the same way is winter. Begin the activity by letting the children look at, and write a story about, a snow painting, such as Caspar David Friedrich's *Winter Landscape with Church* (1811), which is in the Tate Gallery in London. This is a wonderful picture for children, as it shows a snow-covered winter landscape, with fir trees, a church and a figure kneeling by a rocky outcrop. It is only after looking closely that the discarded crutches can be seen, lying by the figure. A miracle has happened. Ask the children if they think it is Christmas. What will the man's family say when he walks indoors? The children could paint their own version of Friedrich's painting, or the celebration when the man arrives home.

An equally intriguing picture that could be used in a seasonal 'spring' theme is Ford Madox Brown's *The Pretty Baa Lambs* in the City Museum and Art Gallery, Birmingham. This picture shows a mother and baby, surrounded by grazing sheep. The baby's clothing could give rise to interesting discussion on costume today and yesterday, as well as the season.
Art: AT1, AT2; English: AT1

Investigating paper

Through the collage activities, the children will have found some of the potential uses of paper. Paper can be explored in other ways.

Crumpled paper patterns

During this activity, lines and shapes will emerge that reveal the qualities of different kinds of paper, and their different reactions to coloured water. Avoid papers that are too thick, as they will crack when crumpled.

What you need

A selection of white papers (tissue, newsprint, lettering paper, kitchen paper, for example), bowls, rubber gloves for the children, plastic sheets, hot and cold water, a range of substances which will stain paper (instant coffee, turmeric, coloured inks, beetroot, for example) two boards and weights (or an old flower press), old newspapers.

What to do

Let the children mix the coffee, turmeric, etc, with a little hot water, then add some cold water and pour the mixture into the bowls. Encourage them to discuss the colours, then let them dip small strips of paper into each colour. Does the colour of the paper change?

Dry the strips of paper on a radiator. What colour are the pieces of paper when dry?

Let the children crumple pieces of paper into balls, then unfold the paper and look at the lines and marks that appear. Let them crumple the paper several times. Does it feel different after being crumpled many times? Let the children repeat the experiment with different types of paper.

Ask the children to dip the crumpled paper balls into the colours – one ball into one colour. Make sure they wear rubber gloves for this part of the activity as some substances, such as beetroot, will stain the skin. Place the balls of paper on to pads of newspaper to drain. Before the balls of paper have completely dried out, unfold them carefully, and compare the colours and patterns. Some papers will have absorbed more colours than others. This method produces surprisingly decorative effects as the colour seeps into the creases and crumples at a varying rate.

Place the paper on a board with a thin pad of newspaper over it. Then cover the sheet with a layer of newsprint. Repeat this until the stack is about 13cm high, then place another board on top and compress the pile with the weights. A flower press also works well.

When the paper is dry, the folds and wrinkles will have flattened and dried into tiny ridges, with deeper tones and lines standing out. Discuss the finished work with the children, talking about the shapes that have emerged and the differences in the paper.

Follow-up

The papers can be used in a collage – many of the shapes and textures suggest natural forms, such as water, rocks or trees. They could be mounted to make a display of different textures, or they could be drawn on, using small felt-tipped pens, to make cards.
Art: AT1; Science: AT3

Resist painting and patterning

Another way of investigating the qualities of paper is through resist painting. This also demonstrates the reaction of water to wax.

The technique of using wax resist on paper and cloth is very ancient. The tradition of blocking the spread of dye colour through material by means of wax originated in the Far East. Javanese batik is still produced by traditional methods, and is used for wall-hangings as well as cloth. Samples are available from sources such as Oxfam, and are usually reasonably priced. Examples of batik work could form part of a school's resource area. In the activity that follows, they could form part of a display on cloth, pattern or water and water-resistant materials.

The use of cloth for batik is difficult with young children, as the wax has to be kept hot. For this reason it is better to use wax resist on paper; the principle is the same as that of the more advanced methods.

What you need

White candles or wax crayons, sugar paper, paints, marbling inks, a tray.

What to do

Explain the need for the wax to be pressed firmly on to the sugar paper, and show the children how to use the crayons or candles to make a variety of thick, thin, scribbly and spotty marks, not just an outline. For example, if the children were drawing a tropical jungle scene, the large leaves could be long strokes, with the underbrush made up of small, broken marks; the sun could be a solid shape, figures could be drawn in outline and the ground could be suggested by dots and small circles. The children could then wash diluted paint in bands across their picture, using darker and greener shades as they got lower down the page and further into the vegetation.

This activity could lead to an investigation into the effect of oil on water, which could be demonstrated by marbling. Here, marbling inks are floated on the surface of a tray of water, stirred, and a sheet of paper gently laid on top. The result is a print of the swirling pattern formed by the mixture of colours.
Art: AT1, AT2; History: AT3; Science: AT3; English: AT1

Exploring fabric

Cloth is a material that is in use all the time. Its decoration and structure make up an area of human activity that crosses cultural boundaries and reaches back into the past. Even at an early age, children enjoy touching and handling fabrics. The use of a needle and thread and the construction of fabrics enable the children to understand the way in which certain everyday objects are made and decorated.

Fabric and thread

This activity is suitable for Reception and Y1 children. Very young children find the patience and manual dexterity required to sustain work in embroidery difficult, but there are approaches that make experience of stitching and threading beads easy. This activity involves group work.

What you need

Binca (attached to an old picture frame), several tapestry needles (threaded with wool or soft cotton embroidery thread in primary colours), a supply of buttons and wooden beads.

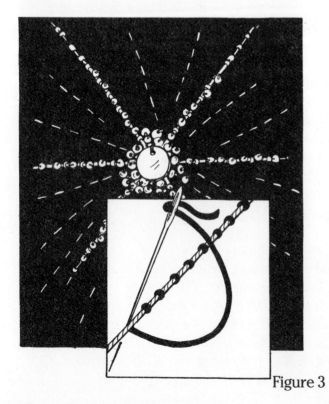

Figure 3

What to do

Prop the binca up in the classroom, with the threaded needles attached down one side at 2cm intervals, knotted on to the background. Show the children how to pass the needle and thread back and forth through the material using running stitch, and how to attach a button and a bead.

Suggest that the children make a striped pattern, and let them take turns to sew when they wish. Some children will enjoy this activity, but others will find it needs too much concentration, and lose interest. Make a point of drawing attention to the progress of the work, and display it when it is completed.
Art: AT1; Science: AT2; Technology: AT3

Embroider a Christmas star

This activity introduces the children to the craft of embroidery in a way that makes success easier to achieve than work on a larger scale. The end result is an attractive card to take home at Christmas.

What you need

Dark blue cotton or polyester fabric with a firm, non-stretch weave, scissors, half-inch gold sequins, small gold sequins, gold beads, a metallic knitting yarn such as Goldfingering, yellow soft embroidery thread, yellow sewing thread, large and small needles, masking tape, white carbon paper, A4 paper, pencils, coloured card, round embroidery frame.

What to do

Ask the children to draw a star shape with rays shining from it. Meanwhile, cut the blue fabric into 20cm squares so that it fits into the embroidery frame, and give one square to each child. The design can be transferred to the fabric by means of the white carbon paper. Let the children use the large sequin to form the centre of the star, and show them how to work the arms in couching, using soft embroidery thread (Figure 3). Tell the children to bring the thread to be couched up from beneath the material and take it through to the back when they have finished the line they are working on. The rays can be worked in running stitch, using the Goldfingering. Show the children how to sew on the beads around the central sequin and at the end of the rays. The smaller sequins can be used to give body to the arms of the star.

When the embroidery is finished, help the children to stretch it out flat on a piece of card, and secure it with masking tape. This can then be window-mounted on to a piece of coloured card scored down the centre line, to form a greetings card. Make sure that the mounting card is sufficiently strong to stand up when the embroidery is attached to it. The message inside could be printed on the computer or handwritten.

Follow-up

After experimenting with embroidery, Y2 children could be taken to visit a museum and see examples of mediaeval embroidery, which was often worked in couching. Many of the copes in the Victoria and Albert Museum in London are pictorial, such as the Syon cope, with its pictures, angels and stories from the Bible.

Art: AT1, AT2; English: AT1; Mathematics: AT1

Using dyes

Dyeing is an ancient method of decorating cloth, easily practised with children. Cheap T-shirts can easily be bought for dyeing or old ones revived. Any plain cotton or silk cloth will dye well, but polyesters are less likely to take deep colour, and the results often tend to be very pale.

Tie and dye

There are many examples of African tie and dye patterns, both in books and in the shops, that could be shown to the children.

What you need

Dyes (cold water dyes are the easiest for the children to work with), dye fix, bowls, elastic bands, clothes-pegs, small pebbles, old T-shirts or small lengths of old sheeting, running water for rinsing the dye out of the fabric, plastic bag, spin-drier, an iron.

What to do

Mix the dyes according to the maker's instructions, and show the children examples of the patterns that can be made by the tie and dye process. Explain that the dye does

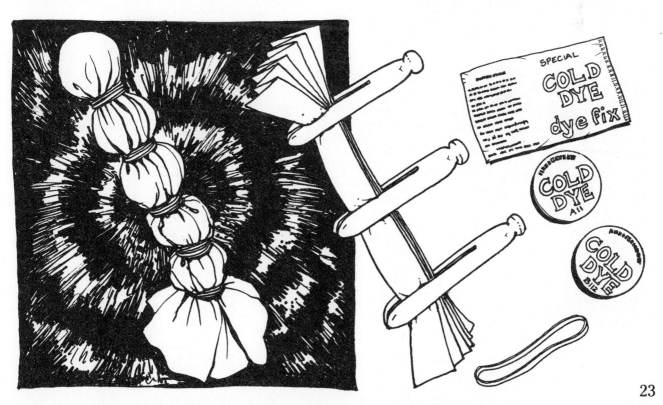

not go into the parts of the fabric that are tied tightly together, so the fabric remains its original colour in these places. Demonstrate some ways in which the material can be tied. For example, the children can create star patterns by putting a pebble in the fabric, and securing it with an elastic band placed tightly underneath. The fabric below the pebble can then be bunched together at intervals with elastic bands, producing lines of paler fabric when they are removed. Check that all the bands are tight before submerging the fabric in the dye bath, and give them an extra twist if necessary.

Another pattern can be made by roughly pleating the fabric, and holding the pleats together with clothes-pegs; this produces a line of small squares when the fabric is unfolded after dyeing.

Wet the fabrics before putting them into the dye bath, and leave them in for about twenty minutes. When they are taken out, run them under a cold tap until the water runs fairly clear, then spin-dry them. The pebbles make loading the spin-drier hard, so do a few at a time. After spin drying, take off the pegs or elastic bands, and unfold the materials. This is an exciting moment for everyone, and is usually pleasantly surprising.

Iron the fabrics while they are still damp,

otherwise the creases stay permanently fixed. It might be easier to take the damp fabrics home in a plastic bag to iron later.
Art: AT1, AT2; Science: AT3

Starch resist

There are other activities that involve the use of fabric. Making clothes for glove puppets is within the range of Y2, as is starch resist. This is a primitive form of batik.

What you need

Fabric, masking tape, starch, washing-up liquid bottle, cold water dyes, brushes, scraper, iron.

What to do

Stretch the fabric taut across a table and fix it in place with masking tape. Make a paste with starch and water and put it in an empty washing-up liquid bottle, then let the children squirt patterns on to the fabric.

Let the paste dry overnight, then let the children paint over the fabric with cold water dyes. When the dye has dried, scrape off the paste. The fabric can then be washed and ironed.
Art: AT1; Science: AT1, AT3; Technology: AT3

Investigating weaving

Another aspect of fabric that can be explored with children is its construction through weaving. The links with other times and places that can be introduced to the children in this area are extensive. The weavings of the Peruvian and Bolivian Quechua Indians are carrying on an ancient tradition, and weaving in Egypt has been revived in recent times. The children may appreciate the story of the Rameses Wissa Wassef Art School in Egypt, where the weaving of beautiful tapestries by local children – telling the stories of village life and tradition – rescued the whole village from acute poverty (*Animals in Art* by Peter Belves and Francis Mathey, Oldham Press).

Weaving is a method of fabric construction using vertical and horizontal elements that hold each other in position. A textile can be made by the horizontal weft threads passing over and under the vertical warp threads. This has to be carried out in a definite order, otherwise the textile will not stay together. Weaving requires manipulative skill plus an ability to understand in advance what is going to happen. Children will therefore need to have some hands-on experience before they can predict an outcome. The following projects are designed as a progressive learning experience, each building upon skills and knowledge from the previous activities.

Simple paper weaving

When introducing young children to weaving, simple methods of holding the vertical warp threads in position need to be devised, so that children learn to pass the horizontal weft threads under and over them. One way of doing this is for the teacher to cut out vertical strips (about 3cm wide) from an area within a paper square, ensuring that when the vertical lines are cut, the top and bottom of the strips are left intact and remain attached to the paper. These then become warp threads. The children can pass additional strips of paper horizontally under and over the warp, making the weft threads.

What you need

Pre-prepared paper squares, strips of paper 2-3cm wide in different colours, paper mats, adhesive, examples of coarse-weave cloth (such as scrim or hessian), a sample of felt, writing materials.

What to do

Give the 'warp' paper to the children and let them select a colour, or colours, from the paper strips. Explain that they are going to make a woven paper mat, made in the same way as some cloths are made. Introduce the words 'warp' and 'weft', and explain that their function is to hold the cloth in place.

Show the children the fabrics and demonstrate the way the warp and weft threads hold the fabric in place by removing some warp threads. Pull the fabric to show the rigidity of the straight grain, and the flexibility when the fabric is pulled crossways. Ask the children if they think all fabrics are made in this way. Let them examine the felt, and explain that there is no warp or weft, as felt is made by pressing the fibres together.

Let the children try a straightforward over and under weave. When they have finished, stick down the ends of the weft threads so that they stay in place.

When the children have finished, ask them to write a description of the method, and draw a plan of the weave construction.
Art: AT1, AT2; Science: AT3; Technology: AT2, AT3

Card weaving

What you need

Card, scissors, a selection of threads and string, thick wool, plastic strips, ribbons, old tights, etc.

What to do

Prepare card looms as in Figure 4 overleaf. Let the children experiment with passing different types of thick and thin threads across the warp. They could use rough or smooth

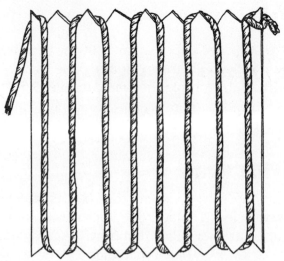

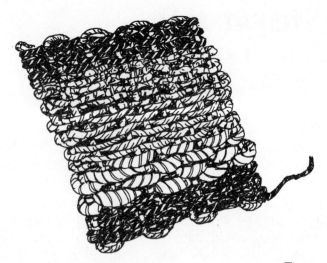

Figure 4

string, bobbly and smooth yarn of various weights, from single ply to rug wool, and strips of plastic or fabric. Alternatively, they could be restricted to two colours of wool, and create striped patterns. Help them to address the problem of tucking in ends and joining pieces of wool together. Help the children to take their woven fabric off the card looms. Let them window mount their work in card frames.

Follow-up

After these experiences, the children will begin to predict in advance what might happen. For example, many of them will now be able to understand how a striped pattern is woven. At this stage they could be shown examples of Indian dhurries, or other coarsely woven striped fabric. They could examine woven fabric patterns under a magnifying glass.

A group-woven wall-hanging

This project builds upon the children's previous experience of construction by weaving.

What you need

Card looms (see previous activity), coloured threads, strings and yarn, a selection of other materials to use as weft threads, such as dried grasses, twigs etc, felt.

What to do

Explain to the children that they are going to make a large wall-hanging, which will take them some time, but that they can work at their weavings individually, once they have decided on a theme for a design. They may choose stripes, or a limited range of colour, or each child might try a different texture of thread. They could choose seasonal colour, or geometric shapes, where, for example, all the weavings could be based on squares. In weaving, it is very difficult to construct a curve because of the limitations of the warp and weft threads. It is as well to bear this in mind when choosing a theme. When the children have decided on a theme, let them use the card looms to make their individual weaving.

Once the weavings have been taken off the card, they can be laced together to make a hanging, or set into a large felt square to enhance the appearance of the work, and then hung. Display the hanging in an appropriate place like a corridor or stairwell. Encourage the children to decide where the wall-hanging should go and evaluate its effectiveness. Other classes could be asked to give their opinion on the work.

The children will begin to understand that group co-operation is required in the production of a larger piece of work. They will develop their manipulative skills, and see the effect of their work in context.

Art: AT1, AT2; Technology: AT3; Science: AT3

Chapter 2
Using three-dimensional materials (Key Stage 1)

Working with three-dimensional materials is important for children, as it develops their knowledge of form, and enhances their understanding of spatial concepts. They also learn how to structure forms that are appropriate to the type of material being used. For example, a model made from boxes and card is constructed in a totally different way to the model made out of a malleable material such as clay. The limitations and advantages of each can only be discovered through practical experience. Before the children embark on a project, they need to become familiar with the materials they are using, so that they are aware of some of their possibilities.

Exploring clay

Clay is both tactile and malleable, and is a fundamental art and craft material that has been used for thousands of years. Once extracted from the earth, it is virtually ready to use. The study of its origins and uses could form an excellent history, geography and science project, and draw the children's attention to the many cultures that have used clay for artistic expression as well as for utilitarian functions.

If it could be arranged, a visit to a pottery would make an exciting introduction to the study of clay. The visit could be supported by a display of clay objects, such as cups and saucers, models of animals, bricks and examples of clay pipes, to which the children as well as the teacher could contribute. Postcards and pictures of historical clay artefacts could be used in the display, such as a Peruvian pot, a Susa vase of 3,000 BC and an Elisabeth Frink bird sculpture. It would be interesting to discover which one the children thought was the most recent, and then to ask them to draw their own version.

The properties of clay

What you need

A grapefruit-sized ball of clay for each child, rolling pins, a selection of mark-making objects (forks, nuts, card, sticks, marbles, small wooden bricks, etc), small pots of water (for dampening the clay when joining pieces together).

What to do

If clay is a new medium for the children, the first part of the session should be experimental, and they should practise pulling and moulding the clay. Ask them:
• How far can it stretch?
• Can you make a tunnel through it?
• Is it cold?
• Can you make a tall thin shape?
    After the children have handled the clay for a time, tell them to roll it back into a ball, and divide it in two. Ask them to roll out one half flat, and make a river shape. Ask them to pattern the river, using the marking tools.

When they have finished, ask them to make a bridge across the water with the other half of the clay. They will realise the need to use solid supports, and find that spidery clay does not hold the weight of a substantial form. Discuss the results with them.
Art: AT1; Technology: AT2, AT3; Science: AT3; English: AT1

Make a tile

What you need

Clay, rolling pins, mark-making objects, pastry cutter, paint, varnish.

What to do

Let the children roll out the clay as before and use pastry cutters to cut it into a geometrical shape to make a tile. Tell the children to choose objects to press into the clay to make a pattern. Ask them to base their patterns on either a circle or stripes, arranging the marks carefully. Allow the tiles to dry slowly, then paint them and varnish them.

Plaster relief

An activity that uses a similar approach is to make a plaster relief. The casting of a relief is a fascinating process for children, as it shows a reverse pattern, changes in materials from liquid to solid and the spontaneous generation of heat as the plaster sets.

What you need

Potters' plaster, small shallow cardboard boxes (such as chocolate boxes), parcel tape, clay, a variety of objects to push into the clay to make a pattern (such as marbles, twigs, etc), bowls, cooking oil, old brushes, water.

What to do

Reinforce the corners of the boxes with parcel tape before the children start work. Ask each child to cover the base of a box with a 2cm layer of clay and to smooth the top with their fingers (a slight rough texture adds to the effect). Next ask them to choose three objects from the selection, and think how they are going to use them to make a picture or a pattern in the clay.
• A cat could be made by pressing twigs into the clay, and then removing them to create an outline. Marbles could be used to make an impression of the eyes, and tabby markings could be indicated by drawing across areas with a blunt pencil or lolly stick.
• A castle could be made by using rolls of clay secured with dabs of water to build up an outline, and creating the effect of stone by making impressions with the marbles.

When the children have finished their picture, check that the indentations and protuberances are clearly defined, then ask the children to brush a thin layer of oil over the surface.

Pour water into a bowl, and sprinkle the plaster on to it, mixing it rapidly with the hand. Plaster sets rapidly, so work quickly, and mix enough for several reliefs at once. Let the children each have a stir. As the plaster begins to harden, or 'go off' as it is called, it gets warm. Mix it to the consistency of single cream, and then pour it into the boxes,

covering the clay to a depth of 2.5 to 3cm. Leave it to set. Overnight is best, although it could be ready sooner.

When the plaster is cool and hard, tear the cardboard away from the sides, and lift the relief out. Discuss the results with the children, and draw their attention to the effects created by the impressed objects. **Art: AT1; Science: AT3; Technology: AT2, AT3**

Make a clay animal

After handling and exploring clay, the children can make a model animal. Familiarity is the key to success in this activity. The children should either choose to model a pet or should study drawings, photographs and other reference materials. One infant class made very realistic and appealing models of the class hamster, including several that showed it with a full pouch or eating a peanut. The hamster was a good subject, as it has a solid shape and small legs.

Remind the children that long-legged animals are best modelled lying down, as the weight of the body causes clay legs to collapse. Legs can be supported by sticks in the centre of the clay, but these cannot be fired.

What you need

Examples of models of animals, a ball of clay for each child, lolly sticks or modelling tools, a small pot of water, blunt knives, kiln (optional), paint, brushes, varnish.

What to do

Show the children some examples of simplified animal form, such as Inuit carvings, and point out their solidity and simple shape.

Ask the children to make their own clay animals, modelling the large shapes first from one piece of clay before going on to add details such as ears, fur texture or shell patterns. Encourage the use of modelling tools to create textures. For example, terrapins have very pronounced shell patterns, which could add interest to a model.

(Even a worm has varying ring marks, although, popular as they are with beginners, they are rather too easy a subject!)

If the model is to be fired, emphasise to the children the importance of modelling as much as possible from one piece of clay. If not, there is a strong probability that the various parts will come apart during the firing, possibly damaging other pieces of work in the kiln as well. Clay used for firing needs to be as light as possible, so when the children have finished their animals, show them how to hollow out the interior from the base, using the blunt knives.

Dry the model animals slowly, and when they are completely dry they can be fired, or painted and varnished, using non-toxic varnish.

These types of models look effective when displayed on a textured surface made from sand or dried leaves.

Art: AT1, AT2; Technology: AT2; Geography: AT5; Science: AT3

Design and make a container

This activity is suitable for Y2 children, and offers further opportunities to discover the malleable and porous qualities of clay, and helps them to relate their own work to the functional use of pottery in everyday life.

What you need

A selection of clay containers (including a clay flowerpot, vases of different types and a utilitarian domestic object like a teapot), clay, modelling tools, kiln (optional), two small plastic bags, small plate, small plastic flowerpot, water, paper, pencils, round and square pastry cutters, small bowl.

What to do

Show the children the clay collection, and discuss the design of the objects, and their uses. Ask the children if they know why the flowerpot has a hole in the bottom when the vase for cut flowers has not. Explain that

growing plants have roots, and drown if they have too much water. Show them the plastic pot, and point out the hole in it. Ask them if they think the water can escape from the plastic pot any other way except through the top and base. Is there another way that the water can get out of the clay pot?

Block the hole in the base of both pots with the plastic bags, stand them on the plates, and pour water in. The children will soon notice the change of colour caused by the porous quality of the clay pot. Encourage them to feel the pot and observe how it feels damp. Explain that the pot has not been glazed, but has been fired once in the kiln – a biscuit firing. Pour water into a vase and demonstrate the difference. Make a tiny thumb pot from the clay, and pour water into it, so that the children can see that clay is soluble until it is fired.

Explain to the children that they are going to make their own containers. If the clay is to be fired, the children can make a plantpot holder; if not, a container for a toy, such as a garage for a small toy car would be suitable. Ask the children to draw their designs for their container, and suggest some decoration for it.

When they are happy with their designs, let them make their containers. The base of the container can be cut out using the pastry cutters; the sides can be modelled, or rolled out then cut and joined. If the children are making a plantpot holder, let them use the small flowerpots to check that the size is correct.

Designs can be imprinted on the sides of the clay, or coils and cut-out clay shapes can be stuck on, using slip or water as an adhesive agent. Adult help might be necessary for this.

Discuss the results with the class and allow the containers to dry before firing. If no kiln is available, paint and varnish the containers once they have dried.

This type of work can look attractive displayed on dark sugar paper, with each model positioned on a sprinkling of sand.

Art: AT1; Technology: AT1, AT2, AT3; Mathematics: AT1, AT3; History: AT3; Science: AT3

Model a figure

This is another activity involving the use of clay, and is suitable for Y2 children. Here, the children try to make their own version of a sculpture. Show them a simple figure sculpture with distinct movement, such as a T'ang Dynasty model of dancing women. These models have a simple, swirling movement and defined drapery that children find easy to understand, and re-interpret in their own versions. Another interesting example of sculpture could be a picture of one of the 2,000 or more terracotta warriors found near Mount Li in China, in the burial mound of the Emperor Shi-Huangdi, first ruler of the Qin Dynasty. These figures have simple poses, and a patterned surface that would appeal to young children. Draw the children's attention to the different features and dress styles. There is a replica of this army at the Bournemouth Exhibition Centre, Dorset.

What you need

Pictures of models of figures, paper, pencils, clay, modelling tools.

What to do

Tell the children to look at the pictures of the figures, and then draw and model their own versions. Tell the children to mould or roll pieces of clay into sausage shapes, and lay them flat on the table, bending and squeezing them to form the body shape. They can then add other sausage shapes for arms, and pull and indent the main body shape to suggest folds in clothes. Let them use small pieces of clay for hair, ears, hands, etc.

Although the results may seem out of proportion or just a lump of clay to an adult, remember that to the young child, the model is a person. This is the beginning of understanding the workings of the whole human form in three dimensions, developing knowledge of space and the relationships between forms. It also helps the child to realise the structure of their own body, and can be used to support a project on 'Ourselves'.

Art: AT1, AT2; Science: AT2

Exploring dough

Dinner time

This activity can form part of a project on food. Discuss and investigate the subject with the children, then explain that they are going to make a model of their favourite dish. Look at and discuss pictures of food. Before starting the activity, gather together a selection of plates with decorated rims. This activity should take place over at least two sessions.

Before the activity, prepare some salt dough for the children to use. A recipe is given on page 143.

What you need

Dough, paints in black, white and primary colours, brushes, cooker (optional), decorated plates, white paper plates, table, tablecloth, plastic knives and forks, a selection of food pictures from magazines, serviettes, felt-tipped pens.

What to do

Tell the children that they are going to make a model of their favourite meal and decorate the plates on which the food is served, before finally role-playing a family eating dinner. Children will happily model the dough into mashed potato, chops, sausages or ice-cream, and even if the modelling is not totally accurate, their enjoyment and understanding of the modelling medium will have been enhanced.

Give the children a good-sized lump of dough to work with. As they model, go round and remind them of the reference pictures if they are not sure of the forms. When they have finished, either lay the dough aside to dry overnight, or bake it in an oven on a low heat.

In the next session, let the children paint the model food, again looking at pictures if they need to remind themselves of colours and textures. When they have painted their food, give out the paper plates, two for each child, and ask them to decorate the rims. Show them the plates with the patterns on, and ask them to try out various designs on one of the paper plates using felt-tipped pens. Ask them to choose the best design and copy it neatly on to the second plate.

Get the children to arrange the model food on their plates. They can then lay the place settings, and act out having a meal.

Art: AT1, AT2; History: AT1; Science: AT1, AT3

Follow-up

This idea could be developed to make the contents of food shops, to produce food for a historic banquet or to see what a week's rations during World War 2 would have looked like.

Using Plasticine

Plasticine is a medium well suited to small, detailed modelling. It is ideal for making flowers and small bushes that are part of a large-scale model. The following activity could form part of a science project on minibeasts.

A model snail and its home

Before the activity, take the children outside to collect snails and leaves. Ensure that the snails are returned to their environment after the children have studied them.

What you need

Plasticine, snails, dishes, modelling tools, a box with the front and top removed, a selection of papers, a collection of different leaves, 4B pencils, scissors, PVA adhesive, spreaders, A4 white drawing paper, magnifying glasses.

What to do

Place the snails in dishes and let the children look closely at them. Point out the snails' shape to the children. Draw attention to the patterns and spirals on the shell. Tell the children to draw the snails, after examining them thoroughly with the magnifying glasses.

The children can then build a snail from the Plasticine, using a roll shape for the body, and fine rolls to form the shell; the patterns can then be scratched into the Plasticine. Show the children how to fashion the antennae from small rolled shapes, and attach bobbles to the ends.

Ask the children to turn the box into a home for the Plasticine snails. Get them to cover the sides of the box with adhesive and stick on paper leaves and Plasticine stalks. Encourage the children to look closely at real leaves for reference before making the paper leaves. Put paper leaf shapes on the floor of the box, and tell the children that their snails

would like some dead leaves to feed on, as well as the green vegetation.

Follow-up

Different groups in the class could make a different insect or mollusc environment, using the same method. They could form a minibeast zoo, experimenting with its construction until they find one that affords visitors the best view. Other staff and children could be asked to visit it.
Art: AT1; Science: AT2

Using imagination

In the previous activities, the children have based their work on observation or the exploration of materials. In the following activities, they draw from their imagination. The children will enjoy making imaginary animals from clay, and adding details with marbles, bottle caps and feathers. Even very young children will benefit from this activity.

Imaginary animals

What you need

Clay, modelling tools, a collection of feathers, toothpicks, straw, bottletops, marbles etc, paint, paper, pencils.

What to do

Ask the children to squeeze, mould and twist the clay into a shape that feels good to handle. Tell them to look at the shape that they have made, from the top and from the sides. Ask them if they can think of ways to turn it into an animal. Stress that this does not need to be a real animal, but that it can be a creature from another world. Let them use their imaginations. Let them decorate the animals with scrap materials.

When the models are finished, suggest they paint a picture, showing the creatures in the world where they came from. Get them to write a story about their creatures.
Art: AT1, AT2; English: AT3

Drawing with wire

Most people think of a pencil or pen when they think of drawing, but drawings can be done in many different ways. A drawing is essentially marks and lines that record what is seen or imagined. One medium that uses space in its form is wire sculpture.

Although young children will not be able to build large wire sculptures, they can make small-scale outline models, which can be made to stand up on a Plasticine base. Some wire is very pliable, and can be cut with scissors, but it is not suitable for large-scale work. Millinery wire, pipe cleaners and soldering wire of a fine gauge are suitable for the following activities.

As a preliminary to this activity, the children could be shown pictures of the *Wire Circus* (1926-32) of Alexander Calder.

What you need

Millinery wire, scissors, ruler, Plasticine.

What to do

Let the children experiment to find out what shapes the wire can make. Tell them to take a piece of wire, 40cm long, and try to make as many shapes and lines as they can. Show them how the wire can be bent, pinched into small shapes and wrinkled and curved round to make loops and circles. Ask them to crunch the wire into a ball, and see if the shape suggests a subject.

When the children are happy with their shape, let them stand it up on a Plasticine base.
Art: AT1, AT2; Technology: AT3

A wire animal

What you need

Millinery wire, pipe-cleaners, scissors, Plasticine, coloured paper, thread.

What to do

Tell the children to think of an animal, then start at one end of a length of wire, and bend it to form the outline of the animal. Remind the children to think about the textures of the animals, and suggest that they can add wriggles and bends to depict, for example, the long hair of a Persian cat. (For a particularly fluffy effect, they may like to use pipe-cleaners instead of wire.)

The models can be stood on Plasticine bases, or exhibited against a coloured paper background. They also work well as shadow puppets if they are attached to a straight piece of wire, or are dangled from a thread. Lighting the models with a reading lamp or a spotlight can make some interesting shadows, which could support work in science.
Art: AT1, AT2; Science: AT3

Using boxes

Boxes are a useful and easily available resource for model-making, and can be used on both large- and small-scale work, and for group projects. Large boxes from the local supermarket can be assembled to make trains, boats and aeroplanes, which children can sit in and use in role-play. For individual work, small boxes can be made into a variety of animals or buildings. Larger boxes can be stacked to form a tower, and then drawn from different angles.

Boxes can be used to hang from the ceiling, with a pattern based on a number or letter on each side. These can look very attractive painted in contrasting primary colours, such as vermilion and green, or yellow and bright blue.

Assemble a totem pole

This activity could form part of a project on the American Indians, and be linked with a visit to a museum, such as the Horniman Museum in Forest Hill, South London, which has a totem pole erected in the grounds, or the Sainsbury Centre for the Visual Arts, University of East Anglia, which has an Amero-Indian collection. This could be a class project, with the children working in groups of four.

As a preparation for this activity, tell the children about the use of tribal symbols by the American Indians. Discuss which animal the totem pole is going to represent, and look at the way some animals have been used in the design of totem poles.

What you need

Boxes (choose ones that will stack one on top of another, getting slightly smaller as they reach the top), a supply of small boxes, paper-backed foil, charcoal, white emulsion paint, house decorating brush, paint, PVA adhesive.

What to do

Before the activity, paint the boxes white, to obliterate any lettering or colouring.

Tell each group of children that they are going to decorate a box to form part of a class totem pole. Ask them to decide how they are going to decorate their box, and remind them that all four sides and the top have to be decorated. Discuss ways of deciding on the colours. Do they think the boxes should be painted in the colours the American Indians used? These would be colours that were based on local materials – dark red, yellow ochre and black and white.

Ask the children to draw the outline of their designs in charcoal, then let each member of the group paint one side of the box. Once dry, the boxes can be stacked. If further decoration is needed, highlight some of the features, such as a bird's beak or claws, using pieces of foil stuck in place with PVA adhesive.

The totem pole can then be drawn, either by itself, or as part of an illustration for a story.
Art: AT1, AT2; Geography: AT2; History: AT3

Make a pram monster

If it is possible to obtain an old pram or push-chair, this can form the base for a box model that can be pushed around. The mobility of the model can give rise to some imaginative play, especially with reception children. At this age, children can show great ingenuity if asked to construct a monster out of boxes and a pram.

What you need

Stories about monsters, an old pram, large and small boxes, cardboard tubes, paints, brushes, PVA adhesive, scissors, a selection of coloured paper, string.

What to do

Read the children some stories about monsters, such as *Where the Wild Things Are* by Maurice Sendak, or *Not Now, Bernard* by David Mckee. Explain that they are going to build a big monster that they can move around. Help the children to cover the body of the pram with a large box. Cut a slot in a smaller box to drop over the handle to make the head of the monster. Make sure the children will be able to see clearly over this when they push it along. Smaller boxes can be glued on to the 'head' to form eyes and ears. Hair can be made from raffia or wool, and the mouth and nose built up from segments of cardboard tubes.

Let the children decorate the body with patterns, and help them to construct movable arms and feet using smaller boxes threaded together with string. These too can be decorated.

This activity will help children to learn about simple construction, and some of the difficulties that can arise.

Although some help will be needed from the teacher, let the children have as much freedom as possible, as they often have an original and imaginative approach to this type of work. For example, one group of nursery children built a ferocious and much-loved monster, using an old pram as a basis, and this activity resulted in a great deal of language development. The monster was played with, and figured in many drawings. It eventually disintegrated, and was decently interred in the rubbish bin, to be replaced by a pram-based travelling shop.

Art: AT1; English: AT1, AT2; Technology: AT3

Other three-dimensional materials

There are many ways of using three-dimensional materials with infant children. Glove and finger puppets can be used to add a further dimension to their experience. These are included in Chapter 4, under cross-curricular themes.

Simple raised reliefs can be made from corrugated paper, cut in strips, curled and stuck (edge-on) to a coloured background. Cardboard egg boxes are also useful; they can be built up into geometric shapes, such as pyramids and squares, and can help children to count and estimate. Cut into individual sections, and stuck down with the hollow side uppermost, they can build up into animal and fish shapes. These can be painted, and patterns made by repeating the shapes **(Art: AT1; Mathematics: AT4)**.

Using a variety of different materials that can be shaped and moulded contributes to the children's knowledge of proportion, and to their understanding of everyday materials.

Chapter 3
Artists and the environment (Key Stage 1)

During the early years children learn most easily through personal experience, as they are still exploring their world, and trying to create order from what they discover. The more they can experience through their own ways of personal expression, and through observation of reality, the easier it becomes for them to understand ideas and think in the abstract. Although children learn through experience, they can be encouraged to leap beyond their own boundaries by seeing examples of art and craft that show different ways of using similar subjects to their own.

Using the environment

Looking, comparing and recording the world around them leads to children developing a greater understanding of the environment. Connections between disparate things become apparent and memorable. Children are thrilled by personal discoveries – the resemblance of the veins on a leaf to those on our hands, or the fact that the pattern on the back of the common garden spider, studied through the magnifying glass, looks like a design for a rug or an embroidery. They feel the same excitement when they realise that artists, designers and craftsmen have produced work that in some way resembles their own.

The relationship between their own work and that of others begins the ongoing process of developing a sense of history and cultural pluralism in society. It also gives children an understanding of continuity. The language that arises during teacher-led discussion can support the teaching of language, history, geography and mathematics.

The school environment

The school building is used as the basis for this work, but the same approach would be equally applicable to a study of the local church or a shopping centre. This series of activities could be part of a history project based on the recent past, or a science project on materials. School provides plenty of opportunity to find out about texture, colour, line and form.

Some time before starting the following activities, collect together a selection of photographs, drawings or paintings of buildings, such as Bryan Wynter's *Carn Cottage* (1946), a simple line and wash drawing that clearly demonstrates the textures and forms of the building, without being over detailed. It also shows a traditional granite Cornish cottage which could lead to a discussion about the varied use of building materials in different parts of the country. Another good example, which would make a complete contrast and give rise to a discussion on the function of buildings, would be Peter Dunne's photograph *Boy in Glasgow*, showing tenement blocks in a derelict condition, with a boy sitting on an empty upturned dustbin in the foreground. Contrasts of this type can make the children

aware of different lifestyles, and lead to discussion about the way different people live. This photograph could help to make children aware of the fact that the design of buildings is not always successful.

A collection of photographs of local buildings could be displayed, and their architectural styles compared. The children could be asked the following questions:
• When were they built?
• Why do you think they were built?
• Would you like to live there?
• Which is the oldest building?
The answers may be a surprise!

During a piece of historically based research, one of the authors was surprised to find that a group of infant children thought 1930s semi-detached houses were very old, and that a Georgian terrace was quite recent. Upon investigation, it was found that the children were judging by the cars in the photograph (Georgian terrace) and the knocker on the front door (30s semi). We feel that this indicates that there is a need to teach children how to look at pictures.

If modern buildings were included in the selection of photographs, there could be a discussion on the way materials have been used at different times. For example, the amount of glass, the use of flat as opposed to the pitched rooves, or the use of concrete rather than brick, could all be discussed.

Today, most children think of tower blocks as old, and post-modern red brick as new. Even young children see the different shapes of windows and are aware that some buildings look older than others. They will, however, need guidance as to which clues to look for to estimate the age.

Art: AT1, AT2; Technology: AT1, AT4; Science: AT2; History: AT1; Geography: AT5

Textures of the school

Touching and feeling their surroundings can make children more aware of the textures in their environment. Texture is a tactile experience: it is felt through the fingers or hands. It can be recorded by rubbings, which introduces a new dimension to ordinary materials, often revealing marks and patterns invisible to the naked eye.

Before experimenting with rubbings, the children can be introduced to texture in various ways. The 'feelie box' is always popular. In this, objects of contrasting textures are enclosed in a box attached to an old sleeve. The children put their hands through the sleeve to feel the textures of the objects inside and describe what they can

feel. Children enjoy this, and often guess what the objects are, as well as describing the textures. Another approach would be to make a 'feelie wheel' from an old cardboard roll. This could be covered with a variety of textured materials – satin, velvet, blotting paper, glass-paper, etc – and turned against the hand.

Before beginning the following activity, collect together a selection of textured objects, such as bark, shells, bubble plastic, an orange and nylon fur, and pass them round among the children, asking them to close their eyes and feel the surfaces. Ask for words that describe the texture of the objects. Suggest that they touch their clothes, and ask them how many different textures they can find.

Two problems may arise during the following activity; firstly, the children may not rub hard enough to get a good image, or secondly, they may rub so hard they make a hole in the paper. Watch out for this in the practice sessions and advise them. It is also important to check that the paper is firmly fastened to the surface, otherwise the image will be blurred. Four tabs of masking tape on each corner of the paper solves this problem.

What you need

A4 textured wallpaper, A4 newsprint, masking tape, heelball (cobblers' wax – available at craft shops or brass rubbing centres) or large black or brown wax crayons, neutral coloured card, adhesive, examples of artists' work where the use of texture is important.

What to do

Explain to the children that they are going to look for texture and pattern in the school, and record it with rubbings. Demonstrate the rubbing technique, using the textured wallpaper, and emphasise that they must hold the paper firmly, as well as securing it with masking tape. If the children are going to use wax crayons show them how to use the

side of the crayon. Let them practise rubbing using the textured wallpaper.

Ask the children to form pairs and let them try to find textures in the classroom before

looking for them outside the school. There are many unexpected patterns and textures to be found in the playground – for example, manhole covers, brick bonding, tree bark, door planks. Explain that one child should hold the paper still while the other takes the rubbing. Make sure that both children have a turn at making a rubbing.

Back in the classroom, let the children try to guess where the various marks came from. Language skills can be reinforced with the introduction of new words to describe the texture. Ask the pairs to select their favourite rubbing and mount it. (Keep the discarded rubbings for subsequent activities.) Neutral colour mounts are more complementary to the black and brown textures than coloured ones.

Have ready examples of the way artists use texture in their drawings, and discuss them with the children. For example, Van Gogh's drawings use a lot of texture; the children could see if any of their rubbings were similar to the marks he used.
Art: AT1; Science: AT3

Pictures from rubbings

There are usually surplus rubbings left after this activity; these can be cut up, or cut out, and made into a collage, adding other textures and colours. The transformation of the textures into other images helps to develop the children's imagination and organisational skills, since they have to divorce the textures from their original source. The process of cutting and sticking improves both their manual dexterity and their knowledge of materials.

This activity can be performed with a large group of up to 16 children, or the whole class.

What you need

Examples of work by artists who have used the rubbing technique, reference material, A2 newsprint, A2 sugar paper, coloured heelball or wax crayon, Pritt Sticks, scissors, textures to rub (for example, corrugated card, backs of leaves, string stuck to card or wound round a billet of wood, paper doilies, crumpled foil).

What to do

This activity could be based on a class project, or the children could illustrate a story or poem, provided it had plenty of suggested texture. *The Tyger* by William Blake would be a good stimulus, or Tennyson's *The Eagle*:

> He clasps the crag with crooked hands;
> Close to the sun in lonely lands,
> Ringed with the azure world, he stands.
>
> The wrinkled sea beneath him crawls;
> He watches from his mountain walls,
> And like a thunderbolt he falls.

Show the children examples of artists' use of rubbings and textures. The *Histoire Naturelle* (1926) by Max Ernst is full of imaginary plants and animals made by rubbing textures. The children could be encouraged to discuss the way he has made up his subjects by combining unlikely objects, for example, the fantasy insect that has leaves for wings.

Demonstrate to the children how new patterns can be made by turning the object that is being rubbed in different directions, and rubbing again on top of the first impression. For example, if this is done with corrugated card, it creates a cross-hatching effect.

Encourage the children to think of the effects of the different textures. For example, if they decide to portray the eagle, have some reference materials ready, such as feathers, photographs or drawings. The smoothness and the ordered pattern of the bird's feathers could contrast with the 'wrinkled' sea, which could be rubbed from folded net or crumpled paper. The eagle's feet could be made from string, thus creating a further texture contrast.

After they have made enough rubbings on to the newsprint, ask them to draw the shapes that they are going to represent on the back of the relevant rubbings, cut them out and carefully arrange them on the sugar paper. When they are satisfied with the arrangement, let them stick the pieces in place with Pritt Stick.

Offer the children a selection of coloured mounts and let them choose the colour they think suits their picture. Remind them that mounts should not make the picture look less important. Encourage the children to evaluate the effectiveness of both the pictures and the mounts, and to talk about the arrangement. Discuss the effects of the different textures, and compare the way colour works with rubbing; they may prefer the effect of plain black or brown.

Art: AT1, AT2; English: AT1

Colour-matching the school

Children of this age group need practice in colour-matching and mixing if they are to extend the use of basic colours in their own work. This activity gives the children confidence in mixing colours, and encourages them to look carefully at the way some artists use colour. It helps them to overlay colour, without reducing the painting to a soupy mess, and they begin to understand colour theory through practical experience, observation and discussion. At this age the formal theory of colour has little meaning except as a practical experience.

Some time before starting the activity, display reproductions of artists' work that use simple colour mixes. Abstract paintings are the best, as they do not distract from the colours by using subject matter. One example that uses clear, defined colours and mixes is Patrick Heron's *Horizontal Stripe Painting, November 1957-January 1958*. This uses warm tones of red and pink at the top of the canvas, painted across in varying widths, and shading into orange, then lemon yellow and white as we progress down the painting. Near the bottom there is a mauve strip surrounded by white, with glimpses of vermilion behind. The whole effect is warm, reminding the viewer of the seaside. It suggests a sunny day and a hot sea, although there is no blue and no subject matter.

Another good example of an abstract work is Nicolas de Stael's *Composition 1950*. This painting is a complete contrast; it is predominantly white with blue and black tints and one black shape – like the inlet of a creek between rocks – jutting up from the bottom of the canvas. The effect is stonelike and rugged, the shapes suggesting slabs of rock. Both paintings have an organic quality, both show limited but subtle use of colour.

Draw the children's attention to the work of the artists, and ask them:
• Which do you like best, and why?
• What colours have they used? (Have some colours out on the table for them to point at.)
• Does either of the paintings make you feel hot or cold?
• Do they remind you of anything – a story, a season, a place, an object?

What you need

Paints, brushes, palettes, paper.

What to do

After discussion, ask the children to try to colour-match something in the classroom, or a section of wall or grass in the school grounds. When they are confident with colour mixing, let them paint a picture using the colours they have found, based on the shapes they have seen in artists' work. Alternatively, they could be asked to paint a picture of the school, matching the artists' colours as closely as they can.

Art: AT1, AT2; Science: AT1; English: AT1

Drawing geometric shapes

To draw a building, children need to have some understanding of space and geometric structure. This activity and the ones that follow it are planned to be progressive, starting with a small-scale exercise designed to help children realise that looking at things from different eye-levels changes the way we see shapes. This is hard for many adults to grasp, as anyone who has tried to teach perspective knows. Not surprisingly, young children find it a difficult concept to understand.

The infant child's use of space in pictures is limited, but at about six years of age, a fascination with detail develops. They will happily draw bricks and ironwork on a building, but are less happy trying to portray three-dimensional shapes on a flat surface. The use of perspective is not of interest to this age-group, but the idea of shape changing with viewpoint can be grasped, and helps with mathematics and geography, increasing their understanding of map-making.

In the earlier years, backgrounds to pictures are often omitted altogether, or indicated by a base line, so this activity is probably best used with the older infants in Y2. It is a useful introduction to map-making and drawing plans, as well as buildings. It introduces the children to the idea of a bird's-eye view. The results are not usually visually exciting, but the success or failure of the exercise indicates the child's stage of spatial development. The child who understands that shapes alter when your eye-level changes has grasped a basic fact about placing and space.

Before starting the exercise with the children make sure there are places where they can safely sit looking down (from the teacher's desk, for example).

What you need

A4 sugar paper, 4B pencils, clipboards, pencil sharpeners, three-dimensional geometric objects from the classroom, such as bricks, boxes and toys.

What to do

Let the children look at, handle and talk about the objects they are going to draw. Discuss the shapes with them, and ask them the following questions:
• How many sides are there?
• What shape is the object?

• If this is put on the floor, how many sides can you see?
• Can you see more of the top?
• Have the shapes of the sides altered?
• Can you see more or less of them?

Let the children start by drawing the objects at eye-level; remind them of the shapes, the shadows and the tones. As each child finishes their first drawing, reinforce the introductory discussion and place the object below the child's eye-level, so that they are looking down on it. Ask them to draw it again. If some children find it hard to grasp that when looking down on an object more is seen of the top than was seen when it was at eye-level, let them draw as they wish and try again a month later.
Art: AT1; Mathematics: AT1

Follow-up

• Follow this activity with introducing the concept of map-making or by asking the children to make a plan of the classroom. One infant teacher tried this approach to map-making with great success.
• Take the children into the playground to draw climbing frames and bikes, from various viewpoints. They could then model the subjects in Plasticine back in the classroom.
Art: AT1; Mathematics: AT1, AT4; Geography: AT1, AT2

Seen through the peep-hole

In this activity, which is suited to all infant age-groups, the children observe their surroundings through a geometric viewfinder attached to the classroom windows. This reinforces their developing concepts of space and distance. It also helps them to realise that the sky is *behind* the view, if they have not reached that stage of development in art.

There are many landscape paintings that would help the children observe variations in the colours of the land and the sky. John Constable's *Leaping Horse* (1825) shows a sweeping, flat East Anglian landscape, suggesting distance, and revealing the changing effects of the sky. The children would enjoy painting their own version of this. If the school were in an urban area, L.S. Lowry's *Coming out of School* (1927) might be appropriate as it shows a cloudy sky behind rather schematic buildings, and tiny, expressive figures that would appeal to this age-group. The pastoral scene of Constable could be compared with the Lowry. Ask the children:
• Which do you like best, and why?
• Were the pictures painted recently or long ago?

A selection of Lowry's paintings can be seen at the Salford Art Gallery, Manchester, while several works by Constable can be seen at the Christchurch Museum, Ipswich, Suffolk.

After discussion, introduce the art activity by reading *Peepo!* by the Ahlbergs. Tell the children they are going to peep through a hole as well. Work with a group of eight to ten children at a time.

What you need

A2 sugar paper, black felt-tipped pens, wax crayons, masking tape, coloured manila with holes cut in geometric shapes (diamonds, triangles, squares, etc).

What to do

Label the geometric peep-holes with the name of the shape, then attach them to the classroom windows with the masking tape. Check that the children have a clear view through the peepholes, and ask them to observe the scene. Encourage the children to count the number of chimneys, trees, etc.

Ask the children:
• What shapes can you see?
• Can you see lines – are they straight or curved?
• What colours are in the sky?
• Do the colours nearest to us look brighter than those that are far away?

After looking and describing what they see, ask the children to draw from memory, using the felt-tipped pens and the sugar paper. If they forget, or want to have another look, allow them to do so. When they have drawn their pictures, ask them to use the wax crayons to colour the items that they think are the most important.

When all the pictures are finished, display them, and ask the children to tell each other what they remembered best about the view. Discuss the mounting with them. Should the pictures be mounted in the peep-hole shapes?
Art: AT1; English: AT1, AT2; Science: AT1; Geography: AT2, AT5; Mathematics: AT4

The shapes of our school

In this activity, the children look at the geometric shapes that underly the basic structure of the school building. This reinforces work on shape in mathematics, and helps the children with concepts of structure, proportion and direction of light, through the observation of shadows, supporting work in science.

Many young children begin drawing from reality by recording the details of what they are looking at. To help their understanding of underlying structures and to develop their sense of scale and proportion, it is useful to draw their attention to the geometric shapes that are fundamental to the structure of buildings.

The drawings of buildings could be compared with photographs and drawings of other buildings in the locality. These can sometimes be obtained from estate agents. A selection of old and new styles could be compared, showing a range of details that could be studied for clues as to their age.

Before starting the activity, preliminary photographs of the school, taken from varying angles and distances, could be a good basis for class discussion. Taking photographs of the building at different times of day could lead to observation of and discussion about shadows and the changing angles of the sun's rays striking the earth, thus reinforcing science as well as art. This activity can be undertaken with the whole class.

What you need

A2 sugar paper, thick and thin charcoal, rags, clipboards, a simple camera, paints, brushes.

What to do

Discuss the various shapes of the building with the children; view it from several different angles. Point out that buildings are like boxes with lids. Ask the children:
• What shapes can you see – squares, rectangles, etc?
• How many different shapes can you see?
• Which is the largest shape?

Each child could take two photographs – one a close-up of a detail, and one from further away – to use as a reference when they work on their drawings back in the classroom.

Ask the children to draw the school building, only putting in the biggest shapes, and not the details such as cornices and architraves. Provide them with clipboards to hold their paper secure as they work. Encourage the children to use the side of the charcoal as well as the tip, and to use the thick and thin sticks to get varied lines. Ask them not to turn their paper over if they make mistakes, but to draw on top of incorrect lines after smudging them out with the rag. When this is done, a shadow of the removed line will remain. Explain that this is not a problem; in fact, this is a method often used by artists. (Henri Matisse used this method; his work could be shown to the children.)

Encourage the children to look closely at the relative proportions of the shapes and to reproduce them as accurately as possible. When they have done this, the details can be added back in the classroom. Remind them to put in the shadows and a ground line, then let them paint into them if they wish.

Discuss with the children the problems of depicting space. Ask them:
• Do the darkest parts of the pictures look furthest away?
• Do the thicker or thinner lines make the buildings look more solid?
• What shapes are there in your own homes?
The paintings could later be used as a basis for an imaginative composition, such as 'My Granny's School at Playtime' or 'We are Playing Football in the Playground'.
Art: AT1, AT2; Mathematics: AT4; History: AT3; Science: AT3

A box model of a school

After their investigations into aspects of the school building, the children can be encouraged to offer their own version of how they would like a school to look.

The hands-on experience of cutting and sticking boxes and paper increases the children's knowledge of materials. The role-play of being an architect and presenting ideas to other pupils helps the children connect their own art and design activities with those that happen outside the school.

The school is an ideal building for the children to design and model, as they are already familiar with its function. The children could be asked to suggest changes they would like in the school exterior, and these could be printed out on the computer and displayed with their photographs. Some technical language could be introduced into the children's vocabulary, such as 'roof ridge', 'bonding', 'casement' or 'sash'.

The teacher needs to check that the scissors work properly, and that there is a private supply of strong glue and a cutting knife. Work with groups of six to eight children at a time.

Before the activity, paint over the boxes with white emulsion paints to cover up trade names, etc.

What you need

Photographs of architects' models, modelling clay, pencils, paper, painting equipment, boxes, scissors, PVA adhesive, spreaders, a selection of coloured papers such as tissue, foil, etc.

What to do

Explain that buildings are designed by architects, who make models to show what their buildings will look like. These are then discussed and often put on display. Show the children some photographs of architects' models, and discuss them. Tell the children they are going to pretend to be architects, and build box models of a school. Explain that they should think about the shape and the playground. Do they want a tall school or lots of buildings? Do they want some kind of shelter in the playground?

Help the children to stick together the boxes to make a model of their school. Let them paint the boxes or stick on coloured papers to represent windows etc. Encourage them to make a playground area from card and to add trees and hedges made from modelling clay. The models could be lit from various angles and photographed or drawn by the children. They could display their models outside the classroom and ask other classes for their comments. Each child could be asked to draw and write a description of their ideal classroom to display beside the model.
Art: AT1, AT2; Mathematics: AT4

Minibeast project

Projects in art should progress sequentially, from observed drawing to imaginative work, through a series of activities that take place over a period of time. In the following series of activities, the children start with an observed drawing of a plant, go on to make leaf prints, collect and draw the minibeasts that live on, under or near the plant and, having gathered information and researched the area, either make a collage of an imaginary plant and its inhabitants or make a monoprint of a minibeast in its home.

Most of the following activities are closely connected with science; they give scope for language development and include some aspects of history and geography.

Observing plants

If you are undertaking a science project, there may be plants already growing in the classroom. If not, dig up common weeds, such as willow herb or dock, from waste grounds.

Work with groups of ten to twelve children at a time.

What you need

A4 white paper, A2 sugar paper, paints in primary colours, large and small brushes, magnifying glasses, pens, black or sepia ink, pots of water, examples of plant paintings (try to include Van Gogh's *Sunflowers* (1888), Anne Pratt's *Ten Vetches* (1854), or any other Victorian plant engraving) photographs from a plant catalogue, adhesive, cardboard, scissors.

What to do

Show the children the pictures, explaining that plants have always been a favourite subject with painters and illustrators. Compare Van Gogh's use of paint with the fine outlines and tints of Victorian prints. Explain that they were made for different purposes. The Van Gogh is painted in shades of yellow, because the artist thought yellow represented sun and happiness. He lived in an area where the fields were full of yellow sunflowers, and he tried to express, in the painting, the happiness he felt when he saw them.

The intention behind the Victorian engraving by Anne Pratt was to show people as much as possible about the plants. Explain to the children that in 1854 cameras were new, and, although they could take photographs of plants, it was difficult to make more than one print. Nowadays we use photography for pictures like this. Show the children the pictures from the plant catalogue. Ask the children:
• Which picture gives the most information about the plants?
• Which makes them feel as though they would like to touch the plants, etc?

This introduction can be performed with the whole class, then ask the smaller groups to decide whether they are going to paint their plants thickly, like Van Gogh, or make a pen drawing, tinted with colour, like Anne Pratt. If they choose to paint the plants, let them use the sugar paper and the big brushes, otherwise let them use the white paper, pens and small brushes. Ask them to start by observing the plant through magnifying glasses. Draw attention to the way the leaves grow from stems or bulbs. Look at and count the number of petals, the variety of greens and the shapes of leaves.

Show the children how to mix delicate shades by diluting the paint with water. Demonstrate that to mix many of nature's greens it is better to use black and yellow, rather than yellow and blue. Tell the children that whichever style they choose, the colours should be correct. Suggest they use a strip at the side of the page to try out the colours they mix.

Go round as the children work, and encourage the painters to use thick paint and expressive brush strokes, and the illustrators to use subtle colour mixes.

Double-mount the work for display: a darker inner mount emphasises the rich colours of the plants. Point out that the painter's work is best seen from a distance, the illustrator's close to.

Art: AT1, AT2; Science: AT1, AT3; History: AT3

Plant structures: leaf prints and patterns

This activity introduces a different way of using parts of plants to make patterns and designs. If you are unfamiliar with this kind of activity, produce a print yourself first before working with the children.

During this activity, two problems may arise. Firstly, if too much ink is applied, the print will not reveal the delicate tracery of veins and leaf shapes. Secondly, the organisation of the print table needs planning, as it can become messy. If either of these problems arises, stop, clear the inks and old newspaper, and start again.

Work with a group of six to eight children at a time; the children can work in pairs. Leave plenty of time for clearing up. Find somewhere to dry the prints – a clothes-line is useful.

What you need

A selection of leaves with firm textures and strongly marked veins, some leaves on twigs (such as cotoneaster), some large leaves (such as horse chestnut), a large table, Redimix or water-based printing ink, print rollers, inking tray, a good supply of old newspapers, A4 newsprint, old cloths, eight dessert spoons, examples of leaves used in design (for example, William Morris prints), a collection of objects with similar structure to leaves (for example, Fan of Venus coral, a peacock's feather).

What to do

Lay out four places on the print table. Each of these should have an inking tray, two rollers, a tube of ink, two newspapers (folded in half), a supply of newsprint, leaves, twigs and a spoon.

Demonstrate the following procedure to the children. Squeeze a 3cm strip of printing ink on to the inking tray and roll it out with a roller until it is smooth. Place a leaf face down on the pad of newspaper and roll the inked roller over it.

Place a sheet of newsprint on a pad of clean newspaper. Carefully remove the leaf, and place it ink-side down on the sheet of newsprint. Cover the leaf with another sheet of newsprint and roll over it with a clean roller to make a print. Discard the inky newspaper. For a good finish, burnish the print gently with the back of a spoon. Lift the top paper, remove the print and allow it to dry.

Let the children work in pairs, firstly printing single leaves to get used to the method, then choosing leaves and twigs, and printing them to form a pattern. A simple repeated pattern would be the easiest to start with. Ask the children:
• Which leaves printed the best and why?
• What other activity has been similar? (rubbing).

Show the children examples of leaves used in design – for example, wrapping paper decorated with William Morris prints.

Show them the coral and the peacock's feather. Ask the children to point out similarities with the leaves.

Art: AT1, AT2; Science: AT2; Mathematics: AT3

Minibeast collection

Take the children on a minibeast hunt, before the activity. This helps them to appreciate the variety of smaller life-forms in the locality.

Asking children to draw the minibeasts ensures detailed observation of their structure, colour and the way they move.

Read up on the private life of minibeasts, not just the biological facts. The knowledge that some ants 'milk' greenfly or that earwigs are good mothers seems to make them more acceptable to the children. This activity can be done with the whole class.

What you need

Jars with holed lids, sea shells, reference books, magnifying glasses, trowels, A4 drawing paper, 2B pencils, ballpoint pens, writing paper, board or flipchart.

What to do

Remind the children of their work on plants. Ask them:
• What minibeasts live on the plants?
• Do they know of any that live under the ground?

Write the names of the various minibeasts on the board or flipchart. Help the children to think of ways in which minibeasts are helpful to us. Which ones are helpful (for example, spiders eat flies)? Which are not (for example, slugs eat young plants)?

Place a variety of minibeasts in the jars with holed lids so that the children can look closely at them. Compare the shell of a garden snail with the sea shell. Note the difference in thicknesses (they are made for different conditions) and note the similarities.

Ask the children to draw the minibeasts in ballpoint pen or pencil, observing them closely through magnifying glasses. Ask them to draw larger versions and to put in details such as texture and pattern, as well as shape.

Suggest they include some objects to indicate the minibeasts' habitat, such as dots and shading to show that a worm lives in the earth, or stalks and leaves for the ladybird or caterpillar.

Let the children arrange their drawings on backing paper and stick them in place.

Make sure that the minibeasts are carefully returned to their natural environment after the activity.

Follow-up

Let the children draw an imaginary plant with its minibeasts or make a monoprint of a minibeast in its natural environment.
Art: AT1, AT2; Science: AT1, AT2

Make an imaginary plant

This activity gives the children an opportunity to use the shapes, forms and textures that they have discovered during the previous activities, applying their own form of visual language and expression.

Before starting the activity, show the children some examples of imaginary plants: for example, Max Ernst's *Histoire Naturelle* or animals and insects from Jacobean bed-hangings like those of Abigail Pett at the Victoria and Albert Museum in London. This activity is best carried out with a group of eight to ten children at a time.

What you need

Stories about tiny people (such as Mary Norton's *The Borrowers*), A2 coloured sugar paper, Pritt Sticks, a selection of papers (such as tissue, sweet wrappers, magazine pages, paper-backed foil), scissors, paper, pencils.

What to do

Read the children an appropriate story, such as *The Borrowers* by Mary Norton, or a children's version of *Gulliver's Travels* by Jonathan Swift. Ask the children:
• What would it be like to be as small as a minibeast?
• What would you see as you looked through the stems and leaves of the plants?
• What would it be like if you were climbing a stalk?
• If you were so small, how would you like your plant to look?

Tell the children they are going to make a collage plant, and fill it with minibeasts. Explain that the plant and the minibeasts could be imaginary and that the minibeasts could either live among the leaves or under the plant, in the roots. Ask the children the following questions:
• Do they want their plant to be a fat plant, like a cabbage? If so, how are they going to show the minibeasts?
• Will the minibeasts be hiding in the plant?
• Will the leaves have to curl back to show the minibeasts?
• Do they want to make a plant with big leaves that minibeasts can shelter under, or one with slim stalks that minibeasts can climb on?

Show the children the different effects that can be obtained by tearing and cutting paper, and demonstrate sticking different types of paper. Ask them why foil needs more glue than tissue paper.

Let the children make rough designs for their plants before making the final collages. Make sure that they apply enough adhesive to stick the heavier papers.

The plants could be mounted side by side to make a frieze.
Art: AT1, AT2

A minibeast at home

In this activity, the children explore use of line – thick, thin, wavy, straight, broken – through print-making. Their attention should be drawn to the fact that the print is the reverse image of the drawing.

It would be wise to try the activity first, if it is a new technique.

What you need

Inking trays, rollers, water-based printing inks, A2 newsprint, lolly sticks, pencils, paintbrushes, somewhere for the prints to dry (for example, a clothes line), card or backing paper, adhesive, a printing surface such as a plastic table-top.

What to do

Remind the children of where they found the minibeasts. Explain that they are going to make a print showing a minibeast in its home. Show them how to use the roller to roll out the printing ink from the inking tray on to the printing surface, then demonstrate using the lolly sticks or the wrong end of a brush or pencil to draw or scratch their pictures into the ink. Encourage them to use a range of lines and marks.

When the drawing is completed, lay a sheet of newsprint on top and gently roll over it with a clean roller. Lift the paper off when a shadow of the image appears through the back of the paper. Point out the reverse image to the children before allowing the print to dry. The prints are best hung up, pegged to a line.

This is a rapid method of printing. Let the children try several prints, and let them experiment with colour by, for example, rolling two colours together.

Mount the prints chosen by each child for display, and ask each group to describe to the class the print they liked best, explaining how they made it.
Art: AT1, AT2

Conclusion

The children will have explored a sequential development in art during these activities, providing a grounding in shape, colour and form that they can then apply to their imaginative work.

Chapter 4
Cross-curricular projects (Key Stage 1)

The primary school's curriculum is already crowded with the demands made by the National Curriculum for the core subjects, so it is probable that art will be taught as part of projects that cross subject boundaries. Art can be useful in capturing children's imagination and arousing their interest in a project. Although the time allowed for art is not defined in the statutory requirements, the assumption has been made by the Art Working Party that there will be two hours a week at Key Stage 1 and slightly less at Key Stage 2. If art is used as a support subject for other areas, this time will expand. Art, design and craft are already widely used in this way in primary schools, particularly with the younger age group. Many of the topics suggested here are suitable for use in an assembly, or for a performance before governors and parents.

Puppets

Projects that include puppets are a useful way of motivating children. They capture their interest and anyone can make them. They appeal to children with different backgrounds, ranges of skills and abilities. Puppets fit naturally into cross-curricular work; language, science, technology, art and drama are all involved in their construction and use. Stories can be told and performed, and the children can use them to act out their own imaginings. Even the youngest children enjoy making simple finger puppets. The most basic puppets can be made from rolled paper fitted over the finger, with a face drawn on, or from a sock worn over the hand, with a piece of felt for a mouth and buttons for eyes.

Puppets have been in use since ancient times; they have been excavated from the

Figure 1

ruins of ancient Egypt, Greece and Rome. Punch has been beating Judy and avoiding punishment in England since 1662, when he arrived from Europe; there he was known as Pulcinello, a character in the *commedia dell'arte*. There is a history of Punch and Judy in Bedford Museum.

Punch and Judy are glove puppets, worked with the hand. These puppets are made by fixing a hollow head to a glove that goes over the hand to form the character's body. A thumb operates one arm, one or two fingers the other arm and two fingers move the head. Quite young children can make effective glove puppets using cardboard rolls for the neck, a paper bag stuffed with newspaper for the head, with fabric sewn or stuck together to make the glove. The face can be painted, and the hair made from wool, raffia or string (Figure 1).

Another type of puppet is operated by a rod; these again are ancient in origin. They are still in use in Japan, where the *Bunraku*, or doll theatre, has had plays specially written for it in the past. The *Bunraku* puppets are operated by two rods, and have flexible joints; they often look very real, especially as they are about 120cm tall. For young children, a satisfactory version of a rod puppet can be made with a card silhouette attached to a small dowel rod, and dressed with silhouette clothes made of firm paper or thin card. These simple puppets are excellent for young children, as they are less complex than glove puppets, and can be used to cover a wide subject area. They can represent trees,

clouds, birds, cars etc. In a performance, the puppet could perform on a tabletop or a bookcase covered with a cloth.

Movable puppets controlled by simple levers are fun for children to construct. It is important that equal attention is given to the visual effect of the puppet as well as to ensuring that the mechanical parts work. If the puppet does not work visually as well as mechanically, the potential for imaginative play is lost.

The traditional Jumping Jack toy is an example of a puppet whose arms and legs are joined to the body with pivotal joints. String levers are attached to the puppet's arms and legs so that they move upwards when the string is pulled. It is not as easy to make as may at first appear, as it involves constructing four pivot joints and four levers, all of which must work well. Young children will need experience of making simple movable puppets before they try these more complex ones. It is useful, however, to have a puppet of this type available so that the children can operate it and see how it works (Figure 2).

Art: AT1, AT2; English: AT1, AT2; History: AT1, AT2; Technology: AT1, AT3, AT4

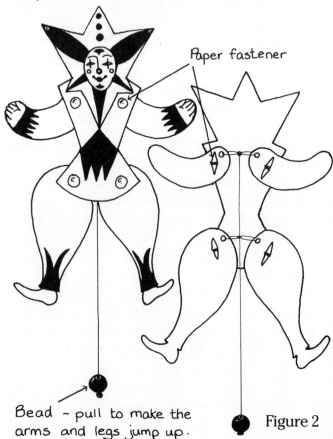

Paper fastener

Bead – pull to make the arms and legs jump up.

Figure 2

52

Using puppets for visual interest and language reinforcement

Puppets can be a useful device for accompanying a story, song or poem as they help to focus the children's attention. They are particularly useful with the youngest children, when a collection of home-made puppets can be used to bring stories to life. For example, a Jumping Jack character could accompany the following poem:

Elastic Jones had rubber bones.
He could bounce up and down like a ball.
When he was six, one of his tricks
Was jumping a ten foot wall.

As the years went by, Elastic would try
To jump higher, and higher, and higher.
He amazed people by jumping a steeple,
Though he scratched his behind on a spire.
(from 'Elastic Jones' by John Foster in *A Second Poetry Book*, compiled by John Foster, OUP)

Pivot puppets: make a hungry crocodile

This is a good way to introduce a simple jointed-puppet activity to the children.

A good range of puppet movements can be obtained from one pivot joint. Demonstrate the basic principle to the children by showing them a pair of scissors. Explain how the movement of the scissors is made by a pivot joint, which joins the two halves of the scissors together, but allows enough flexibility for the two halves to move when they are opened or shut.

A simple pivot joint suitable for puppetry can be made by joining two pieces of card together. Punch a hole in both pieces of card where the join is to be made, and fasten them together with a round-headed paper-fastener and bend the ends back. Care has to be taken that the head of the paper-fastener is bigger than the punched hole, and that the ends of the clip are not bent back so tightly as to restrict movement.

What you need

A copy of *Animals Matter* (Puffin), two strips of cardboard 15cm × 5cm, hole punch, paper-fasteners, wire, masking tape, manila paper in various colours, scissors, sequins (optional), photographs of crocodiles.

What to do

Read 'The Crocodile' by Bryony Mackenzie in *Animals Matter*, and tell the children they are going to make their own movable crocodile puppets, which will open and shut their mouths like the crocodile in the poem.

Show the children how to shape one strip of card to form the bulge of the crocodile's head, as in Figure 3. Have photographs available for them to look at. Make sure they keep the other piece of card straight. Then help them to join the two strips together with a pivot joint, to make the movement of the crocodile's mouth. Teeth can be cut out of the manila and stuck on to the mouth. Scales, eyes and nostrils can be added, using the card and sequins. This basic design can be adapted for many animal puppets. They can have legs attached to the card if it is extended, although not to the movable part.
Art: AT1, AT2; Technology: AT1, AT2, AT3, AT4; English: AT1, AT2

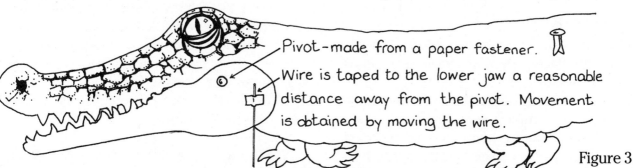

Pivot-made from a paper fastener.
Wire is taped to the lower jaw a reasonable distance away from the pivot. Movement is obtained by moving the wire.

Figure 3

Shadow puppets

These are suitable for use on dark winter days, as a light source has to be placed behind the puppets so that their shadows project on to a wall or screen.

Making the screen for shadow puppets

It is relatively easy to make a screen for use with shadow puppets, and once made it could go into the stock cupboard for use as a school resource. Perhaps a parent could be asked to help out with its construction.

What you need

Four pieces of wood batten (cross section 2cm × 3.5cm, length roughly 36cm), sufficient white sheeting to cover the wood when it is fixed together to form a frame, staple gun, drawing pins, G-clamps (obtainable from carpentry shops), wood adhesive, wood tacks, hammer, sandpaper.

What to do

Cut a section out of the ends of the pieces of wood and stick them together to form a frame (see Figure 4). Nail them through, for extra strength. Allow the wood adhesive to dry, then sandpaper them smooth.

Secure the sheeting tightly across the frame with drawing pins; it is best to start attaching the fabric from the middle of two opposite sides of the frame. Make sure the weave of the fabric is straight, otherwise it will not stay flat. When it is well positioned, staple it to the frame. The frame should then be attached to a tabletop with G-clamps.

Lighting the screen

Once the frame is made, it needs to be lit from the back. There are various ways of doing this.

The screen should be backlit from only one source. The simplest way would be to use a torch, but a reading-lamp gives better results. A slide projector can also be used, and has

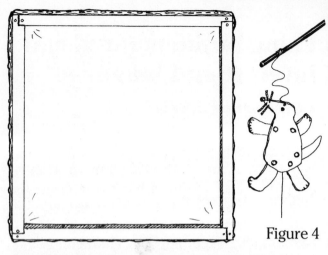

Figure 4

the advantage that slides can be projected as a backdrop to the puppet drama. Characters can then be made to appear to be sitting in a room, walking through the countryside or flying through the air – whatever you wish. The best light source, however, is an overhead projector; this will not overheat and small puppets can be projected, much enlarged, if they are placed on the light box. Colours can also be projected by placing clear plastic or acetate on the light box.

Make shadows on the projector

To ensure that the method of operation is clear to the children, start the activity by allowing them to practise making shadows. This could be part of a science project on light. It is easy for children as young as five or six years old to place their hands on the light box of the overhead projector and discover what forms they can make from the shadows. For example, everyone knows the way to make a rabbit! The children can progress to finding out what other things make patterns and shapes when put on the light box.

Everyday objects like leaves, lace and shoes can be tried out for shape and effect, and the children can be asked to describe what shapes are made. They can also experiment with the effect of placing pieces of different coloured acetate on the light box to find which produce the best colours on the screen. They could see which materials are transparent, and which opaque.

Nursery rhymes make good subjects for simple shadow puppet plays.
Art: AT1; Science: AT1, AT4; Technology: AT2, AT3

The Old Woman who Lived in a Shoe

This rhyme could easily be used as a subject for a shadow puppet play, even by the youngest children.

What you need

Overhead projector, a shoe, paper, pencils, scissors, thread.

What to do

Give the children each a piece of paper and ask them to draw one of the Old Woman's children. One child can be asked to draw the Old Woman. Let them cut out the figures.

Lay the shoe down sideways on the light box. Attach thread to the characters that the children have drawn, and let the children place them in the shoe, holding the threads so that their hands are not projected on to the screen. As they chant the rhyme, ask the children to draw the figures slowly out of the shoe to projected them on to the screen.
Art: AT1; Science: AT4; Technology: AT3

Follow-up

The children could work in groups, illustrating different stories or rhymes to each other, such as Little Miss Muffet, Incey Wincey Spider or Rapunzel.

Alternatively, they could make up a story based on images they have discovered from placing objects on the light box. For example, a hair curler could become a caterpillar, a string of round beads can be made to resemble a snake and some crumpled string could become a giant spider.

This work stimulates the children's imagination, encourages them to think of descriptive words and makes them aware that things can become transformed in certain conditions. It is a good way to draw their attention to the idea that images can be manipulated.
Art: AT1, AT2; English: AT1, AT2, AT3; Science: AT1, AT3; Technology: AT2, AT3

The Wooden Horse of Troy

This activity describes a puppet play for Y2 children.

Using simple stick puppets, the children can make a legend into the basis for a shadow puppet play. There are many other stories that would be suitable – Icarus, Jonah and the Whale, Noah's Ark, among many others. At this point, it would be beneficial for the children to see examples of the beautiful and elegant stick shadow puppets made in Malaysia. These demonstrate the need to cut holes for eyes and mouths in their cardboard shapes. Discuss the decoration on the puppets, and the way the figures are cut to suggest movement.

Making the Wooden Horse

The horse itself needs to be the biggest puppet, as the figures of the Greeks need to be able to hide behind it.

What you need

Manila, scissors, newsprint, felt-tipped pens, paper-fasteners, wire, garden sticks, masking tape.

What to do

Tell the children the story of the Wooden Horse, and suggest that it would make a good puppet play. Ask them how they would make the Greeks appear to come out of the horse. Could they do it by making a flap in the side of the horse attached to a stick, or should it have a back that lifted up? Perhaps it could just be a silhouette for the Greeks to hide behind? Remind them that the audience will only see the shadow on the screen.

Ask the children to draw some of their ideas, using newsprint and felt-tipped pens. Tell them to work out how big the figures would have to be to fit behind the horse.

Moving scenery can be made by drawing on plastic and rolling it across the light box.

Figure 5

Discuss the results and select a suitable horse shape. Ask the children to choose a method to turn it into a shadow puppet cut from manila paper. The horse can be moved along behind the screen using another stick or wire attached to its body with masking tape (Figure 5).

Odysseus, Hector and Achilles

These figures could be slightly larger than the other warriors, and identified by individual silhouettes. For example, Odysseus has often

been depicted with a beard, Hector could have horsehair plumes in his helmet and Achilles could be tall and slender, or have a large shield attached to his arm.

Again, the children could be asked to draw these figures, and the most effective examples could be cut out of card to make the three main characters. The rest could be used to make up warriors on both sides. Remind the children of the running and walking movements of the Malaysian puppets, and tell them that all the figures would be carrying swords. The figures could be moved across the screen using wires or sticks.

The scenery

Start by showing the children photographs of the Lion Gates of Troy and of Agamemnon's golden mask. They may also find the tale of Schliemann's discovery exciting – how he draped the golden head-dress and the necklaces round his wife's neck.

The scenery can also be made from cut-out card. The great walls of Troy can be on one side of the screen, moving slowly across to allow the horse to enter the gates. Then a window could open at the top of the screen, with the figure of Helen looking down on the Greeks defeating the Trojans in the courtyard.

The final scene could show the Greeks sailing away in a boat, on a sea of blue net, with a tiny image of Troy in flames near the top of the screen. The flames can be made from red acetate.

Performance

The timing and use of the figures and the horse will have to be rehearsed, and care taken that everyone has a turn at operating the puppets. The puppet play should be accompanied by sound effects and words; the children could pre-record these on a tape recorder. The play could then be performed for another class or the whole school.

Figure 6 illustrates the cross-curricular applications of this project.
Art: AT1, AT2; Technology: AT2, AT3, AT4; English: AT1, AT2, AT3; History: AT1, AT2, AT3; Geography: AT4; Mathematics: AT1

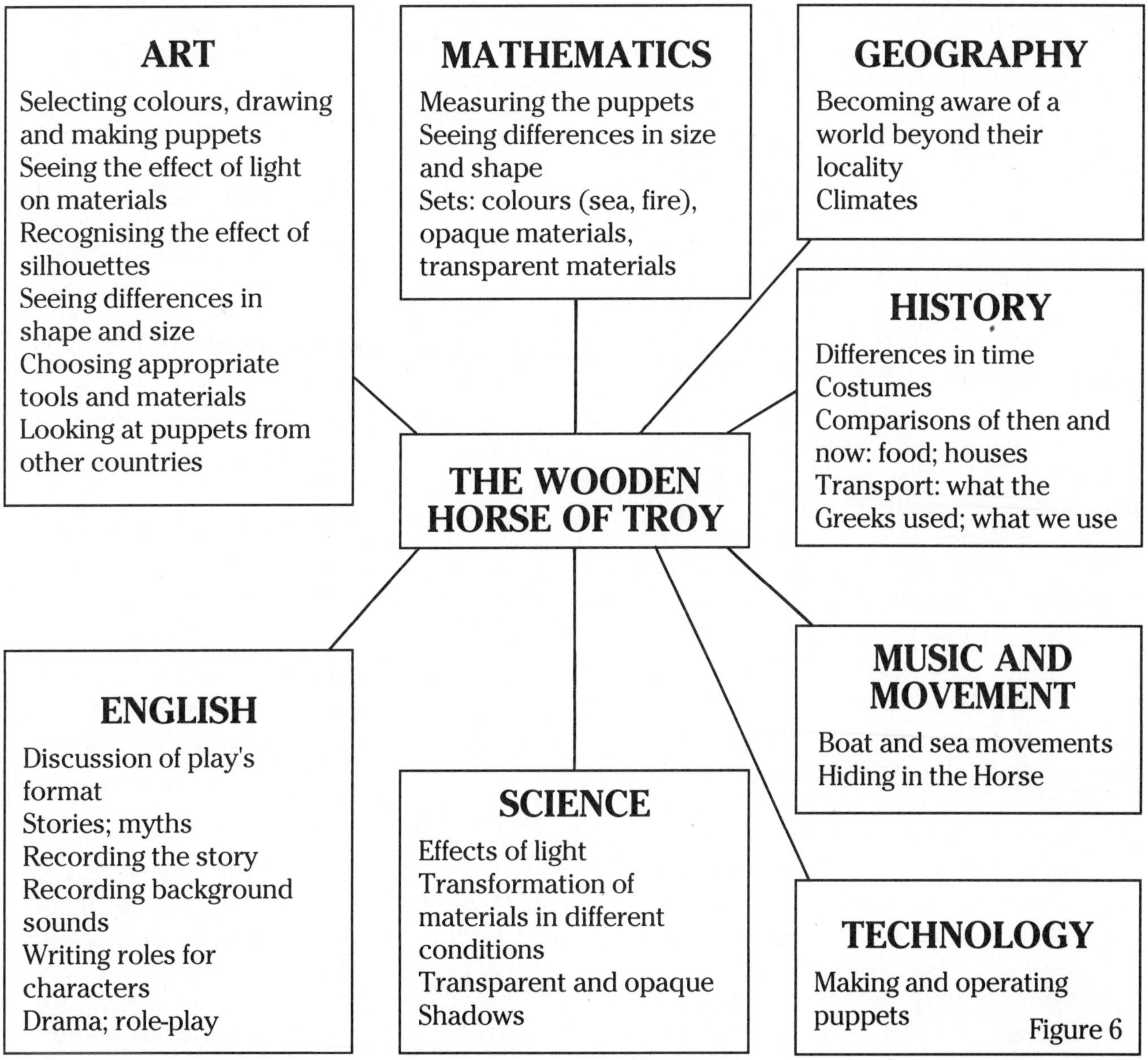

The Wooden Horse of Troy (topic web)

ART
Selecting colours, drawing and making puppets
Seeing the effect of light on materials
Recognising the effect of silhouettes
Seeing differences in shape and size
Choosing appropriate tools and materials
Looking at puppets from other countries

MATHEMATICS
Measuring the puppets
Seeing differences in size and shape
Sets: colours (sea, fire), opaque materials, transparent materials

GEOGRAPHY
Becoming aware of a world beyond their locality
Climates

HISTORY
Differences in time
Costumes
Comparisons of then and now: food; houses
Transport: what the Greeks used; what we use

THE WOODEN HORSE OF TROY

ENGLISH
Discussion of play's format
Stories; myths
Recording the story
Recording background sounds
Writing roles for characters
Drama; role-play

SCIENCE
Effects of light
Transformation of materials in different conditions
Transparent and opaque
Shadows

MUSIC AND MOVEMENT
Boat and sea movements
Hiding in the Horse

TECHNOLOGY
Making and operating puppets

Figure 6

Art and the past (the Stone Age)

Concepts of time develop slowly in the young child's mind, and can be encouraged by finding out and imagining what life was like both long ago ('ancient times') and more recently ('in your nan's day'). The following two projects suggest ways of investigating, firstly, 'ancient times' and secondly, the recent past. Both have elements of science, English, history and geography, as well as art.

Stone Age hunters

All young children are fascinated by the idea of living in caves and hunting for food.

Graham and Lynn (one of the authors and a colleague) discovered this interest while investigating children's reactions to images of the Third World. The infant age-group, in particular, were keen to read the hunter-gatherer lifestyle into every situation, even unlikely ones.

'The extent of the hunter-gatherer image surprised us, and we sought some explanation. The media was an obvious source. Several children referred to programmes about "tribes", especially when discussing the scene in Bangladesh... there had been a programme on Aborigines in Australia which... was frequently mentioned as a primitive place with a primeval lifestyle.' ('Mud Huts and Flints', *Education 3 to 13*, June 1989)

This quote highlights the importance of helping young children place events into some historical context, so that they learn to distinguish reality from unreality.

The project on Stone Age hunters could be introduced by showing the children pictures of the cave paintings of bison, horses, mammoths and deer at Lascaux and Altamira. Tell the children how these pictures, painted deep in the labyrinth of caves, were only discovered in Queen Victoria's day, and that people could not believe that they were painted long, long ago, before man could make metal tools. Cave paintings are still being found – the discovery by a diver of an undersea grotto containing hundreds of prehistoric paintings was reported in *The Guardian* newspaper on Saturday, 19 October 1991. The paintings, like those found at Lascaux and Altamira, dated from the late Palaeolithic era. This event would make a stirring introduction to the project. The children could be told how the diver was swimming in the warm Mediterranean Sea, looking at the seaweed and fish, when he found a cave entrance and swam in. After a long swim of about one hundred metres, he came to a beach in the cave, and when he stood up and looked round he saw a wall covered in paintings. Ask the children:
• Why do you think the cave entrance was underwater? (The sea level was lower in the Mediterranean in those days.)
• Who painted the pictures?
• Are there animals like these nowadays?
• Are they painted in the same colours that we would use?
• Where did the cavemen get the colours from?
• What did they paint with?

Paint a cave picture

The children could make the tools, mix the colours from natural sources and paint a picture of the caveman at work. They could make hand prints, which have been found beside the cave paintings in some places. No one knows if they were signatures or made purely for fun.

Make your own painting tools

What you need

Young green twigs from a bush or tree, feathers, bamboo canes, cut to 16cm lengths, raffia, cord or rope, PVA adhesive, rolling pins, string, scissors, charcoal, moss, straw.

What to do

Tell the children that they are going to make their own tools for painting, like those made by the cavemen. Let them make their tools in any of the following ways.
• The end of the twigs can be pounded with the rolling pin, so that they fray out, and then trimmed to a straight end. Explain that if the pounding is too energetic, the fibres in the twig will be destroyed, and will fall apart as it is used.
• The rope can be frayed at the end, and bound with string above the frayed area.

• Trim a feather at the thick end of the quill and insert it into a bamboo cane. A little adhesive poured into the hole at the centre of the cane will secure it.
• The raffia can be bound together with string and trimmed.

Other local resources include charcoal taken from an extinct bonfire, moss gathered from local trees and dried or straw treated in the same way as the raffia.

Art: AT1, AT2; Science: AT2, AT3; Technology: AT3

Make your own paints

Children enjoy making dyes and paints using local materials, and it is an area that relates well to science. There are several colours that can be made from everyday materials, depending on your geographical location.
• Chalk can be grated and mixed with a little water to make white.
• Clay can be mixed with water to get a reddish colour. If it can be heated, it will produce a darker red-brown.
• Soot from an oil lamp could be used to make black, but care should be taken in showing the lamp to the children.
• Many berries, such as blackberries, can be used to produce red or pink. (The children must take care that they do not stain their clothes.)

What you need

Bowls, water, chalk, clay, soot, berries.

Making the painting

After exploring the possibilities of making their own tools and colours, and trying out methods of working, the children could go on to produce their own version of the cave paintings. Alternatively, they could paint a cave family sitting round their fire, making the painting tools or eating mammoth or bison meat. The cross-curricular applications of this activity are shown in Figure 7.

Art: AT1, AT2; Science: AT1, AT2; Technology: AT3

Follow-up

A comparison could be made between the way the cavemen recorded their pictures, and

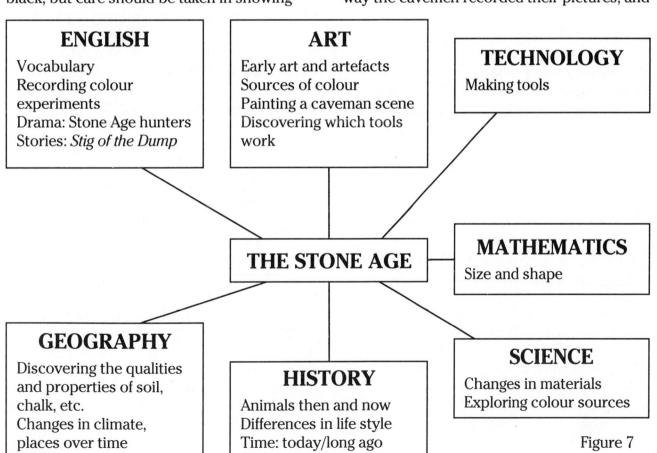

ENGLISH
Vocabulary
Recording colour experiments
Drama: Stone Age hunters
Stories: *Stig of the Dump*

ART
Early art and artefacts
Sources of colour
Painting a caveman scene
Discovering which tools work

TECHNOLOGY
Making tools

THE STONE AGE

MATHEMATICS
Size and shape

GEOGRAPHY
Discovering the qualities and properties of soil, chalk, etc.
Changes in climate, places over time

HISTORY
Animals then and now
Differences in life style
Time: today/long ago

SCIENCE
Changes in materials
Exploring colour sources

Figure 7

the advances that have been made in relatively recent times with the invention of the camera. Ask the children:

• How do we record our pets and events in our lives?
• What pictures do they think a caveman would have taken, if he had had a camera?

Attention could be drawn to the many uses of photography today – recording events, illustrating stories and advertising products. Ask the children what was it like before the camera was invented and became popular. Point out that it was only in their great-grandmother's time that it became widely used, only in their grandmother's time that television arrived and only in their mother's time that video became widespread.

Art: AT1, AT2; History: AT1, AT3; Geography: AT1, AT3, AT4; Science: AT1, AT2

Art and the past (the recent past)

Photography and advertising

Photography can be a powerful means of communication as is apparent in the many media images projected at society. Children are subject to these pressures, and they can be made aware of advertising by drawing their attention to the packaging of toys. Ask them if they have ever felt disappointed when a toy's packaging has turned out to be more impressive than the actual toy inside.

Developing children's critical awareness of images

In order to develop young children's critical awareness of the images portrayed through the media, ask them to bring in some toys and their packaging. Encourage the children to compare and contrast the pictures on the packaging with the real product. The children could be asked to discuss what they like and dislike about the products. Ask them:

• Why do some toys not stand up or move about in the way depicted on the packet?
• Do they think it right that the packets can be so misleading?
• Should playthings be targeted at both boys and girls?

Art: AT1, AT2; Science: AT1, AT2; Technology: AT1, AT2, AT3, AT4; History: AT1, AT2, AT3

Packaging a toy

What you need

Envelopes, scissors, paper, pencils, felt-tipped pens.

What to do

Ask the children to make a drawing of a toy they would like to buy, and cut it out. Get them to make a cover design on the front of the envelope, and place the drawing of the toy inside it. Encourage the children to discuss and display their toys and their packaging.

If feasible, a visit to the Robert Opie Collection of Packaging and Advertising in Gloucester would enable children to gain a historical perspective.

Art: AT1, AT2; Technology: AT2, AT3; Mathematics: AT1; English: AT1, AT2, AT3

Portrait photography

A technique often used to support media images is photography. Young children can learn a little of the history, science and uses of this medium, both by operating a simple camera and by scanning the results, and by experiencing photography as it was in their great-grandparents' day.

An important role of photography is to record what people look like. The technology that makes this possible evolved during the first part of the nineteenth century. Before that time, only the rich could afford to have their portraits painted. Photography has made portraiture available to many more people, and has given us vivid records of recent history, such as the earliest family portraits from Victorian times or the snaps of the flappers of the 1920s, cavorting at the seaside.

Most children will have photographs of themselves at home; they could be asked to bring one into school. These could be pictures of themselves when they were babies. The photographs could be displayed beside a recent school photograph of the same children. The pictures could be discussed and any changes in appearance noted. This could lead to a discussion about the changes that take place as we go through life, leading to an imaginary self-portrait of themselves as old people. Point out that the camera is a useful tool for recording these changes.

As a progression, the children could be asked to bring in photographs of their parents and grandparents to display beside a selection of Victorian photographs. The children could be encouraged to discuss the difference in dress style, while noticing that people's faces look much the same. To reinforce the concept of 'a long time ago', look at postcards of Egyptian and Roman portraits, and compare them with the modern and Victorian photographs.

To reinforce understanding of distance, to give practice in scanning pictures and to familiarise the children with the use of a simple camera, each child could take two photographs of their friend.

What you need

A simple camera loaded with film, examples of portrait photography.

What to do

Preferably on a clear sunny day, take the children out to the playground and ask them to think about the photographs they are going to take of their friends. One photograph should be a close-up, and the other a distance shot.

When the photographs have been developed, ask the children to look closely at them:
• Are there things in the photographs that are a surprise?

• Which photograph looks most like your friend?
• If you came from a far away country, what could you see in the photographs that would tell you what our life was like?

Portrait photographs from magazines and books could be shown to the children, for example, the work of Cecil Beaton, or the pictures of children taken by Bill Brandt in the 1940s. Discuss and compare these examples with photographs from advertisements.
Art: AT1, AT2; History: AT1, AT2, AT3; English: AT2; Science: AT2; Technology: AT4

Take a Victorian photograph

This project could be used as a follow-up to the previous activity. The people in early photographs often look very stiff and serious. This is because it took a long time to take the portraits, and often the sitters had to hold

their positions, unmoving, for between two to five minutes, depending on the light. Sometimes, heads were held still with clamps. In comparison, modern cameras take photographs very quickly.

What you need

Victorian-style clothes (long skirts and straw hats for the girls, stiff collars made from white manila for the boys), small table, tablecloth, potted plants, upright chairs, a camera, a tripod.

What to do

Ask a group of children to dress up in Victorian-style clothes and explain that they are going to pretend to be photographed. Tell them that this means that they will have to sit still, without moving, for about two minutes.

Arrange a formal setting with potted plants, a little cloth-covered table and a group of chairs for the children to sit on. Set up the camera on a tripod in front of the group, and take photographs at the beginning and end of the sitting. When the photographs have been developed, children compare them to see just how much movement, both voluntary and involuntary, has taken place during this time.
Art: AT1, AT2; History: AT1; Science: AT1

Make a family tree

To follow up the photography activity, and to support a project on their families, the children could make their own family trees. The information needs to be clearly written, and could be made to look attractive by using coloured pencils to tint the branches of the tree. Explain to the children that coloured pencils produce a pale tone and would not dominate the written information as would felt-tipped pens. The children could draw from family photographs, and paste their drawings into position on the tree.
Art: AT1, AT2,; History: AT1, AT3; English: AT1, AT2, AT3; Mathematics: AT1

Light-sensitive materials

In this activity children can learn about the ways in which light can change the colour of some objects. For example, if a polished silver spoon is left in a bright light, it tarnishes after a few days. This is close to what happens to black and white photographic paper when it is exposed to light. This can be demonstrated to the children by means of photograms. This is a method of making photographic pictures of objects without using a camera.

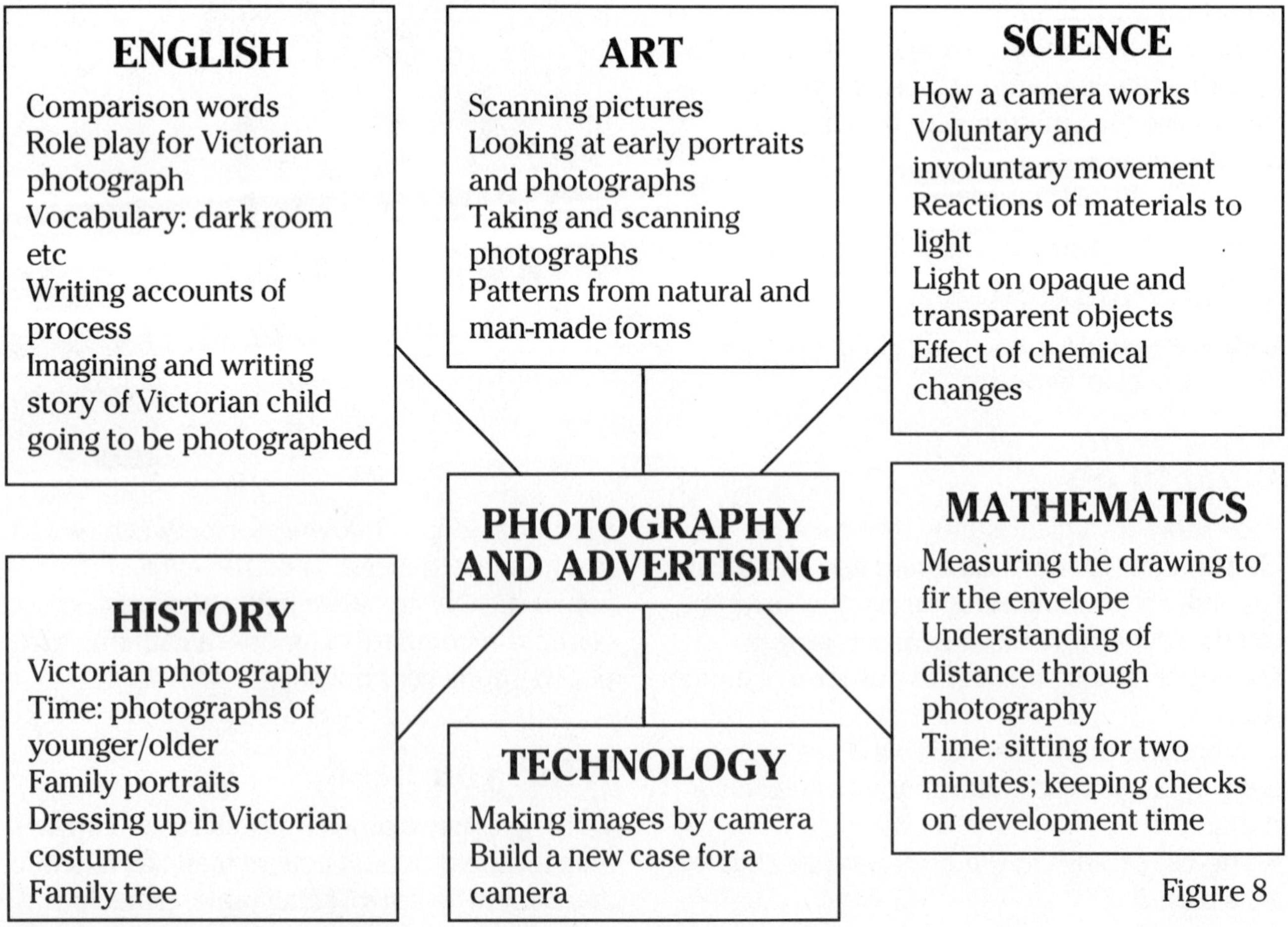

ENGLISH

Comparison words
Role play for Victorian photograph
Vocabulary: dark room etc
Writing accounts of process
Imagining and writing story of Victorian child going to be photographed

ART

Scanning pictures
Looking at early portraits and photographs
Taking and scanning photographs
Patterns from natural and man-made forms

SCIENCE

How a camera works
Voluntary and involuntary movement
Reactions of materials to light
Light on opaque and transparent objects
Effect of chemical changes

PHOTOGRAPHY AND ADVERTISING

MATHEMATICS

Measuring the drawing to fir the envelope
Understanding of distance through photography
Time: sitting for two minutes; keeping checks on development time

HISTORY

Victorian photography
Time: photographs of younger/older
Family portraits
Dressing up in Victorian costume
Family tree

TECHNOLOGY

Making images by camera
Build a new case for a camera

Figure 8

Photograms were made by children in a reception class, with excellent results. Several attempts were made to find the correct length of time to expose the photographic paper to the light from the torch. Then the teacher put the paper through the chemicals, while the children sat in a circle and watched. They were not allowed near the chemicals. The class found that the correct exposure time was one minute; the children counted out the 60 seconds. After developing several photograms, all the children knew that 60 seconds made one minute, and could count up to 60. Photograms could be part of a science project on changes that take place in materials.

What you need

Black and white photographic paper (do not open the paper container except in the dark, or under safe-light conditions), chemicals for processing the photographic paper (developer and fixative which can be purchased from science educational suppliers and photographic companies such as Kodak and Ilford), dishes to hold the chemicals, cold water, a measuring jug, two torches (one with the face covered with red Cellophane to make a safe-light, the other with an ordinary light), a darkroom (this could be adapted from a cloakroom or backstage in a hall, which can easily be blacked out), a collection of objects (such as pieces of lace, a glass, leaves, paper shapes, tracing paper, scissors, and pressed flowers) food dyes, felt-tipped pens.

What to do

Take the objects into a darkened room and place them on top of a piece of the photographic paper. Shine some light on to the paper for a short time, using the torch with the ordinary bulb. Remove the objects from the paper, and process it in the appropriate chemicals. (The proportions of the chemicals will vary according to the make, and will be clearly indicated on the container.)

The children will be surprised to see that the shape or pattern of the object appears on the paper, but in negative form. Some objects, such as those made of glass, will let the light through, and the transparency will create new forms and shadows within it. With opaque objects, only the shape appears in white on a black ground. Attractive shapes and patterns can be made, and the white areas can be coloured afterwards, using watered-down food dyes and felt-tipped pens.

The cross-curricular applications for this series of activities are given in Figure 8. **Art: AT1; Science: AT6**

Pattern

The desire to repeat shapes and make patterns comes naturally to the young child, as anyone who has seen small children draw will know. The radials that emerge from the circular shapes made by children in their early scribbles are full of rhythm. For example, legs, wheels and hair often turn into a rhythmic repetition that is enjoyed for its own sake, rather than for its pictorial value.

As children progress towards the use of symbolic representation in their art work, they become deeply involved in depicting details accurately. In *Creative and Mental Growth*, Lowenfeld and Brittain show drawings by children where the right number of buttons on the clothes are so important that they have overlapped the drawn boundaries of the figure. This interest in detail suggests that most children understand pattern-making, once the element of repetition is clear to them, as it is essentially concerned with small shapes.

Basic pattern is the repetition of shape to make decoration on paper, cloth, stone or any suitable surface, so that it becomes pleasing to the eye. The desire to decorate both functional objects and ourselves, in order to create an effect that is aesthetically pleasing, is reflected in some of the earliest artefacts produced by the human race.

Some 10,000 years ago, in the Magdalenian culture, spirals were used to decorate shaped pieces of bone in a way that would be both acceptable and recognisable to us today. In the Danube basin, pottery was decorated with sweeping curves and ribbons in the third millennium BC. The use of pattern is universal, and often both the patterns and the objects that are decorated take similar forms, familiar to us today, wherever or whenever they were made. This is a useful point to make when promoting equal opportunities within the classroom. To give an example, the curves decorating a Megalithic pot from the Danube are similar to those on a Chinese Neolithic pot, and to the Art Nouveau glass of Tiffany, the psychedelia of the 1960s or the shapes used by Aboriginal artists such as Michael Jackson Tjakamarra today.

The basis of pattern is repetition. This involves mathematics and the organisation of shape, even in the simplest exercise. The process of organising pattern can become more and more elaborate, involving complex layers of form and line, with depth suggested through colour. It might be interesting for the children to examine and talk about the complexity of more advanced designs, such as that on an Indian carved box, available in most stores, or on replica Kurdistan rugs, again available in local markets at minimal cost.

With Key Stage 1 children, the practical work should start at the most basic level, and progress through several stages to a more complex form, such as a reverse repeat pattern. In this way the children can understand the building blocks of pattern and design, begin to predict results and offer suggestions for the development of their work. They will thus be learning the formal elements of this area of art.

Pattern from natural form

This is a simple form of pattern-making that offers a good introduction to the subject for any age group. Children enjoy the process and it easily evolves from random marks into a simple repeat pattern.

What you need

A collection of fruit and vegetables, a knife, squares of sponge or a pad of cloth, paint, dishes, A4 newsprint and sugar paper, old newspapers.

What to do

Let the children examine and talk about the vegetables and fruit, comparing their colours, textures and shapes. Slice some of the fruit and vegetables in half, cutting some in different directions, to show the change in pattern. (A tomato, an apple or a Brussels

sprout reveal completely different patterns depending on whether they are cut open lengthwise or across.)

Place the sponges or cloth pads in dishes and soak them thoroughly with paint. Let the children take turns to press a piece of cut fruit or vegetable on to a pad, twist it and blot it on a piece of newspaper, before printing on to a piece of newsprint or sugar paper. Explain to the children that they must put the fruit or vegetable back on to the paint pad after every print, otherwise the subsequent images will be pallid and incomplete.

After the children have familiarised themselves with the process by making random prints, ask them to print in rows, trying to get an even spacing. Some Reception children will find this quite difficult, and this may be sufficient for the first session of pattern-making at this age.

If the children can space and order the shapes, ask them to choose two shapes and print them alternately, using a different colour for each. After this has been successfully completed, ask the children to print the shapes again, but this time to reverse every third shape. This is a useful mathematical exercise; let the children continue until the page is full.

Follow-up

The papers can be used to make decorative book covers for children's topic books.
Art: AT1, AT2; Science: AT2; Mathematics: AT4

Junk patterns

This is a progression from the previous activity, and involves utilising and making patterns from scrap objects. These can be printed overlapping, and joined together to make stripes and pictures. This activity requires both thought and imagination.

What you need

A collection of scrap objects that are easily manipulated, either with a pattern on them or of a clear shape (for example, the collection could include old jar lids of varying sizes to provide a range of open circles, corks for solid circles and cotton reels for patterned circles; scraps of card can be printed sideways on to make lines; corrugated card can be printed in blocks, or rolled up and printed end on, which gives a rippled circle), paint-impregnated sponges or cloth pads (see previous activity), dishes, old newspapers, newsprint or sugar paper, pencils, ruler, examples of repeat patterns.

What to do

Ask the children to try stamp printing the various objects, and then tell them to arrange the prints to make a flower or a striped pattern. Let them try out a print on scrap paper, and experiment with ways of arranging the pattern. Ask them:
• Is the design going to cover the paper, or is it going to alternate with a spot or a circle?
• Are they going to print their pattern so that every other space is left empty, like a draughtboard?

Show them some examples of flat pattern. Good quality wrapping paper is useful, and there are many books on design, such as Owen Jones's *Grammar of Ornament* or *The Justema Book of Pattern*.
Art: AT1, AT2; Mathematics: AT4

A card block

As a final activity in exploring flat pattern, Y2 children can construct a card block. This takes pattern-making further, as it requires preplanning and involves the children working with reverse images (the print is the reverse of the block). With a card print, it is also possible to produce reverse repeat patterns, and half-drop patterns, once the children have understood the reverse repeats. This gives scope for the development of an original, simple image into something far more complex.

The construction of the card block is based on the principle that the raised areas can be inked up to make a print. The block comprises:
• a background (a piece of firm card);
• the raised areas (pieces of card cut to make a design, which are then stuck to the background block).

What you need

Firm card, pencils, scissors, adhesive, paint, paper.

What to do

Ask the children to cut out a square from card, then to make some slightly smaller designs with pencil on another piece of card. Ask them to cut out the designs and stick them carefully on to the card squares.

When the children make their card blocks, remind them that if the shapes forming their pattern are too far apart, the background will print. If they are too close together, the spaces between shapes will fill with ink, and the design will blur. A simple, bold design is best, with about 0.5cm between shapes.

The design of the card block could be based on a project that the class was involved in, or it could be used to reinforce work in mathematics using geometric shapes.

The cross-curricular applications of these activities on pattern are shown in Figure 9.

Conclusion

Young children's interest can be aroused and sustained by a mixture of theoretical and practical knowledge. Cross-curricular projects present both similarities and differences within topics and enable the children to combine both academic and practical aspects of education.

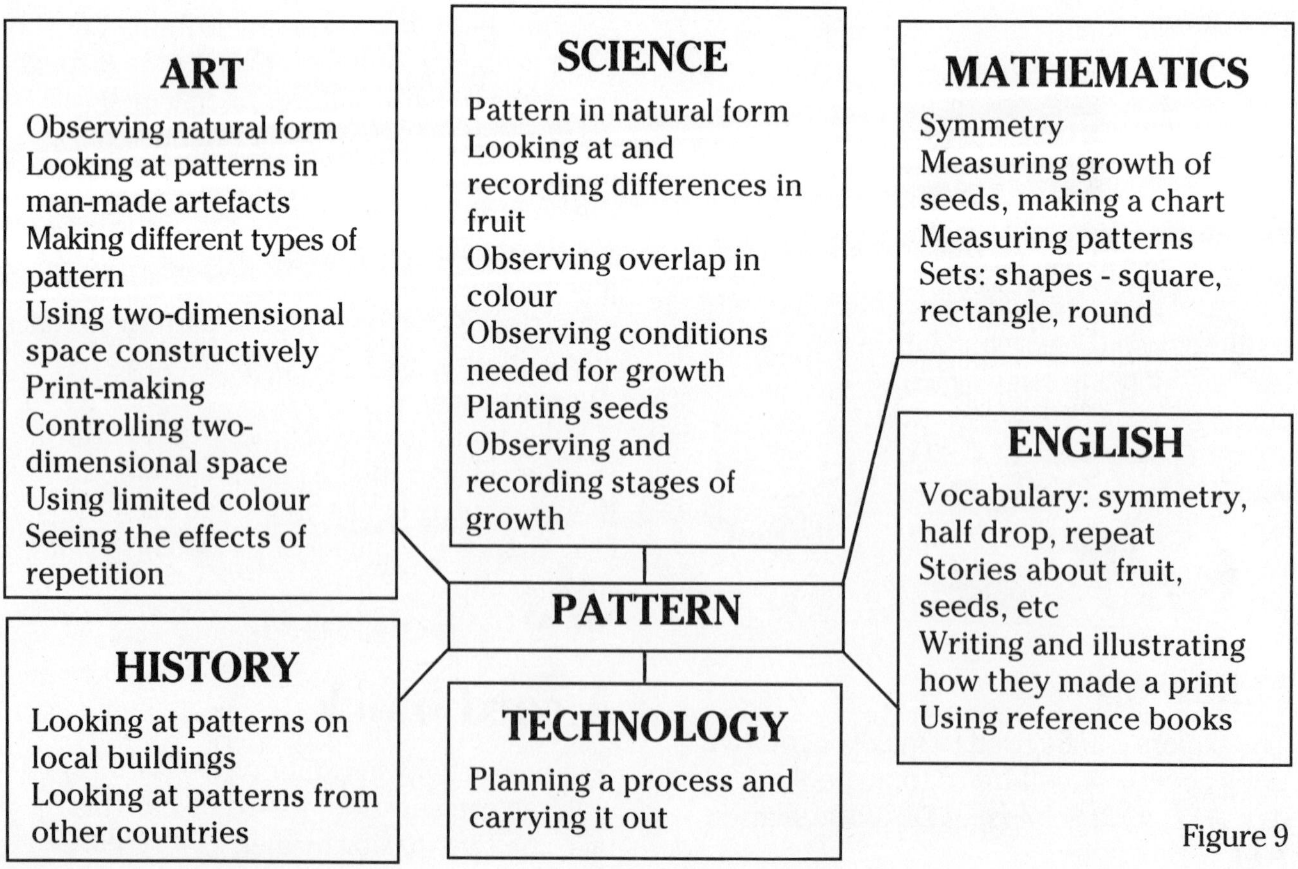

ART
Observing natural form
Looking at patterns in man-made artefacts
Making different types of pattern
Using two-dimensional space constructively
Print-making
Controlling two-dimensional space
Using limited colour
Seeing the effects of repetition

HISTORY
Looking at patterns on local buildings
Looking at patterns from other countries

SCIENCE
Pattern in natural form
Looking at and recording differences in fruit
Observing overlap in colour
Observing conditions needed for growth
Planting seeds
Observing and recording stages of growth

PATTERN

TECHNOLOGY
Planning a process and carrying it out

MATHEMATICS
Symmetry
Measuring growth of seeds, making a chart
Measuring patterns
Sets: shapes - square, rectangle, round

ENGLISH
Vocabulary: symmetry, half drop, repeat
Stories about fruit, seeds, etc
Writing and illustrating how they made a print
Using reference books

Figure 9

Chapter 5
Using two-dimensional materials (Key Stage 2)

As the children reach Y3, they begin to understand and make connections between their own work and that of their peers, as well as wanting to draw with greater realism. At this stage in the development of their visual literacy, the role of the teacher is of particular importance, as children often suffer a loss of confidence in their own ability in art. The teacher's interest and suggestions can prevent this happening, even though she may not be an art specialist. The role of the teacher is to develop in the children an experimental and adventurous approach to art, to show them the ways in which other artists have solved similar problems and to help them realise that there are no 'right' or 'wrong' images in art.

If the children are offered stimulating and progressive programmes of work, and encouraged to enlarge their knowledge of the elements of art through sketching and drawing, they should be confident and happy in their work, and continue to draw, paint and model unselfconsciously.

At Key Stage 2, children make use of the same tools and materials as those at Key Stage 1, developing their skills, and expressing a wider range of ideas and emotions. These basic materials can be supplemented by more advanced methods of print-making and modelling. Many of the activities suggested in Key Stage 1 can be adapted for use at Key Stage 2 (for example, the puppets in Chapter 4, the use of drawing tools for a stormy day in Chapter 1, page 14 and the clay tiles in Chapter 2, page 28).

In this chapter we suggest some ways of developing previous ideas to fit the children's capabilities, and introduce more techniques, suitable for Y3 to Y6. If any of the activities or projects are more suited to Y5 and Y6 only, this is indicated in the text.

Screen printing

Save the whale

This project is suitable for Y4, Y5 and Y6. At this age, children begin to become aware of issues beyond their immediate environment, and are often deeply concerned about partially understood images and messages received from the television, or overheard from adult conversation. Teachers can both clarify the issues and explain what action can be taken and what is being done to remedy the situation, by setting projects that deal with issues like pollution, conserving resources, famine or endangered species.

As part of a science project on the variety of life, the children could produce posters, etc, for a 'Save the whale' campaign. This would increase their knowledge of the effects of human activity on the natural world, and encourage them to care for other forms of life. It should also help their geographical knowledge as they map the path of the whales around the world, as well as helping them to realise the need for careful thought and preparation when designing and making an article for a particular purpose, such as a poster or a badge.

Before the work begins, collect a selection of 'Save the whale' T-shirts, badges and posters. These are available from Greenpeace or Friends of the Earth (see Resources, page 192). Ask the children to arrange these for a display, and discuss their reactions. Ask them:
• Do they think they are effective?
• Would they make them look at the message and feel any sympathy for the whales?

Find out what the children already know about whales, and read some myths and stories about them, such as Jonah and the Whale or a selected passage from *Moby Dick* by Herman Melville. If possible, play a recording of the whale's song. (They could later be allowed to compose their own whale song.)

This could be accompanied by a visit to a museum of natural history to look at whales and their skeletons. The children could draw and record their observations in their sketch-books for reference back at school.

Tell the children that they are going to start their own 'Save the whale' campaign and that they need to devise publicity material that will draw people's attention to the whales. Explain why we should take care of the whales. Talk about their unique qualities, as well as their size. The children will be fascinated by facts such as the female killer whale living for up to a hundred years, and the blue whale being able to make a sound louder than a jet plane.

Discuss the ways in which the campaign could be mounted. The children could investigate goods that are made from the whales, or learn about the harmful pollutants that are present in the sea.

The children could be encouraged to design posters and badges, print T-shirts and produce information leaflets. If the children have seen model whales or whale skeletons in a museum, let them use their sketches as the basis for a poster picture. If not, provide them with plenty of reference books. Before they begin, remind them that posters need to put across their message simply, using a clear picture and few words, carefully placed.

What you need

Sketch-books or A4 paper for preliminary planning, pencils (HB to 4B), rubbers, a selection of lettering samples or templates, tracing paper, reference books, soft and hard brushes, paints and painting equipment, A2 brushwork paper in assorted colours, newsprint, silk screens (see Chapter 9, page 148), cloths, squeegees, water-based printing ink, plastic-covered print table, pins, card, newspaper, plain T-shirts, stencil brushes, fabric crayons, masking tape, scissors, computer with an art package and a publishing package, safety pins.

What to do

Ask the children to use their sketch-books or the reference books to help them make small drawings to use for the poster. Talk to them about the design or shape of the picture.

Explain how it ought to fit comfortably with the lettering, so they need to think about the position of the lettering in relation to the picture, and whether it conveys a clear message. Ask them:

• Are they going to have one whale or a school, or maybe a whale family?
• Can they think of any ways of making people realise that whales are not fish, but warm-blooded mammals?

Ask the children to try out several ideas in their sketches, and allow them to work together in groups. Encourage them to discuss their work with each other, and suggest that the best design should be carried out by the group, organised so that each child has a defined task to carry out.

Discuss the colours with the groups, and ask them what colour should dominate. As the whale lives in the sea, should the main colour be blue? Or should it be green, as this is thought of as a conservation colour? Or should it be red, because that stands out?

Ask them to try out several different colour schemes of their favourite sketch, and indicate where the lettering is going to go. Suggest that it would be less complicated to print using one colour on to a coloured background paper.

Printing the poster

The children will need a demonstration of the printing process, so that they see how important it is for the stencil to be made from clear, simple shapes. Choose another endangered animal, such as the anteater, for your demonstration print. Show them the whole process, through to the cleaning stage, and tell them to keep detailed notes and diagrams of the method. Let them try a 'pull' (a test print) of the anteater before the design is removed, to practise using the squeegee.

Point out that screen printing is an industrial technique, although industrial printing machines are computerised. Explain some of the jobs that can be found in screen printers. For example, as well as the printers, there are designers, photographic printers and developers, tracers, dye mixers, etc. Ask the children to organise themselves into teams, as they would in a printing firm, with two printers, a cleaner and a stencil cutter. Explain that two printers are needed, one to hold the screen steady and one to pull the squeegee across. Encourage the class to work out a rota, so that each group makes one test print, and then four good prints, trying out the various tasks in turn.

Explain that the groups' first task is to make stencils for the whale and the lettering. The children can make their stencils out of newsprint. The whale can be drawn directly on to the newsprint and the lettering can be traced from newspaper headlines and then cut out.

Ask the children to place the stencils in position on a sheet of practice paper on the print table. Help them to place the screen carefully on top of the stencils, pour the ink in at one end, and pull the squeegee across from the other. The stencils should adhere to the screen, which can then be used to print the posters. Suggest that each group uses either different coloured inks or different coloured paper to print on. Lay the posters out before putting them to dry, and discuss the different effects.

Point out the fact that in screen printing, unlike linocut or monoprint, the image is not reversed. Show examples of the different uses for screen printing, such as a scarf, a plate or a picture. Images such as Roy Lichtenstein's *Whaam!* (1962) and Andy Warhol's *Liz Taylor* (1964) or *Elvis Presley* (1964), are good examples of the use of screen-printing techniques. Tell them that many modern notices and posters are screen printed.

Other campaign material

If the designs are the correct scale, the same screen could be used to print on the T-shirts. The T-shirt needs to be stretched out flat and pinned to the plastic on the print table, but the method of printing is the same. Alternatively, the children could cut a stencil out of card, and stencil the design on to the fabric, using transfer printing inks and stencil brushes, or draw directly on to the material with fabric crayons, which are fixed by ironing.

As part of their campaign to raise the school's environmental awareness, the children could make badges, using such programs as *Paint Spa*, *Draw Mouse* or *Paint Pot* on the computer, and cutting out the printed motif, sticking it to card and fastening the card to a safety-pin with masking tape. A more interesting activity would be for the children to produce a news-sheet about their campaign, using a publishing package on the computer, such as *Caxton*. The leaflet could be distributed and possibly sold to parents and governors, or used in fund-raising at the school fete.

Art: AT1, AT2; Science: AT2; Geography: AT2; Technology: AT1, AT2, AT3, AT4; Mathematics: AT1; English: AT4, AT5

Stencils

Birthday card project

Screen printing can be used to produce attractive cards in combination with the stencil technique, and lovely colour effects can be obtained by printing one colour on top of another. The children could make cards based on numbers or letters.

This project involves carrying out research to find out how many parents and pupils would buy birthday cards if they were sold at a school fair or local shop. The children would have to cost the cards, and decide whether selling them would be a viable proposition.

Research could be carried out among the children's families; they could be asked what their favourite subject matter was, and what price they thought it reasonable to pay. This information could be noted, and later recorded in graph form; it could be used as a basis for the design content and method of making cards.

A collection of commercially made cards could also be made and displayed in the classroom.

What you need

Examples of commercially produced greetings cards, magazines and newspapers, examples of medieval Books of Hours, scissors, pencil, card, felt-tipped pens, black drawing pen, rulers, selection of envelopes, lettering paper (for envelopes), scrap paper, sketch-books, photocopier, cartridge paper, calculator, Pritt sticks.

What to do

As an introduction to this activity, show the children some examples of cards, the designs of which are based on numbers, and also some examples of designs that are based on letters. These could include examples of figurative work, such as Richard Doyle's decorative letters, used in *Punch* in the 1830s. Compare these with examples of styles of lettering found in today's magazines.

Medieval Books of Hours are another kind of reference that could be used. The *Très Riches Heures du Duc de Berry* (1340-1460) and *Les Grandes Heures de Rohan* contain both figurative and patterned illuminated capitals. The Rohan master painted his book for John the Good, King of France, (1319-1364). The effects these medieval painters achieved were beautiful, with jewel-like colours and complex patterns. Tell the children that in those days often even the kings and queens could not read, so the Books of Hours were made to give them plenty to look at on the cold and draughty winter evenings passed in their smoky castles.

Both numbers and letters could be treated similarly by the children. Tell the children to think of someone for whom they would like to design a card, and explain that they are going to base their design on either the age or the initial of that person. Suggest that the simplest way to do this would be to make a template of the letter or number. Ask them what sort of letter or number they are going to use. Suggest that they look at newspaper headlines, and in books, to find out the different typefaces that are available. Show them how to draw the outline of the letter or number on to card and cut it out to make the template.

When they have made their templates, ask the children to think about the size of envelope that will be needed. Show them a variety of envelopes and allow them to unfold a few to see how they have been made. Help them to cut out their own flat shapes for envelopes and fold them and stick them together, using Pritt Sticks.

Ask the children to make some rough designs for their cards in their sketch-books, using the templates they have made as a basis. Show them how the template can be moved round and overlapped to form a design. Alternatively, it could be used just once and the shape decorated with tiny figures, animals or plants. When the children are happy with their designs, let them trace them in black pen and photocopy them, colouring in some of the shapes using the felt-tipped pens.

The finished work should be mounted on to white or coloured card that is twice the width of the design, including any border. Mark the centre of the card in pencil, and then run the corner of a ruler along the line, on the inside of the card. This should not cut through the card, but leave a shallow groove to make it easier to fold.

Before the cards are put in their envelopes, the children can arrange a display, grouping the cards according to subject matter, and talking about the designs. Ask them:
• What do you think these cards would cost to make?
• Do you think we would make a profit if we sold them?

Make a costing sheet, with a list of the various materials used, and ask the children to fill it in and calculate the prices; let them use a calculator if necessary. The time it took to make the cards and the cost of labour should be included on the sheet. Children are usually very surprised to find that their own products would cost a large proportion of their weekly pocket-money.

The children now have to decide how much they are going to charge for their cards, and which is the easiest way to produce them. For example, one school has a selection printed annually, and sells them through a nearby bookshop; the money goes into the school funds.

Art: AT1, AT2; English: AT1, AT2, AT3, AT4, AT5; Mathematics: AT1, AT2, AT5; History: AT3

Expressing movement

To introduce children to the idea of depicting movement, show them the work of artists who have used movement and circles as a basis for their paintings. These could include examples of work by Robert Tyro, who uses circles in his *Homage to Bleriot* (1914) to show the movement of propellers and distant aeroplanes behind a dancing array of brightly coloured circular shapes. Another suitable artist would be Giacomo Balla, whose *Young Girl Running along a Balcony* (1912) is influenced by time-lapse photography, and shows another way of dealing with movement by the repetition of shapes.

These artists belonged to the Italian Futurist movement and, according to the *Futurist Manifesto* (1909), were interested in 'the dynamism of modern life'. Other artists who dealt with mechanical themes were Fernand Leger (1881-1955) and Jean Metzinger (1883-1956).

The following series of activities all use the theme of bicycles to look at different ways of expressing movement.

A bicycle project

Children at Key Stage 2 often enjoy looking at, understanding and drawing functional objects that they use themselves, such as skateboards, roller-skates and bicycles.

In this project, the children examine the construction of a familiar mechanism, use it as a basis for design, and discover that shapes drawn from original source material can be made into paintings that suggest movement. The children could start with a thorough investigation of the bicycle, drawing it from various angles, using thin felt-tipped pens. Encourage them to look in particular at the proportions and the basic structure of the frame, wheels, saddle and handlebars. It would be useful to have an old bicycle that could be taken apart, so that the children could use labelled drawings to record in their sketch-books the way the parts fit together. They could also make prints and rubbings of the tyre patterns, and draw the details of the links on the chain. This would provide a good basis for pattern-making.

Once this preliminary investigation has taken place, the children could choose a shape that they found interesting, and translate it into a repeat pattern or a model made from Plasticine and wire. This activity suggests an abstract design to be undertaken by Y5 and Y6 children. The design could be based on bicycle wheels, using the spaces between the spokes, as well as the wheel shapes, and positioning the shapes on the page to create a feeling of movement.

What you need

Photographs and diagrams of bicycles, an old bicycle, coloured paper, stencil brushes, paints, rulers, soft and hard brushes, scissors or craft knives, thin card, pencils, thick and thin felt-tipped pens.

What to do

Discuss with the children, any paintings they have seen which suggest movement. Point out how they can use the sections, segments and shapes of the wheel to try to make their own picture move in the same way. Ask them:
• What shapes are there in the wheel, apart from the circle?
• Are there any triangles?
• What happens to them when the wheel moves?

The children could attach triangles of coloured paper to the spokes of the bicycle, and revolve the wheel at different speeds to observe what happens to both the colours and the shapes. Ask the children:
• How could they paint this effect?
• How have the artists done it in the pictures they looked at?

Ask the children first to design a pattern, concentrating on simple bold shapes that can be overlapped. Let the children cut templates of the main shapes made by the spokes and stencil colours round the shapes, later adding lines using paint, felt-tipped pens and a ruler. Suggest they may like to draw a bicycle, a pair of handlebars or a saddle in part of the picture; they may like to include feet on the pedals.

The children could then write an account of an imaginary journey to a distant place, draw a map of their favourite local cycle routes or design a cycling outfit the colours of which would help cyclists to ride in safety. There would be an opportunity here to discuss safety on the roads, and the advantages of using cycle lanes in the locality. This could lead to further map-making.

The children could be shown pictures of the uses made of bicycles in other parts of the world, such as the elaborately decorated rickshaws of Java, or the bicycle taxis of Peru, with their huge grocer's-style metal container on the front for the passenger.

Follow-up

Ask the children to design and make their own version of a foot-powered vehicle, using small boxes, axles, cotton reels and an elastic band.
Art: AT1, AT2; Technology: AT2; Geography: AT1

A lino print design

This activity can be undertaken with Y3 and Y4 children.

Ask the children if they like cycling, or ever watch the *Tour de France* on television. There is a good opportunity to reinforce safety aspects here.

What you need

An old bicycle, Blu-Tack, small brushes, black paint or Indian ink, newsprint, PVA adhesive, scissors, paints, lino and lino equipment (see Chapter 9, page 147), cloths, cardboard, string, viewfinders cut to different geometric shapes.

What to do

Turn the bicycle upside-down, so that it stands supported by the handlebars and saddle. Attach the viewfinders to different parts of the bicycle frame with Blu-Tack, ensuring that interesting sections of the bicycle can be seen through them.

Ask the children to draw the shapes they can see in their sketch-books.

These shapes could be turned into either a card block (see Chapter 4, page 65) or made into a lino print (see Chapter 9, page 147). Encourage the children to arrange the prints in a way that suggests movement.
Art: AT1, AT2; Technology: AT2

Paint a bicycle race

This activity could be a development from either of the two previous activities. It is a group activity, again emphasising movement.

What you need

An old bicycle, a video or photographs showing moving objects, mural paper, paints, Blu-Tack, sponges, scissors, paper, charcoal, PVA adhesive.

What to do

Discuss the different ways in which artists portray movement and speed. Look again at the bicycle wheels, and, if possible, look at a video or photographs that show the blurring effect of movement on objects. Ask the children to use charcoal to draw a series of cyclists, and to paint and cut them out. These can be attached to the mural paper with Blu-Tack, possibly overlapping.

Ask the children how the picture can be made to look at though it is moving. Suggest that the background would be blurred. Let them detach the figures from the mural then, using the sponges dipped in diluted paint, try to suggest movement in the background by extending the colours used on the figures, but in a paler version. When the paper is dry, let them stick the figures back in place, then sponge some of the colour from the figures on to the background to enhance the effect of movement.

Art: AT1, AT2; Technology: AT2; Science: AT3

The human form

Having explored movement and machinery, the following project encourages the children to explore ways of depicting the human form and introduces techniques of portraiture. It could be part of a history project, or a science project on 'Ourselves', lasting over several sessions. It introduces positive aspects of equal opportunities and can be taught to the whole class, with groups working on different aspects of the theme.

Preliminary studies

The children need to acquaint themselves with variations in skin tone, with the details of facial features, and with the proportions of the head and shoulders, before they attempt to paint a portrait. As a simple introduction, ask the children to try to colour-match the skin on their hands. Point out that no one is only one colour, and that our skin tones change according to the light, the veins under the skin and the thickness of the skin. Most hands have at least six colour tones. Make sure that the children are aware of the following points.
• The skin stretches and changes colour as we clench our fists.
• The colour on the palm of the hand is different to the skin on the back of the hand.
• The colour at the base of the thumb is usually darker, as it covers many small veins.
• Often the skin at the base of the nails is a different colour.
• The colour also varies in the lines of the hand.

When they have finished this exercise, ask the children to draw an eye from memory. Many people draw eyes like buttons, flat circular shapes floating in a sea of white. Eyes are not like this, unless the person is a victim of terror or strangulation! Usually it is only possible to see the lower circle of the iris, as the eyelid overlaps the upper part of the eye.

Accept the children's first attempts at drawing an eye, and then ask them to draw their own eyes while looking into a mirror,

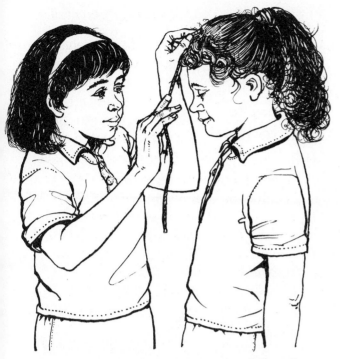

and see how correct their original drawing was. Make sure that they observe with care. Help them to be aware of details, such as the tear duct in the corner of the eye. This observation encourages self-confidence in children's drawing, and goes some way towards eliminating the copying of stereotyped facial features derived from cartoons and toys.

After drawing the eye, ask the children to look in the mirror again, and draw their mouths. Show them good examples of drawings of mouths, such as those by Hans Holbein. Explain that the most important line to draw in the mouth is the line made by the two lips coming together. This is the darkest and strongest line. Holbein draws this line clearly, and suggests the shape of the upper and lower lips. Look, for example, at his drawings of Sir Thomas Moore or Queen Jane Seymour, both in the Royal Collection at Windsor Castle. Tell the children that the outer line of the lips is only pronounced when the subject is wearing lipstick, so they should try to avoid this effect in their drawings.

The children should also make a close study of their noses in the same way. These are more difficult to draw, as they are a less defined form, but the children should try to convey the curling flaps of the nostrils in their own way.

Art: AT1, AT2; Science: AT1; History: AT2

Measuring proportions

Using string, the children can measure the proportions of their heads and compare the distance from the top of the head to the eyebrows with the distance from the eyebrows to the chin. Show them how to mark the string with chalk, and lay it along a ruler to measure the sizes. Ask them to use the same method to compare:
• the size of the ears to the length of the nose;
• the width at the base of the nostrils to the width of the mouth;
• the width of the face from the tops of the ears to the length from crown to chin.

The proportions of the body could be measured in the same way. Compare, for example, the length from shoulder to elbow with the length from the shoulder to waist.

Children have a much bigger head-to-body size than adults (Figure 1), and this could be demonstrated if comparisons were made with a participating adult. At this point, it may be interesting to the show the children examples of paintings by early Renaissance artists, such as Coppo di Marcovaldo. His *Madonna*, painted in 1261, clearly shows the infant Jesus as a miniature adult, with adult proportions.

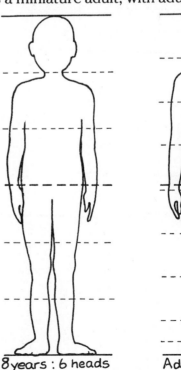
8 years : 6 heads

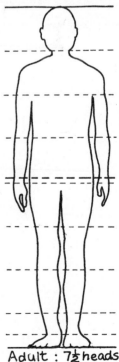
Adult : 7½ heads

Figure 1

The effect is odd to modern eyes. Another painting that shows the same oblivious approach to the differences between adult and child proportions is Giovanni da Milano's *Birth of the Virgin* (1365). Children would be interested in this, as apart from the child's curiously aged look, it shows the dress, the hairstyles and the attendants at the birth. Point out how no doctor is present!

These could be compared with works from the late Renaissance period, such as *The Nativity* by Federico Barocci (1580), where Jesus is shown in his crib, with a correctly proportioned baby's head. Although this is a sentimental painting, the details interest children (the cow looking at the manger, the straw, the figure observing from the doorway). It is a picture with more action than many Renaissance nativity scenes. As well as the proportions, point out to the children that the later painting includes a setting, unlike the earlier paintings where the figures were displayed on a gold background. This could be followed up with a visit to an art gallery to look at portraits, both past and present.

Art: AT1, AT2; History: AT2; Mathematics: AT1; Science: AT1

A portrait of my friend

After these preparations, the children should be ready to paint portraits of their friends.

What you need

Paints (thickened with PVA adhesive), brushes, easels, cloths, A2 paper (coloured and white), charcoal, bamboo garden canes (hollow in the centre and cut into 40cm lengths), a reproduction of Matisse's *Portrait with a Green Stripe* (available from the Tate Gallery, London).

What to do

Carefully insert pieces of charcoal into the ends of lengths of bamboo garden cane. Give one to each child and explain that they are going to use them to draw with. Explain that they are going to make a portrait of a friend, starting with a charcoal drawing. They are to stand up and hold the cane at arm's length while they draw. Explain how this loosens up their arm movements, and ensures that the form is kept bold and simple.

Encourage the children to work on a large scale, with big shapes. Point out that any small details will disappear when they paint. Explain that they can draw over incorrect lines, or erase them lightly with the cloths: the paint will cover any mistakes.

Ask the children to decide whether they are going to paint their friends in realistic colours or in colours that express the way they feel about their friends. Although they have already seen the pictures from the Renaissance period, explain that this is not the only approach to painting the face. Show them a copy of Henri Matisse's *Portrait with a Green Stripe* (1905) and tell them that as this very famous artist could put a bright green stripe down a nose to make it stand out, there is no reason to worry about the colours they use. Stress that it is their picture, and they can use any colours they like to make it sad,

happy, pretty or lively, if they feel this makes it more like the person they are painting.

Tell them to paint in all the large shapes and background before putting in any details, such as the pupil of the eye. Point out that most painters leave out a lot of detail – not many put in eyelashes, for example. Encourage the children to use the paint freely, and not to worry about the final effect until all the paper is covered. Then they can pin the picture up and see if more work is needed.

Follow-up

Follow this activity with a portrait of a historical figure, using costume books and portraits for reference. The Tudors or Stuarts are visually rewarding subjects, and comparisons could be made between their clothes and ours, in matters of style, materials and hygiene.
Art: AT1, AT2; Science: AT2; History: AT3

Tone and colour

In the portrait sessions, the children have explored line and colour. In the following activities, they use tone, and then move on to develop a section of the image on computer, using colour.

Make a picture grow

What you need

A selection of black and white newspaper photographs (cut in half, but containing at least some recognisable people, scenery, vehicles or events), HB-6B pencils, A1 drawing paper, Pritt Sticks, sketch-books, magnifying glasses, viewfinders (with 3cm viewing window), copies of work by Roy Lichtenstein, a computer with an art package.

What to do

Ask the children to select a half-picture from the newspaper clippings, and decide what the scene depicts. Tell them that they are going to stick the clipping on to their drawing paper,

and, using the pencils and tone, but no lines, extend the image out until they have a picture. Allow them to try out some rough ideas first in their sketch-books, including areas of tone made with the pencils. Explain that when they have finished extending their pictures, it should be hard to see the newspaper clipping, which should have disappeared in the middle of their drawing.

When they have completed this exercise, ask them to scan over the picture, using the viewfinders, for a section that makes either a pleasing pattern or an interesting picture. Let them make notes of these in their sketch-books, and finally choose one to work on.

Point out the Ben Day dots on the newsprint, and explain that the image was put through a fine mesh screen, so that the final picture was made up of many dots; how many depended on the screen's mesh. Show them paintings by Roy Lichtenstein (1923-), which use greatly enlarged Ben Day dots, either silk-screened or hand-painted. Explain his work was based on the comic strips. Ask the children which comics they read, if any, and ask them to see if dots are still used (comics are differently produced nowadays).

Tell the children that they are going to transfer their designs or picture to the computer. Then, with the use of a paint package, they can try enlarging the design and using different colourways. Encourage them to try a variety of colourways, and print out the ones they like best.
Art: AT1, AT2; Mathematics: AT3

Experiments with paint

Taking their favourite computer print, the children can enlarge their design and turn it into a painting, experimenting with the effects of texture and thick paint, and comparing this with the original flat print.

What you need

Computer print from the previous activity, A2 manila, rollers, cloths, sawdust, sand, grit, palette knives, paint, brushes, PVA adhesive.

What to do

Talk to the children about the way an image can change according to the medium used. Point out the even, flat quality of the computer print. Tell the children about Jean Dubuffet's *D'hôtel Nuance D'Abricot* (1947), which is a portrait of a friend from a series called *Better Looking Than They Think*. In this series, the artist emphasises the most curious features of the friend, such as large spectacles or a wide mouth, and uses extraordinary techniques to do so. He applied his paint with a spatula, like icing a cake, and then sprinkled ashes on the wet canvas, followed by a layer of sand and coal dust. He then trickled runny paint over the surface, using a mixture of yellow ochre, white and crimson, and

brushed it in. The whole surface was covered with black paint and a layer of ashes and dust. He then scratched his image into the surface of the picture, painting the outlines he had made in white. The children may think his images funny, and his techniques odd, but point out that he is a very successful artist, and does succeed in capturing the spirit of his sitter. Some of his works are in the Tate Gallery in London and in the National Gallery of Scotland, Edinburgh. Show the children how paint can be mixed with a little PVA adhesive, so that it can be applied thickly, with the palette knife. Demonstrate the effect of mixing sand or sawdust into the paint. Ask them to paint a big version of their computer print, using different textures of paint, thickened with PVA, and applied to manila.
Art: AT1, AT2; Science: AT3

Follow-up

Ask the children to apply the same techniques to a landscape, based on a local scene that they have previously sketched.

Paper-making

Making paper gives the children an idea of the operations involved in carrying out an industrial process. It can give rise to discussions on conservation, recycling and the need to protect the earth's resources. Many children have no idea where paper comes from or how it is made, and find it exciting to produce their own instead of buying it from a shop. The process of making paper also makes it plain that production depends on planning, and following a defined order of tasks.

Handmade paper often has a coarser, more textured quality than commercially produced papers. It can be coloured by adding food dyes, paints or inks to the pulp. Texture and pattern can be created by mixing in scraps of paper torn from magazines or coloured tissue paper. Small seed heads, leaf skeletons, grasses and straw can add interest to the paper if they are laid on the wet pulp, or sandwiched between two layers in the mould.

Recycling paper

What you need

A bucket, water, wooden spoon, liquidiser, paper mould, sketch-books, pencils, a selection of seeds and grasses (such as straw or birdseed, etc) food dyes, coloured magazine pages, paper for recycling (newspapers, brown paper bags, computer paper, wrapping paper), newspaper for draining the paper before drying.

What to do

Talk to the children about the origin of paper as wood pulp, and the need for recycling to preserve the world's forests. Explain that they are going to make some recycled paper, and use it for a card or a picture.

Get the children to tear the paper into small pieces (about 6cm square), and put it to soak in the bucket of water. Let the children give it a stir, and leave it to soak while they make drawings of the process.

Liquidise the paper, and show the children how to pass their mould through the pulp, adding food colouring, seeds, etc, if they wish. Remove the paper from the mould, and let it dry. This process is described in detail in Chapter 9, page 145.

Art: AT1, AT2; Science: AT1, AT3; Technology: AT1, AT3, AT4; Geography: AT5

Floral cards from handmade paper

If the children's handmade paper is coloured, or has had textures or seeds added to the pulp, it can be made into a pleasing card, mounted on manila.

What you need

Handmade paper, scissors, paper adhesive or double-sided tape, watercolour brushes, diluted paint or food colouring, pressed leaves and flowers, examples of commercially produced greetings cards showing pictures of gardens.

What to do

Ask the children to look closely at the pressed flowers and leaves, then ask them to use the paint and food colouring to make a picture on their handmade paper, based on the shapes they have seen in the flowers and leaves. Suggest that they make a garden background, using pale colours. Show them examples of cards with pictures of gardens.

Ask if they would like to add a selection of dried flowers and leaves to their work. Let them experiment by laying out arrangements of flowers and leaves. When they are satisfied with the design, let them stick the leaves and flowers in place with paper adhesive or double-sided adhesive tape.

Finally, let them choose a contrasting piece of manila trimmed to size, and let them mount their work.

Art: AT1, AT2; Technology: AT2, AT3

Follow-up

The paper that has been made has many other uses. The children could use it for drawing, make simple books from it and use it for relief and paper sculpture. It could also be used in the following activity.

Using the computer

Make a storyboard

In the process of making paper, the children were made aware of the need to conserve the earth's resources. In this activity, they investigate one of the ways in which a major influence on our thinking is designed – television or film production. This investigation of the media is developed from discussion about their own experiences, and moves on to examining a commercial method of presenting designs for a moving image and introduces the use of computer technology.

As an introduction to the storyboard, organise a class survey of the children's favourite television commercials, and suggest that they investigate how these are made. This could be accompanied by a visit to the Museum of the Moving Image on the South Bank in London or The National Museum of Photography, Film and TV in Bradford. During the course of their research, the children will learn about the uses of the storyboard. This method of presentation is used by the graphic designer to show a client the sequence of frames for television commercials.

What you need

A2 white drawing paper, tracing paper, HB pencils, black felt-tipped pens, erasers, sketch-books, computer with publishing and animation packages, scissors, stapler, thin card.

What to do

Tell the children that they are going to work as a graphic designer would in order to make a television advertisement. Ask the children to devise a sequential set of images to sell either a toy, or to support the anti-smoking campaign. Tell them to use their sketch-books to rough out their ideas in miniature drawings. These are known as 'thumbnail sketches', and are used by most artists, not just graphic designers, to work out their ideas; they often have notes attached. Explain that even though these are roughs, each little drawing should indicate clearly what is intended, and be enclosed in its own space. Ask them to draw a line all round to indicate the shape of the finished design. Sketches should never be stuck to the top or sides of the page, and should never be joined together. There must always be a space in between each drawing, otherwise the drawings read as a long, single strip.

Tell the children to use four pictures to convey either the attributes of their chosen toy or the horrors of smoking. Show them how they can divide the drawing paper into four equal squares, separated by margins. Once the children have decided on the main features of their advertisement, they may need to trace them, to ensure continuity through the scenes on the storyboard. Remind them that the backgrounds must be in sequence as well, unless they change logically.

Lettering can be incorporated into the sequence, and the children could try out

several typefaces to find one that they like. This could be done using a publishing package on the computer, and printing out trial letters to cut out and lay on their pictures. Discuss how some messages are best conveyed by dramatic use of a caption, carefully placed – this could be true of one picture in the anti-smoking sequence, for example.

If an animation package like advanced *Logo* for the Applemac were available, the main theme of the storyboard could be animated against a background. The story could then be printed in a series of movements, and made into a flick book, so that the image moves as the pages are run through the fingers. These can be made up very simply by stapling the pages together between two strips of thin card. They work best if they are quite small – about 8cm by 4cm. This is the simplest form of animation, and could lead to a project on the way images were made to move in previous centuries.

Display the results, and ask the children for their comments – if they were the client, which one would they choose? In this activity, the children will have learned how to order their ideas into a sequence and have begun to understand a media process. They will have had to consider the images that they put in

their sequence to make the message clear.

This could be followed by a session where they watch videos of television commercials, to see what the designer has done to enhance the client's product. This media education is important in a world where instant selling messages are viewed daily, often uncritically. **Art: AT1, AT2; English: AT1, AT5; Technology: AT2, AT3; Mathematics: AT1**

A shape poem

This activity helps to make the children aware of presentation and design, and the use of words or letters to form designs.

As a follow-up to the storyboard, the children could be asked to write a poem, based on either smoke or their favourite toy. Suggest that they think of a list of descriptive words, and also think of an appropriate shape. For example, if the chosen toy was Barbie, the poem could be in the shape of her hair or her eye.

Show them examples of the way this manipulation of shape has been used in poetry and children's stories. The classic example is 'The Mouse's Tale' in *Alice in Wonderland* by Lewis Carroll. Another poet who has used the shapes and design of words is Roger McGough. In *After the Merrymaking*

(Cape Poetry, 1980), there is the amusing and highly visual 'Pantomime Poem', and in 'Sunday Before Christmas' McGough describes the weather, and a dreary winter street scene thus:

```
RAIN   a dog      RAIN
RAIN   runs the   RAIN
RAIN   gauntlet   RAIN
RAIN   of drop    RAIN
RAIN   ping trees RAIN
```

The poem has a third verse which runs:

DRIZZLEDISMAL
DRIZZLEDISMAL
(Reprinted by permission of the Peters Fraser and Dunlop Group Ltd)

Point out to the children that words can be combined and their size altered to express the meaning. For example, if they used the anti-smoking theme, you could point out that smoke takes on many different shapes – curls, rings, long misty strands, stifling fug and branches like a tree. Suggest they draw all the smoke shapes they can think of in their sketch-books, and try arranging the words to fit the shapes. In the same way, a favourite toy must have shapes that the children associate with it. If the favourite toy is a bicycle, they could try to make the words suggest speed. Maybe by using loooooooong repetitions, or

varYING the size and s-pa—c—i—n——g?

The poems could be roughed out by hand in the children's sketch-books. A hand-produced version could be tried, followed by a paste-up.

What you need

A selection of magazines and newspapers, A4 white paper, paper paste, spreaders, fine drawing pens (such as the Edding 0.5), rulers, HB pencils, scissors, compasses, photocopier, computers with art and graphics package.

What to do

Tell the children to select a design for their shape. If the shape is angular, encourage them to use rulers to make the outline; if it is curved let them use compasses. Tell them to place the words of their poem carefully on the lines; they may need to rule a top line for each word if the size varies, to ensure the right shape. Suggest that they select some large letters from the newspapers and magazines to cut out and paste on to their poems, to draw attention to the important parts. The finished poem should make a pattern, so the balance and appearance needs to be well thought out, as well as the content. When the children are happy with their shapes, let them experiment with printing out their shape poems on the computer. Variations in size and shape of font can be utilised to form the poem. Photocopy the end results and make them into a class book of shape poems.

Using programs such as *Paintspa* on Nimbus, *Macdraw* on the Apple and *AMX* on the BBC and Nimbus Computers, the children could draw and colour illustrations to their poems.

Art: AT1, AT2; English: AT1, AT2, AT3

Conclusion

The discovery and enjoyment of using new and more advanced two-dimensional media should be accompanied by a similar experience in three-dimensional design, which is described in the next chapter.

Chapter 6
Using three-dimensional materials (Key Stage 2)

In the infant years, the children will have experienced the malleable qualities of clay, dough and Plasticine. They will have discovered through practical experience that these materials respond to manipulation quite differently from the rigid hard forms created by card. They will know that ordinary objects, such as boxes, can be transformed into other things, and they will also have found out that boxes are not malleable, but static, and have to be cut and bent to make form.

In Y3 to Y6, as they reach greater maturity, they can make use of and build on their knowledge, applying it to familiar and new media. They will make new discoveries, and develop more advanced designs. By Y4, Y5 and Y6, there should be a new completeness in their work, and the children should be expressing themselves more fluently in their art, as they are expressing themselves in spoken and written English.

Provided the children have had a good grounding in the use of basic tools and materials, and have experimented with a variety of ways to express themselves, the exploration of a new medium should be exciting and stimulating. The children still need to continue their work in familiar media as well as discovering the potential of new ones, so that their visual education broadens and deepens.

Using clay

In the following activities, the children learn to make practical and decorative artefacts by using clay in a traditional way. Discuss the importance of clay. For example, chinaware is an area of craft in which clay is used – the teapot, cup, saucer, vase and ornament all form a familiar part of our daily life. Point out how plastic cups are considered less desirable objects than china ones; it may be constructive to explain briefly to the children the difference between the natural source of clay and the man-made production of plastic. Point out also that once clay is fired and glazed, it is as hard to dispose of as plastic; it becomes a permanent and lasting part of the earth's accumulated detritus, even when it is crushed or broken. This should help the children to understand that firing a piece of work that is not of good quality is wasteful. Before it is fired, clay can become soil or mud; it can also be reused.

As an introduction to the following activities, the children could be shown a video on the making of pottery, and the various uses of clay. These uses include pantiles for roofs, ceramic inserts used as damp courses, land drains, bathroom tiles and lavatory pans. A visit to a local studio or a commercial pottery would help the children's understanding of the medium's potential.

A professional or amateur potter could be invited into the classroom to give a demonstration of the simple techniques the children are going to use. Photographs could be taken during the visit or demonstration, and displayed in the classroom. These would assist the children when they write an account of the visit or demonstration.

Once the preparatory work has been undertaken, the children can then go on to make their own pots, using one of the following methods. These techniques are widely used today and do not involve the use of a potter's wheel. Some of the most beautiful African pots (for example, those in The Museum of Mankind, in London) are coil pots, smoothed and decorated by impressing sticks into the clay.

Pinch pots

The children should have had some experience of clay before embarking on this activity. If it is a new medium, refer back to the clay activities in Chapter 2, page 27. Making a pinch pot appears simple, but it may need two or three preliminary attempts before a satisfactory result is attained. Most people find handling clay in this way a soothing and satisfying experience.

What you need

Clay or self-hardening clay, water, modelling tools, kiln (optional), paints, brushes, varnish.

What to do

Demonstrate to the children the way to make a pinch pot by taking a small ball of clay, slightly larger than a table tennis ball, in your left hand, and cradling it in your palm. (If you are left-handed, hold the clay in the right hand.) Push the thumb of the opposite hand into the centre of the ball of clay, until it is near the bottom of the ball. To thin and form the sides of the pot, rotate the ball of clay in your hand while exerting a gentle pressure with the first finger and thumb of the other hand.

Try to build up a rhythm in the rotary movement, as this helps to keep an even

thickness all round the sides of the pot. Leave an extra thickness of clay at the rim, to prevent cracking – this can be thinned out later.

Heat from the hand tends to dry out the clay, so it may be necessary to moisten it. However, take care it does not become soggy, or it will turn into mud. Red terracotta is the best clay for this process, as it retains moisture better than other types.

Once the children have made their own pinch (or thumb) pots – and they can become very adept at it – the form can be used to build objects other than pots, such as hedgehogs, fish and other animals.

A dinosaur

A single pinch pot can be used as the basis for a dinosaur, such as triceratops or stegosaurus, with the neck and legs emerging from the flattened pot; plates and a tail can be added, and the whole model dried, painted and varnished.

Pebbles

These are easily made by moulding and shaping the pinch pot, and can look very effective. Flatten the pinch pot by gently pressing on a flat surface. When pebbles are dry, they can be painted and varnished. This could form part of a geography project.

Fruit

Many different types of fruit can be made by joining two pinch pots together. Show the children how to flatten and roughen the rims of two pinch pots (Figure 1) brush them with slip (a clay and water mixture) and put them together (Figure 2), smoothing them off and gently fashioning the pebble into shape. Get the children to try matching the texture of a fruit such as an orange. Other fruit, such as apples, can have leaves and stems added; peppers would need careful shaping.

Half-fruit can be made from a single pinch pot base. (The interior of a pepper, for instance, contains a variety of interesting shapes.)

Seed heads

Large seed heads, such as thistles and poppies, can be formed from one pinch pot. Insert rolled clay or, if the model is not going to be fired, other materials such as thin card, to suggest the interior of the seed head in cross-section. Stems for the seed heads could be made out of garden canes or wire, and pushed into the moist clay; again, these could not be fired.

Art: AT1, AT2; Technology: AT1, AT2, AT3, AT4; History: AT3; Geography: AT3; Science: AT1, AT3

Figure 1

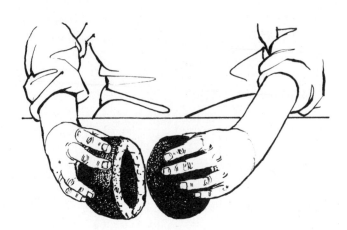

Figure 2

Slabware buildings

A widely used technique for pottery is slabware. This is clay that is rolled flat, and moulded or cut to form the required shape. Slabware is also used for making tiles. (For full instructions on how to roll out the clay, see Chapter 9, page 142.) There are many two- and three-dimensional objects that can be made with slabbed clay. It is a medium that produces good results from relatively simple methods.

This activity could support a history investigation, and would need preliminary work on the structure and appearance of the buildings the children were using as source material. Ideally the children should have the opportunity to visit, draw and photograph the buildings, supporting their art work with written descriptions of the colours and textures they can see, and including notes and maps of the locality. The children could use the local houses, and each model a specific building as part of a larger model of the locality. If this project is undertaken, the houses need to be built to a set scale.

What you need

Clay, modelling tools, kiln (optional), reference books or children's sketches of a building they have studied, A4 drawing paper, pencils, rulers, plastic bag, paints, brushes, varnish.

What to do

Ask the children to draw a plan of the building. Explain that this should not be a ground-plan, but resemble rather more a dressmaker's pattern, showing the shapes of the walls, etc (Figure 3). Make sure that the children measure carefully the size of the walls in the pattern, so that they fit together when they are cut and built in clay. Help them to understand that the work must be on a small scale, not more than 10cm tall, otherwise the building will collapse.

Tell the children to roll out their clay and explain that the walls need to be measured and cut. Ask them to roughen the edges using the modelling tools, stand the walls on a clay base and join them together with slip. Other details can be added by inscribing texture, or pushing clay through a wire tea strainer to create a moss effect, or through a larger sieve for thatch (Figure 4). Roof tile patterns can be marked with a modelling tool, and ornamental details added by rolling fine coils of clay and attaching them to the model with water or slip. Cut a hole in the base when the building is finished, as the air will expand when it is in the kiln.

If the work takes more than one session, cover the models with plastic bags to keep them damp. Dry the models very slowly, away from central heating or sun, and fire or paint and varnish them.

Art: AT1, AT2; Technology: AT2, AT3; Science: AT3

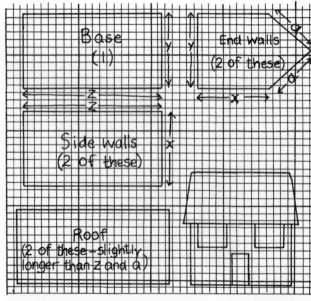

Figure 3

Figure 4

Make a wrap vase

Another simple but effective technique for making a pot is by wrapping clay around a cylinder. Children can make pleasing vases in this way.

What you need

A cylinder such as a cardboard tube, cling film, clay, modelling tools, metal ruler, water, painbrush, kiln (optional).

What to do

Cover the cylinders with cling film and explain to the children that this will stop the cardboard sticking to the clay. Ask the children to roll out the clay, lay the cylinder on it and make marks in the clay at the top and bottom of the cylinder. Show them how to cut two parallel lines across the marks; this will form the top and the bottom of the pot. Lay aside the extra clay. Show them how to cut another straight line down the clay and lay the cylinder on the clay beside it (Figure 5). They should then roll the clay round the cylinder, roughen the edges where the clay meets and join them with a little slip (Figure 6). Ask the children to smooth the join out with the fingers (unless they wish to retain or extend it as a decorative feature. Let the children stand the cylinder upright on a piece of the surplus clay, and cut round the bottom edge of the cylinder to get the correct size for the base, as in Figure 7. The edges of the walls and base need to be roughened and joined together with slip.

Help the children to take the inner cylinder out, and smooth the inside of the pot, especially where the seams join; a small

Figure 6

paintbrush and a little water is useful for the final finish. Any decoration or ornament can be added at this point by using any of the following ideas.
• The clay round the rim of the pot can be pinched and made very thin and wavy, like the petals of a flower, or cut into shapes.
• Texture can be added to the pot by pushing objects such as buttons or badges into the clay.
• Patterns can be created by scratching the surface with a fork, stick or modelling tool.
• Extra shapes can be cut from the spare rolled clay and attached with slip. These could take the form of tree bark textures, leaves, seaweed or the silhouettes of buildings.
Art: AT1; Science: AT3: Technology: AT2, AT3

Follow-up

The pots can be used to make the towers of castles or large houses, and can be combined with the slab construction already described.
Art: AT1, AT2; History: AT3; Technology: AT2, AT3

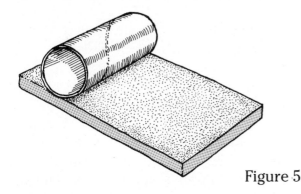

Figure 5

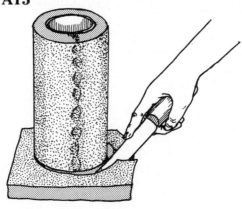

Figure 7

Make a mask

Slabbed clay can be used to make masks, and would provide an excellent follow-up to a museum visit with Y4, Y5 and Y6 children. Some preliminary investigation into masks is needed, perhaps as part of a history project on the Romans or on the Explorers, or as part of an English project involving investigation into the depiction of mythological figures, or the way in which masks were used in Greek drama.

What you need

Clay, modelling tools, cocktail stick, paper, pencils, water, kiln and glazes, paint, brushes, drawings and reference books of masks, newspaper.

What to do

Encourage the children to look at a variety of masks in the reference books, then get them to make a rough design of their own on paper.

Tell the children to roll out the clay, and copy the features and shape of their mask on to it, using a cocktail stick. Help them to cut out the shape, and lay it over a damp mound of newspapers roughly shaped to a mask form. The clay can then be built up on the newspaper base, joining extra pieces to the main form with slip or water to form facial features. Help the children to cut out ovals to form the eyes.

The clay masks can be dried and painted, or fired and painted as decorations. Alternatively, they can be used as a base for papier mâché masks that the children can wear.

Art: AT1, AT2; Science: AT3

Coil pots

Another way of building a pot is by coiling clay. We are told that this was the first method of pottery used by man. (We would have thought that the natural instinct was to stick your fingers into a lump of clay to make a container. We have never seen a young child build a coil pot spontaneously!) It is certainly true that the massive wine and oil vats of ancient Greece were coil pots, and these are still used in the wine-making areas of southern Spain. These pots are large enough for someone to stand in and coiling can reach a huge scale. Pictures of these pots could be shown to the children but it is better for them to start more modestly!

Do not let the children try coiling clay, unless it is soft and has been well wedged (that is, kneaded to remove air bubbles). The whole process works best on a wooden surface, although this is not essential.

What you need

Clay, modelling tools, polythene bag, kiln and glazes (optional), paint, brushes, varnish.

What to do

Ask the children to break their ball of clay up into lumps roughly the size and shape of a wax crayon. Demonstrate rolling the clay out into a long, even coil, by using the fingers, and not the palm of the hand. Tell them to roll the coil right round in one direction only, and not backwards and forwards, otherwise a fold or flat edge will appear. Explain that they should start from the middle of the coil, and handle the clay gently – it is unproductive to roll the clay as though it were under a steamroller!

When the coil is as long, slender and even as the children can manage, let them begin to build the pot. The base can be made either by coiling the clay rolls round in a spiral, or by cutting a spiral from rolled out clay. Explain that in either case, the pot should grow from coils of clay being wound round on top of each other. Tell the children that as the pot grows, they should smooth the inside of the coils together. Stress that it is important to do this as the pot grows because it is impossible to do it well once it is finished. Tell the children that they should not be able to see any light through their pot, otherwise as it dries it will fall apart, like a coiled spring. They should also make sure that the bases are firmly attached to the sides, otherwise they will end up with a coil tube instead of a pot. Tell the children that the pot can be widened and narrowed gradually by altering the position of successive rows of coils. To widen the pot, they should place the coils slightly further out on each row, and reverse the process to narrow it. Try to get the children to form a neat rim – this could be trimmed or narrowed down.

Let the children choose whether to smooth the outside of the pot or leave the coils as they are. If the coils are retained, let the children decorate them by smoothing them out at regular intervals with the fingers or a lolly stick.

Coil pots need to dry very slowly; try enclosing them in a polythene bag for two days to distribute the moisture evenly throughout the pot. Then remove the bags, and allow them to dry in the air. They are then ready to fire in a kiln, or paint and varnish.

Art: AT1, AT2; Science: AT3; Technology: AT3

Follow-up

• The coil technique can be used to form builders' bricks to construct walls. The coils (or rolls) should be cut up into equal lengths. This is good for helping children to understand the various types of bonding used in brickwork and can be included in a study of a particular building or area.
• When modelling historical figures, coiled pots can be turned upside-down and used as skirts. They are much lighter than a solid block of clay.
• Coils are a useful means of decorating slab and pinch pots, especially for the outlines of figures and animals, or for wavy patterns.

Sculpture

All the techniques described above can be combined to build animals, figures or buildings. They use the medium of clay as potters do; the method used by sculptors is described in the next series of activities.
Art: AT1, AT2

Make a clay head

This is an activity for Y3 and Y4 children.

What you need

A ball of clay and baseboard for each child, lolly sticks or modelling tools, cocktail sticks, plastic bags (to wrap the clay and distribute the moisture evenly before drying), mirrors.

What to do

Give a ball of clay to each child, and tell them that they are going to model a head that expresses either sadness or happiness. Ask the children to look in the mirrors and make a happy or a sad face, and then try to mould the features in the clay. The children may be quite content to poke holes in the clay for eyes and draw the mouth on using the cocktail sticks. However, try to persuade them to observe themselves carefully in the mirrors, and point out how the folds of skin by the cheeks vary according to the emotions. The sculptures can become very expressionistic. Make sure that the sculptures are well wrapped up in plastic bags between each session.

Art: AT1; Technology: AT3

A sculpture of my friend

Making a model of a friend's face in clay will give the children experience in viewing objects from different angles as they work. It will help them understand how different textures and shapes can be modelled, as well as increasing their awareness of space. In this activity, work with groups of a maximum of twelve children. The approach is suitable for Y5 and Y6 children.

Ask the children to think of any striking characteristic of their friend's face, such as curly hair, a wide mouth or large eyes. Suggest that they could exaggerate the size of this feature. Show the children pictures of the sculptures of the Swiss artist Alberto Giacometti (1901-66), for example *Monumental Head* (1960), in which the head is elongated. Giacometti was obsessed throughout his career with spatial relationships, and described his own work in this style as 'transparent constructions of human figures'.

There are many examples of his work in the Tate Galleries, both in London and Liverpool, and in the Scottish National Gallery of Modern Art, Edinburgh. Another contrasting approach to portrait sculpture can be seen in the *Portrait of Igor Stravinsky* (1951), by Marino Marini, which shows a pleasing textural use of the clay, and is uncompromising in its presentation of his large ears and nose.

What you need

Examples of classical portrait busts and other ancient sculptures, clay, plastic bags, cloths, modelling tools or lolly sticks, cocktail sticks, a board for each child, blunt knives, jars of water.

What to do

Show the children some examples of classical portrait busts, and explain that bronze sculptures are cast from clay; the *Head of a Berber* in the British Museum in London, is a lively example. It is a Hellenistic bronze, made about 400 BC, with engraved lines added to the hair after casting. Another possible sculpture to show them is the portrait head of *A Man From Delos* of about 100 BC, and also in

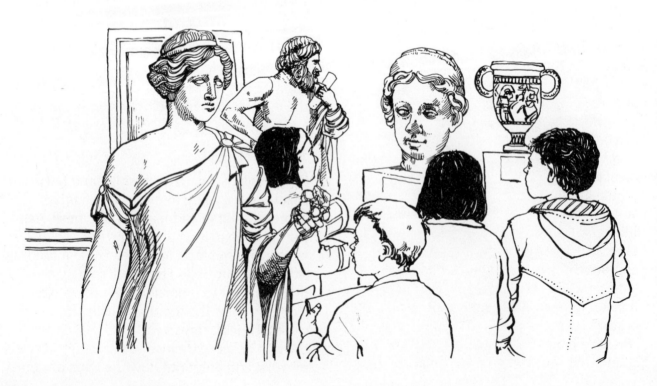

the British Museum. There are many other examples of classical sculptures to be found, such as in the Ashmolean Museum, Oxford, and in the Fitzwilliam Museum, Cambridge.

These sculptures illustrate the classical way of modelling eyes, using glass or jewelled inlay. Ask the children if they would like to paint colour into the eyes of their sculptures. Explain that they will be able to do this when the clay is dry. Point out how the pupils of the eyes of these classical statues were often hollow and tell the children that they will be able to use the cocktail sticks for this effect, if they wish. The cocktail sticks can also be used to form the nostrils and to incise deep lines, such as the centre line of the mouth or strands of hair.

Tell the children that classical Greek sculptures were brightly painted, but over the centuries the paint wore off and only traces of it can sometimes be seen today. There are reconstructions of the original colours in the Ashmolean Museum, Oxford. To our eyes, they are surprisingly like fairground figures. Explain to the children that the ancient Greeks were living before Christ was born. They were pagans so the first Christians disapproved of their temples – where most of the sculptures were to be found – and buried the statues, or threw them into the sea. When the statues were rediscovered, much later, people thought they were very beautiful and copied the way they were made in their own work. As by this time the ancient statues had no colour left, it was assumed for many years in Europe that sculptures should not be painted.

In other countries, colour has often been used on sculptures. The children could be shown examples of these sculptures, such as one of the painted wooden figures of Tutankhamun (Egypt 1352 BC), or an Indian painted sculpture, such as the figure of the Hindu god Ganesa on the Royal Palace of Nepal, which is brightly coloured and decorative in treatment and includes a human being, as well as the elephant-headed figure of Ganesa. (Ganesa is a friendly Hindu god, and his story could be told to the children.)

Provide each child with two balls of clay. Explain that they are going to make the head out of one ball of clay, and use the other for the features and the neck. Ask them to mould an egg shape for the head, and position it on a small column of clay forming the neck and shoulders. Suggest that they think about the position of the head on the neck. (Is it going to be placed so that the person is looking up at you, is bent down or turned to the side?) Make sure the ball and the column are fastened securely together.

Once they have got the head at the right angle, ask the children to draw on the position of the features, using a cocktail stick. Remind them of the proportions of the face, and tell them to indicate the position of the ears. Discuss the results with them before they progress to the next stage of the activity. Remind them to view the head from the front, both sides and the back. They need to think of it as a three-dimensional form.

Demonstrate to the children how to gouge out the features, and then build up the nose and the forehead. The eyes can have eyelids added, made from small rolls of clay. Show them how to indicate the mouth by incising the lines, using a lolly stick or a modelling tool. Once these features have been marked in, the children can build them up, using tiny dabs of clay, and by incising where appropriate.

If the sculpture work is being undertaken over more than one session, make sure the children wrap their work in cloths and polythene bags at the end of each session, to prevent it drying out.

When the portraits are finished, dry them slowly, then paint and varnish them. They could be displayed alongside photographs of the subjects.
Art: AT1, AT2; Technology: AT3; History: AT3; Science: AT3

Casting hands and feet

As a continuation of their study of the human figure, the children could make hollow casts of their hands and feet.

This is an activity for Y4, Y5 and Y6 children. The children could use Mod-Roc for this work. It is a satisfying medium to use, it is easy to manipulate and it looks effective.

The children should work in pairs for this activity. It is probably wise to have only two pairs working at a time.

What you need

Mod-Roc, knife, bowls of water, oil or grease, old newspapers, scissors, sponges, ruler.

What to do

Demonstrate the way to use Mod-Roc by making a cast of two fingers. (This is quicker than covering a larger area, it shows the technique and dries quickly.) Cut the Mod-Roc into 4.5cm squares, making sure that it stays dry. Lightly oil the fingers, as this prevents the Mod-Roc adhering to the hairs and surface of the skin. Place the hand on the table, with the fingers apart, and cover them liberally with the Mod-Roc, which has been dipped in water. Trim off any surplus. Use three or four layers of Mod-Roc, and smooth them down as they are applied; a damp sponge can give a final finish to the last layer. Keep the hand still until the Mod-Roc is set, then lift or slide it off. The Mod-Roc will set, if not dry completely in a few minutes. The cast of the fingers will form a hollow mould.

Let the children cast their forearms and hands, or legs and feet. Make sure they do not totally encase their limbs; they must be able to extract them from the casts! They can measure and compare sizes, and could cast pairs of hands or feet in different attitudes – hands clasped together or feet walking, for example. Alternatively, they could use the forms to make other objects. For example, casts of hands and forearms stood on end could be developed into a tree. Once the Mod-Roc is totally dry, it can be painted or used for a collage.
Art: AT1; Science: AT3

Model an animal

As a further investigation into living forms, the children could study the animal kingdom. This could be purely an art topic or it could form part of a science project on the variety of life, and our similarities and interdependence.

There would need to be preliminary studies made of the chosen animals, which could take the form of photographs and drawings. In the country, local livestock would be a useful resource, and could be supported by showing the children Henry Moore's studies of sheep. In an inner city area, pigeons, cats and dogs are easily observed, or the class could visit a zoo or a city farm.

There are a number of recent or contemporary artists who have used urban and rural creatures in their work. These include Dame Elisabeth Frink (1930-), who has produced a notable series of horses and riders. These could be compared to the horse sculptures of Marino Marini (1901-80).

What you need

Books about animals, white and black paper, scissors, adhesive, Mod-Roc, bowls of water, sponges, preliminary drawings and photographs, old newspapers, brown adhesive tape, fine wire, thick needle, pencils, sketch-books.

What to do

Preliminary studies

After the children have drawn and taken photographs of their chosen animal, tell them to research its inner structure, particularly the bones and muscles. Let them make collages, using white paper on black, of the skeleton and the main muscles. Discuss the way the inner structure affects the outer form, and encourage the children to comment on similarities and differences between their chosen animals.

Tell the children to think of how the animal looks when it is moving or lying down asleep, and get them to make a rough impression of the animal's pose using crumpled newspaper and brown tape. Remind them of the bones of the skeleton and the large muscles of the shoulders and the haunches. Point out any drastic mistakes they may have made. Let the children cover the newspaper with the Mod-

Roc, and mould the form of their animal. Tell them that if they work quickly they can mould and shape the animal while the Mod-Roc is still damp. They can smooth off the last layer of Mod-Roc with the sponges, or use additional strips to suggest the rough, thick fur of an animal, such as a long-haired cat. Whiskers could be made from fine wire, and then pushed into a hole in the Mod-Roc made with a thick needle. Use a blob of spare plaster to keep them in place (plenty usually accumulates at the bottom of the water bowl).

Tell the children to keep notes of any problems that may arise, and to draw the solutions in their sketch-books.
Art: AT1, AT2; Science: AT2, AT3; English: AT1, AT3; Technology: AT3

Modelling with chicken wire

What you need

Chicken wire, newspapers, adhesive tape, baseboard, metal snips, clay, cardboard, Plasticine, twigs, foam rubber, balsa wood, adhesive, paint, brushes.

What to do

Before the activity, cut the chicken wire into manageable pieces using the metal snips. Warn the children that the edges of the chicken wire are very sharp.

Ask the children to model animals, figures or fantasy creatures from chicken wire, by bending the chicken wire roughly into shape, then covering it with newspaper held in place with adhesive tape. Ask them to cover the chicken wire frames with Mod-Roc as in the previous activity, then paint the models when they are dry.

Let the children make an environment for their models. This could be another planet or a dream world, or they could model their local area. Let them experiment with the following ideas for landscape features.
• Buildings can be made from clay or cardboard.

• Trees can be made from Plasticine and twigs.
• Foam rubber can be used for hedges and bushes.
• Park benches can be made from balsa wood.
Art: AT1; Technology: AT3

Making costumes

Another aspect of three-dimensional activity that may arise in school is making costumes for a carnival, festival or school play. Many cities and towns have their own carnivals and street festivals, and many of the colourful and imaginative costumes that can be seen at these events are made from inexpensive recycled materials. Imaginative costumes can also be made for annual religious festivals in the school itself, such as Christmas or Diwali.

Often, parents and other teachers can give practical help with these events, and may even make the costumes. However, the children themselves can become deeply involved in making their own costumes, with some adult help.

Resources

Making the costumes requires a good supply of resources in the form of a selection of materials. Ideally your stock should include the following:
• dress fabrics and sheeting;
• ribbons;
• a variety of coloured papers, ranging from sticky paper strips to tissues;
• wire;
• cardboard;
• cane;
• soft shoes, such as gym shoes and slippers;
• large plastic sequins and tin foil;
• bubble plastic (ask parents and staff to contribute to ensure an adequate supply. The material is easily cut and shaped, and can look attractive as it is; it can also be laid over another coloured fabric or paper).

A good supply of beads is an advantage. They are often expensive to buy from a commercial source, but can also be found

cheaply at local fetes and jumble sales. However, there are also various ways of making beads. For use on costumes, the beads need to be large in scale.

• Beads can be made from clay, self-hardening clay and modelling media such as Cernit or Fimo. Roll the clay into small pellets, make a hole through the middle with the knitting needle or an ordinary needle, depending on the size of the bead, and flatten each end. Leave the beads to dry.

When the beads have dried they will need painting. Thread them on a knitting needle, and stick the end of the needle into a lump of Plasticine, so that the needle and beads stand firmly upright. The beads can then be painted altogether. Beads can be made from dough shaped round any small cylindrical object, dried slowly in a cool oven, and then painted. The dough can be coloured before use with food colouring; this will produce a low colour tone, but is a quicker method of production than painting the beads.

• The coloured casings that go round electrical wiring can be cut up, and threaded to make beads.

• Paper beads can be made by wrapping paper round a knitting needle. Make sure that the paper is three layers thick, and then wipe paste over it so that it sticks together. When the paste is dry, the long cylinder can be eased off the knitting needle and cut into beads. They can then be painted and varnished. (For costumes, the beads can be left long, and then painted in fluorescent paint, if appropriate.)

The children need to be aware that each material has its own characteristics, and that these influence the outcome of the design. They should have had some experience of using the materials before starting a design for a costume. For example they should be familiar with the use of needle and thread, if cloth is being used, and with adhesives, if the costume includes paper or card. Most materials for costume need to be cut, so make sure that your scissors are sharp, and that the children know how to use them safely.

Using paper has the advantage of being easily available and cheap; it has the disadvantage of not being waterproof. However, it is easy for children to cut, stick and colour, and, provided it is kept dry, it will last for quite a while. For stronger or stiffer costumes, several sheets of paper, such as newspaper or wrapping paper, could be pasted together before spraying or painting. Tissue and crêpe paper come in bright colours, and can be effective when wrapped round canes or fine wire, to make wings or head-dresses. Tissue and crêpe paper can also be pleated to make skirts.

The following activity introduces the children to the processes involved in making a costume. They should already have made their own designs for costumes.

Making a costume pattern

What you need

Children's designs for costumes, old newspapers, brown adhesive tape, pins, paper, pencil, sketch-books, scissors, tape-measures, rulers, black felt-tipped pens, dressmaker's pattern.

What to do

Ask the children to work in pairs, and tell them to measure each other's skirt or trouser lengths, the width round the chest, waist and hips and the length of the arms, and write the measurements down. Show the children a dressmaker's pattern for a simple garment. Tell them to try to think what the costumes would look like if they were laid out flat. Ask them to draw the patterns for the costumes in their sketch-books, and then enlarge them on to the newspaper, ensuring they have used the correct lengths and widths of the wearer.

Ask them to cut out the newspapers, leaving a generous edge, and pin them together to see if they work. Extra pieces will probably need to be stuck on, and other parts cut away, but when the patterns are reasonable, they can be used as templates for the final designs.

Art: AT1; Mathematics: AT1; Technology: AT2, AT3

Paper sculpture

Whole costumes can be made by using curled and pleated paper. Curl paper by wrapping it round a pencil, or by running it down the edge of a ruler or pair of scissors. Large versions of the cutlet frill that decorates a crown roast can make effective helmets, wristbands and even trousers and jerkins.

What you need

Large sheets of flexible but firm paper (old advertisement posters are excellent, and can sometimes be found through a local scrap scheme, or be donated by a local printer or billboard agency), scissors, double-sided adhesive tape, tape-measure, pencils, rulers, cutlet frills.

What to do

Give the children the cutlet frills, and let them take them to pieces to see how they are made.

Let the children work in pairs and take each other's measurements. Ask them to mark the measurements on the large sheets of paper, making the length about a third longer than is needed. Explain that margins should be left at the top and bottom of the paper, and regular lines ruled between them, as in Figure 8.

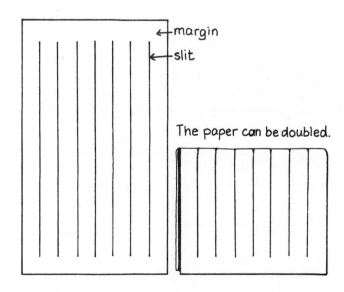

The paper can be doubled.

Figure 8

These lines are then slit, and the paper can be fastened at the back of the wearer, using double-sided sticky tape. The slits in the paper gape apart as it is pulled tight at the wrist, ankle or waist (Figure 9).
Art: AT1; Technology: AT2, AT3; Mathematics: AT4

Fabrics for costume

A collection of discarded clothes and sheets is invaluable for making costumes in the classroom. Woollen garments are also worth collecting. Wash these in very hot water, so that they mat together like felt. In this state, it is easy for the children to cut and shape them, as the wool does not fray, and can be used like felt.

There are also a number of inexpensive and easily manipulated materials which are available from the art educational suppliers. These include:
• tarlatan – a tough net, generally used for the theatre. This is excellent as a basis for clothes, as it does not fray, and children like the bright colours, which look effective in a performance. It can be fastened together by gluing or stitching.
• nylon net – this is cheap, and makes a pretty final layer over other fabrics.

Once you have a selection of fabrics, there are several ways in which they can be decorated or coloured.

Dyeing

Cotton sheeting can easily be dyed to make fabric for costume. However, it may need to be washed before dyeing to remove any remaining starch or dressing.

What you need

Cold water dyes, bowls, rubber gloves, fabric for dyeing, water, wooden spoon, spin-drier, pencils, paper, detergent.

What to do

Ask the children to write down the process of dyeing as they work.

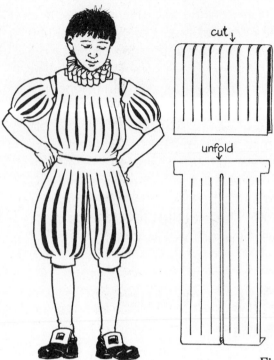

Figure 9

Mix the dye according to the manufacturer's instructions. Tell the children to put on rubber gloves and wet their pieces of fabric. Next ask them to submerge their fabric in the dye bowl and leave it to soak for 50 minutes or an hour. Explain that the longer the fabric is submerged, the deeper the colour will be. Tell the children to stir the material occasionally. At the end of the dyeing process, let the children rinse their fabric in cold water until the water is clear before putting it in the spin-drier.

The fabric should be washed by the teacher in very hot water and detergent before it is used for making a costume.
Art: AT1; Science: AT3

Instant dyes

There are also many instant dyes available that can be drawn or painted directly on to the fabric and are fixed by ironing.

Using wax crayons

A cheap way of colouring fabric, which works quite well and which would be effective for stage or carnival clothes, is to use thick wax crayons.

What you need

Patterns for children's costumes, thick wax crayons, drawing paper, fabric, newspaper, an iron.

What to do

After the children have drawn a design to decorate their costumes, and cut out the pattern, tell them to transfer the shape that is to be decorated on to the drawing paper. The design can be drawn in outline on the paper, and then coloured, using the wax crayons. Remind them that if the design includes words they will have to reverse it as it will be the opposite way round when it is printed. Tell the children that the wax crayons should be applied thickly to the paper.

When the design is complete, tell the children to lay the paper on the fabric, with the coloured side downwards. Put old newspapers beneath the cloth on top of the waxed drawing before ironing, as the wax can stain the iron and the ironing surface. Iron over the back of paper. Colour will then be transferred to the fabric as the wax melts and is absorbed. This method will only create a temporary effect, as it rapidly fades if washed.
Art: AT1; Science: AT3

Other ways of decorating cloth

These include tie and dye, stencilling and appliqué. For a description of these techniques see Chapter 9. Many items for decorating fabric could be collected from parents. These could include:
• all types of braid, cord, ribbons, velvet, satin scraps and buttons;
• feathers and artificial or dried flowers;
• chocolate wrappings;
• wooden beads;
• sequin mesh;
• liquid glitter.

Cardboard and card can be cut and shaped by the children, then sprayed and painted. The teacher should paint the card with white emulsion before the children begin if there are any trade names on it.

Card is useful for making head-dresses and armour. Lacing it together, by punching holes and threading them with string, allows the children freedom of movement.

Making head-dresses

Many head-dresses of elaborate design and shape can be supported by a simple strip of card that sits in a circle round the child's head.

What you need

Strips of card 4cm wide, tape-measure, pencil, scissors, decorative materials for the head-dress, fastening device (such as staples, adhesive or laces and hole punch), paper, paint.

What to do

Ask the children to form pairs and measure each other's heads round the crown, using the tape-measure. Get them to mark the length on the card, allowing an extra 2cm if the card is to be stuck or stapled together; if it is to be laced, it needs to be 1cm shorter than the head measurement. Tell the children to cut the strip out, and fasten the ends together, fitting it to the wearer's head. The headband can then form the basis on to which the decoration can be stuck or stapled.

A central strip of card can be added to the headband, then straight hair can be made from wool, string, crêpe paper, raffia, or from raffene, if a gaudy look is required. Curly hair can be made by curling strips of paper round a pencil, or by running a strip of paper down the side of a blunt knife or scissor blade. The 'hair' is attached to both the central band and the headband, to make it fall correctly, using staples or glue.

The children can turn the headband into a crown by painting it gold, and adding 'jewels' made from plastic sequins alternating with shapes cut from sequin waste and crumpled Cellophane paper.
Art: AT1; Technology: AT3, AT4;
Mathematics: AT1, AT2

Using an armature

Transparent shapes that stand up, such as wings, can be made using an armature or wire structure.

What you need

Soft wire, Cellophane, non-fungicidal wallpaper paste, scissors, sugar paper, pencils, large brushes, pots for the wallpaper paste.

What to do

Before the activity, mix the wallpaper paste according to the manufacturer's instructions.

Let the children experiment with bending a small piece of wire into shapes. When they are familiar with the ways in which wire can be bent, let them make a sugar paper template of the shape they want. Tell them to bend a large piece of wire round the outline on the sugar paper, and twist the ends together.

Give each child two sheets of Cellophane, and tell them to brush the wallpaper paste over the whole of one sheet. Next ask them to lay the wire shape on the sheet of pasted

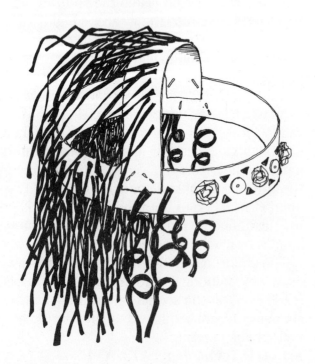

Cellophane, and add any other decorative shapes. Help them to lay another layer of pasted Cellophane on top. Leave the shapes to dry, and then tell the children to trim the Cellophane to shape, leaving at least a 2cm overlap around the edge of the wire. Warn the children not to stick shapes on the outside of the Cellophane as they will fall off.

Follow-up

Wire shapes can also be covered with net, ribbons can be stuck on with PVA adhesive, or sewn with cotton, using just enough stitches to hold the fabric in place.
Art: AT1; Technology: AT2; Mathematics: AT1, AT2

Face masks

Simple face masks can be made from card. These can be either full-face masks or half masks.

What you need

Card, paints, brushes, pencils, raffia, string or wool for hair, rulers, decorations for the mask (beads, sequins, nylon fur, etc), drawing paper, pictures of masks from a variety of cultures (Greek, African, Inuit, depending on the theme for which the masks are intended), chalkboard or flipchart, sketch-books, knife, scissors, elastic.

What to do

Show the children the pictures of masks from various cultures. Ask the children to think about the characters suggested by the mask. Discuss this with them and write descriptive words on the board or flip chart.

Ask the children to draw a design for a mask in their sketch-books, then tell them to form pairs, measuring the position of each other's eyes and the size of each other's faces. Ask them to use these dimensions to draw the basic mask oval on card, and mark the features in. Check the position of the eye holes to make sure that the children will have a clear view, then help them to cut out eye holes. Do the same for the mouth.

Demonstrate to the children how to give the mask depth, by running a knife gently down the centre line inside the mask, and folding it (Figure 10). Encourage the children to give character to the mask by adding hair, eyebrows etc.

The mask can be secured by fixing it to a headband, or with the traditional elastic, but if there are any energetic movements to be performed, a headband is more secure.
Art AT1, AT2; Technology: AT3, AT4; Mathematics: AT1, AT2

The world of colour: a carnival theme

The following activity can be used to incorporate all the previous ideas for making costumes.

Figure 10

What you need

A variety of resources (see pages 93 to 95), videos of festivals, books of costume, adhesives (Polycell, PVA), double-sided adhesive tape, scissors, old newspapers, cardboard boxes, paper bags, notebooks or sketch-books.

What you do

Tell the children they are going to make their own costumes and take part in a festival of colour. Ask them to form groups of roughly eight to ten children, and to decide on a colour for their group, thinking about what that colour reminds them of. Limit the time they have to think about this, and, if they cannot decide, choose colours for them. Ask them to devise costumes based on their chosen theme.

As an example, if a group were to choose yellow, they could associate it with sunshine, which could give rise to some interesting costumes based on the disc and rays of the sun. The children could find out about Ra, the sun god of ancient Egypt, and make costumes based on this myth. They could learn about the Greek god Phoebus, who lived, surprisingly, in India, and sat on a great throne that 'glittered as with diamonds'. On either side of his throne stood the Day, the Month, the Year and, at regular intervals, the Hours. The making of Phoebus' chariot would be a challenge! It could have a great sun mask, like the Roman plaque in Bath, on either side.

Another group might choose red, which would open up many possibilities: the gates of Hades; Orpheus and Eurydice; a Viking burial; the red planet of Mars. The children might choose a different approach, and claim that red signifies danger, fire or anger.

As long as the children have a valid reason for their choice, let them draw the costumes, and begin work measuring and making them up in newspaper.

Demonstrate the paper curling technique (see page 95) and show them how to sew or stick on the beads, etc. Give active help when it is needed, and remind them to consult reference books for ideas on costume. Point out that the costumes are going to be seen from all sides, and that this needs to be considered when they are making them. This should be fun for the children, as well as teaching them a great deal about the way materials behave in a three-dimensional context.

There are many ways of assuming a new character. Large brown paper bags with a face hole cut in them can be decorated and put over the children. The bags can have holes cut in them, from which decorated hands and arms could emerge. Large cardboard boxes can be collected from local shops, and used as a basis for caricatures of specific figures.

Finally, discuss the way their carnival is going to be presented. Ask them the following questions:
• Are they going to have music in the background? If so, will they compose it?
• Are they going to have leaflets explaining what each group represents?
• Are they going to dance, walk, march?
• Who are they going to invite – the governors, parents, other classes, the headteacher?
• Should they offer the audience coloured food and drink?

Many of these aspects can lead on to work in English, and further work in science. The same approach and techniques can be applied to an assembly, in a simpler form.
Art: AT1, AT2; Technology: AT1, AT2, AT3, AT4; Mathematics: AT1, AT2; History: AT3; English: AT1, AT2, AT3

Conclusion

All the work in this chapter has been concerned with the acquisition of spatial knowledge. None of these suggestions are meant to be prescriptive; as in the rest of the book, these are only suggestions of ways to approach certain aspects of visual education. Each class will differ in their levels, skills and needs, as well as each child; all the suggestions in this chapter can be adapted to suit the needs of the children.

Chapter 7
Artists and the environment (Key Stage 2)

In the proposals for *Art for ages 5 to 14* submitted by the National Curriculum Art Working Group in June 1991, the importance of educating pupils of all ages to appreciate the work of other artists and cultures is clearly stated. As the Working Party Report states:

'Young people who are visually literate have more control over their own work and are better able to understand, enjoy and discriminate between the images and objects that appear both in the familiar environments of the home and the neighbourhood, and in less familiar places, such as galleries and museums.'(3.19)

By the time the children are in Y3 to Y6, they enjoy investigating the different methods that have been used by artists in the past and today, producing their own interpretations of the works, and of the styles and techniques. Introducing these to the children could be approached in several ways.

• The class could be split into groups, and each group could investigate the life and work of artists they have looked at in books, museums or galleries.

• They could be told to choose works of art from a specific period of time and find out about them.

• Another approach would be for the children to look at the way different artists have treated a particular theme, such as flowers, people or dreams.

• The children could investigate the way other countries approach the depiction of the human figure, or the use of a specific craft technique, for example *ikat* tie and dye in Malaya. Oxfam provides an inexpensive pack about Alaro textiles from Nigeria for use with primary children.

• They could base a movement lesson on the position of sculptures.

In the following project, which is suitable for Y4 to Y6, the children investigate the work of Seurat, a Neo-Impressionist, who based his paintings on scientific theories of colour. This activity would relate well to a science-based project on the eye, or on light.

Seurat (1859-91)

Pointillism, or Divisionism, as it is sometimes called, came into being at the end of the nineteenth century, and was founded on the scientific theories and discoveries related to colour that had emerged earlier in the century. In part, Pointillism was a reaction by a small group of younger painters against the Impressionists' use of colour, which the younger painters felt lacked form. The two most famous Pointillist painters were Georges Seurat and Paul Signac (1863-1935). The best known is Seurat, who is considered one of the great painters of the nineteenth century.

Seurat was born in France, and spent his short life working in and around Paris. At the beginning of his career as an artist, he concentrated on black and white drawings for a period of two years. During this time, he added deep and velvety tones to his drawings, using conte-crayon and textured paper; these drawings show that he was a great draughtsman. When he decided to use colour, he was influenced by the Romantic painter, Delacroix, by the landscape painters of the Barbizon School and by Impressionists, such as Monet, Renoir and Pissarro. While admiring the Impressionists' use of colour, he felt they were too involved in catching the passing moment on their canvases, and in their anxiety to do this, sacrificed form and solidity in their work.

Seurat set about producing paintings that combined the glowing colours of the Impressionists with planned and regulated composition. To this end, he and Signac used Divisionism, or Pointillism. This system involved placing small regular dots of unmixed primary and secondary colour side by side on the canvas, so that when they are looked at from a distance, they react together and appear to mix, creating a more vibrant effect than each individual colour would on its own. Such a complex system cannot be produced on the spur of the moment; Seurat planned all stages of his compositions with care, making many full-size oil studies for his paintings.

Seurat worked on a large scale, and his painting *Une Baignade* (1883-4), which is in the National Gallery, London, measures approximately 2m by 3m. The painting uses broader brush strokes than Seurat's later work. It uses the Pointillist technique, which is easy to observe and would have an appeal to many children through its subject matter – bathers on a river bank – and its historical content.

The picture has a calm, dreamlike quality, characteristic of Seurat's finished works, as though a warm, hazy summer afternoon has been frozen in time on the canvas. The children may find it interesting to look at the clothes worn for an afternoon by the river – bowler hats, straw boaters, long swimming trunks.

The *Baignade* could be looked at with *La Grande Jatte* (1884-5), also by Seurat. This depicts Parisians taking a stroll on the banks of the Seine. Although the painting contains more activity than the *Baignade*, it also has a stillness, a sense of calm. Again, the children would find the clothes interesting, in particular the parasols and bustles on the women's dresses. Draw the children's attention to the way Seurat has used shadows, which are strongly marked in both pictures, and form an important part of the composition. Ask questions such as:

- Whereabouts is the sun? Can you tell where it is, even though you cannot see it?
- What colours does Seurat use?
- How does he put the paint on?
- Do you think it was painted in this country?
- When was it painted?
- Would you like to go there?

Experiments with Pointillism

When the children have looked at the work of Seurat, they can be allowed to investigate the ways he used to apply paint. The children can try a selection of paints and tools to find which works the best for them. Some patient children can produce beautiful, tiny pictures with fine felt-tipped pens, using Seurat's technique; others may prefer to use coloured pencils or paint.

What you need

Felt-tipped pens, paints and painting equipment, small brushes, A4 cartridge or drawing paper, coloured pencils, postcards of Seurat's work, magnifying glasses, viewing windows, sketch-books.

What to do

Ask the children to look at a postcard of a Seurat painting through a magnifying glass, and note down the colours they see, both in paint and in writing. Encourage them to record which colours are side by side. To make it easier for them to focus, provide small viewing windows. (These can be made from card with a 4cm square cut out of the middle.)

After the children have made a close study of Seurat's use of colour, offer them a choice of tools and subject matter. Suggest they try a small picture, using felt-tipped pens or coloured pencils, or a larger painting, using soft brushes. Tell them to choose a section of a Seurat painting as a basis for their own, but to put the figures in a modern context. For example, they could adapt *Une Baignade* by transferring Seurat's figures to a modern swimming pool.

Remind them to think where the light is coming from, as it will affect the shadows. Explain that these shadows should help with the composition, so their position is important; suggest that they make thumbnail sketches in their sketch-books. Tell them to follow Seurat's colour range as closely as they can.

When the paintings are finished, pin them up and discuss the different effects. Ask them:
• Do the pictures all look the same?
• Do they look still and quiet, like Seurat's? Point out that the pictures are all different, and all are to be valued, if they are well thought out. Discuss the pictures and emphasise the individuality. Every picture should be different, even though they are all using Seurat as a basis.

Any artist's work could be approached in a similar way.

Art: AT1, AT2; History: AT3; Technology: AT2, AT3, AT4; English: AT1; Science: AT3

Picasso (1881-1973)

Picasso was a Spaniard, from Barcelona, and was the most productive and wide-ranging artist of this century. He painted in many styles, innovating all the time; he also designed ballet sets, created ceramics, illustrated books and was a sculptor. His draughtsmanship and genius were prodigious; he always claimed that he could draw like Raphael when he was a boy, and spent the rest of his life learning to draw like a child.

Two paintings by Picasso that could be compared and discussed, depict images of his children; he painted many of these, changing his style often. *Paul in a Sailor Suit* (1925) is a conventional and pretty portrait of his son. This could be compared to *Girl with a Cock* (1938) where Picasso uses a semi-cubist technique on the face, hands, legs and feet. Ask the children why they think Picasso painted his daughter like this.

After listening to their ideas – and they may know the answer, children often do – explain that Picasso was painting more than one view of an object. He included not only what could be seen from the front, but what could be seen when you moved, hence the profile combined with the full face, nose and eyes. Show them a Cubist painting by another artist, and ask them to identify the subject matter. Two easy Cubist paintings are Georges Braque's *Houses at L'Estaque* (1908) and Fernand Leger's *Soldier With Pipe* (1916).

In his earlier work, Picasso used colour to convey atmosphere and mood. This expressionistic use of paint can be seen in the paintings of his Blue Period (1901-04) and the later Rose Period (1905-06). In the Blue Period, Picasso worked almost in monochrome – cool, quiet blues, with an occasional dash of dull green – to convey a feeling of isolation and loneliness. He painted the outsiders of society: the works are mostly of solitary figures, such as *The Old Guitarist* (1903). In this painting, Picasso has elongated the figure. Show the children a copy of the painting and ask:
• Does the guitarist look as though he is enjoying himself?
• How has Picasso made him look sad and hungry?
Discuss the use of the exaggerated form and the position of the figure, and compare it with a painting from the Pink Period, such as *Les Saltimbanques* (1905). This picture shows a group of circus clowns in an empty landscape. Although the figures are of more usual proportions, they are still expressive, but treated in a less melancholy way than *The Old Guitarist*. He used tones of pink and cream giving the figures a warmer, more comfortable feeling.

The two paintings could be discussed, and the children asked to decide how the artist felt when he was painting them, and whether they find one set of colours makes them feel differently to the other. The children could develop this use of monochrome colour to express their own reactions to a current event, or to a historical scene.
Art: AT1, AT2; English: AT1

How do I feel?

In this activity, the children try using colour to express their emotions. They could choose to express their happiness on holiday or their fear of Dracula. (One boy painted a huge bush reflected in the window of his front door, and explained that as he was convinced Dracula lurked in it after dark, he kept a piece of garlic in his pocket. He did, too! Dracula has entered modern mythology, like *Dr Who* or *Thunderbirds*.)

What you need

A2 white drawing paper, paints, brushes, palettes, pencils, paper.

What to do

Remind the children about the Picasso paintings, and tell them they are going to paint a picture using only shades of one colour, and black and white, to suggest their feelings about a dream or an event in their lives. Ask them not to tell each other what feelings they are depicting because, when the work is finished, they are going to write stories about each other's pictures, and then find out if the story matches the feeling that was intended in the painting.
Art: AT1, AT2; English: AT1, AT2, AT3

Narrative paintings

Children love narrative paintings as they usually contain a great deal of detail. There are a wide range of these paintings to choose from, especially from the Victorian period. They could be used to support history and technology projects, involving looking at and drawing domestic artefacts, costumes, toys and transport.

The most famous early picture of children at play is *Children's Games* (1560) by Pieter Bruegel (or Brueghel) (C. 1525-69). This detailed picture is a good source of comparison, both with today's more complex entertainments and with the games that were played in Victorian and Edwardian times, many of which resembled those in the Bruegel painting – the hoop, for example. The Flemish School to which Bruegel belonged is a good source of early narrative work.

Probably the easiest pictures for children to understand are the Victorian narrative paintings, which are relatively recent, and include a large number of clues, both as to content and to period. Many of the pictures deal with social and moral themes that are relevant today – repossession of the home, family breakups, gambling, homelessness. There are also many paintings dealing with an idealised rural England which the Victorians thought existed before the industrial revolution. These could be studied by rural schools, in particular, to see if the children find the pictures realistic; town children may also find them interesting, although some inner London children we spoke to found the rural life boring, after only their first visit.

Another favourite theme of the Victorian narrative painter was the army, as in *The Soldier's Farewell* (1853), by John Callcott Horsley, RA, which is a rather romanticised vision of a maid, clutching her duster and brush, looking at her 'follower' through the window.

The value of narrative paintings in school lies not so much their aesthetic qualities, as in the historical insight they give us into the lives of the people of this time. An example of this is *The Doctor* (1891) by Sir Luke Fildes, which is in the Tate Gallery in London. This picture shows a sick child lying on two chairs, covered with a blanket. The family doctor leans forward, a thoughtful look on his face, while in the background the anxious father hovers.

There are many items of human and historical interest in this picture. For example, it shows the interior of a respectable working man's cottage. Tell the children how Sir Luke Fildes built a mock-up of a cottage interior in his no-doubt extensive studio, so that the painting had an authentic feel. The fact that the chairs do not match, and that the child has to sleep downstairs to keep warm, could give rise to discussions on the changed conditions in our homes. Draw the children's attention to the oil lamp, and the ragged state of the tablecloth. This picture could lead to a discussion on present-day poverty. Ask the children:
• Does anybody live like this today?
• What should be done about it?
• When was the picture painted?
The children could draw and paint the exterior of the cottage, and write a story about the child's schooling or her toys, if they think that she would have any.

A fine painting in the narrative style is *The Last of England* (1855), by Ford Madox Brown, which is in the City of Birmingham Museum and Art Gallery. This depicts a couple emigrating to Australia, and there are many details in the background to indicate the mixed bag of passengers to be found on the emigrant ships. Point out details such as the tiny baby's hand sticking out from beneath the mother's shawl. This painting could bring the reality of emigration home to the children. It could support work in history, geography and technology.

Before showing them a reproduction of the painting, describe the work to the children, and then ask them to paint their own version of the scene. The children could do some research, and find out what sort of ships emigrants would have travelled in and what conditions were like on board. This could lead to model-making and prints based on details of the rigging or galley.

Art: AT1, AT2; History: AT1, AT2, AT3; English: AT1, AT2

Themes in artists' work

Choosing specific themes allows a wider investigation of artists' work, as this does not limit the children's study to a specific artist or period. Themes can be helpful in encouraging the children to use reference books, and to make close observation of pictures, as well as increasing their knowledge and enjoyment of art. In the following section, there are suggestions for themes, names of artists and brief descriptions of appropriate pictures, sculptures or crafts.

Food

Many artists have painted pictures of food, in various contexts. In earlier times, many of the scenes depicted food in a religious context, such as the ancient Egyptian wall-paintings on display in the British Museum, which show food being offered on an altar. Food can also take on symbolic meanings, as illustrated in *The Last Supper* (1495-8) by Leonardo da Vinci (1452-1519).

There are a few pictures of medieval food to be seen in *Les Très Riches Heures du Duc de Berry*. The duke is shown sitting at table, in public, with a lot of activity going on around him. His large status symbol, a gold salt-cellar, is prominently portrayed, and his two little dogs sit on the table beside a plate of food! There is an unusually domestic scene portrayed in *The Luttrell Psalter* (1340) of the lord of the manor and his family at dinner; note the lack of forks, and the trestle table.

The average Tudor farmer's meal is well conveyed in a woodcut from Gringoire's *Castel of Laboure*, printed by Wynken de Worde in 1506, and now in Cambridge University Library. (This could also be included as part of a larger topic on printing.) There are numerous wood engravings of this type, and in most the meals look very meagre! However, this might possibly be just a reflection of the wood engraving technique, as a painting of *Break-fast* (1614) in the Bowes Museum, Durham, is lavish, with fish, cherries, bread, ham and shrimps; again, note the lack of forks.

The children could make models of a medieval banquet or food stall following examination of some of these pictures. Food and figures could be made from Plasticine; the tables could be constructed from balsa wood, carefully measured, cut and stuck together; clothes could be made from a selection of materials. The whole scene could be displayed in a box with one side cut away. The box could be painted and furnished like a period doll's house.

Some children enjoy working on a small scale; others could work on a large scale, investigating and drawing kitchen and farming equipment and the conditions of the same period. Food, tableware and manners could be contrasted with conditions in the nineteenth century or today.

More recent paintings of meals include Henri Matisse's *Dinner Table (La Desserte)* (1897), showing a formal table setting of the late nineteenth century and Edward Kienholz's *The Beanery* (1965), which is set in a cheap diner.

There are other sources that can be referred to as well as paintings. Illustrations, such as the engraving entitled *Our Housekeeping* in Dickens's *David Copperfield*, are funny as well as informative. The soft sculpture of Claes Oldenburg (1929 -) was based on food; there is something disconcerting about six-foot high hamburgers, but they are very realistic.

Art: AT1, AT2; Science: AT1, AT3; History: AT1, AT3; English: AT1, AT2

Animals

In the Middle Ages and the Renaissance period, drawings of animals were gathered together into books called bestiaries. The bestiary of Leonardo da Vinci is in Windsor Castle. In this book, Leonardo accurately draws animals with which he is familiar. The cat, the lion and the horse are shown in movement and in detail, whereas his pictures of the more obscure and exotic animals approach fantasy since he had to rely on travellers' tales. This in itself could give rise to some interesting discussions with the children on modern methods of communication, which have resulted in our greater knowledge and understanding of the appearance of animals and their anatomies.

The nineteenth century Romantics, with their revived interest in nature, produced dramatic and studied animal paintings. Eugene Delacroix's *Lion Hunt* (1855) in the National Gallery in London, is a masterpiece of action and colour, as is Vernet's *The Lion Hunt* (1836) in the Walker Art Gallery, Liverpool. The children could try to make their own version of this picture. The pictures and drawings of the Romantic artists would form a useful reference in any project based on animals, such as the clay work described in Chapter 6.

Another painter and sculptor who studied animals and people was Edgar Degas (1834- 1917), whose bronzes of racehorses and paintings of the racetrack are a true record of events that he had witnessed. Degas belonged to the Realism movement that superseded Romanticism in the last century. The painters of Realism, who include the Impressionists, recorded contemporary events and scenes from everyday life.

A different approach to animals can be found in Max Ernst's Surrealist painting *The Elephant Celebes* (1921), in the Tate Gallery, London, in which an elephant is constructed out of a Sudanese clay grain vessel, with a hollow bull's head and horns. It looks very large on the canvas, standing on a flat plane with tiny mountains in the distance. The whole picture is disturbing, as the usual perspective and logical juxtaposition of objects has been disrupted; but this is what Surrealism is about. The children would find this an interesting picture, and it could be shown to them before a junk-modelling session, as a stimulus to their imagination. They could be asked to make an animal out of plastic bottles, milk bottle tops, egg cartons, cord, raffia, scraps of nylon fur etc.

Other works of art that could accompany Max Ernst's picture are Picasso's animal sculptures, such as *Cock* (1932). Many sculptural works could be shown to the children, to demonstrate that junk objects can be transformed into other and powerful images. *Cast Iron* by Julius Schmidt (1961) is a box-like animal shape, constructed from scrap engineering parts, while the spidery form of *Royal Bird* (1948) by David Smith uses the spaces between shapes to suggest flight.

Art: AT1, AT2; Science: AT2, AT3

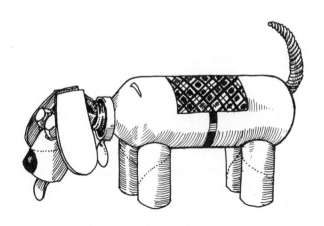

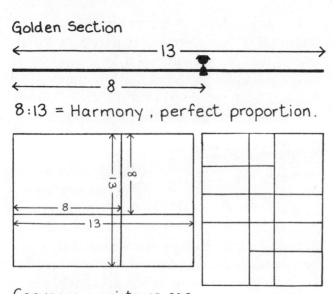

Golden Section

8:13 = Harmony, perfect proportion.

Canvases or pictures can
be divided this way . . . . . . and subdivided.

Figure 1

Mathematics

This may seem an unlikely theme to be linked
to art, but many compositions are based on a
mathematical division of the canvas, known
as the golden section. This divides a line or a
rectangle in two unequal parts, in such a way
that the ratio of the smaller to the larger is the
same as that of the greater to the whole –
approximately 8:13 (Figure 1). It was much
used in Renaissance times, and it is still used
today in certain types of abstract art,
resulting in clear geometric shapes.

Although the children will not need to know
anything of the golden section, they will
appreciate the balance and harmony that
results from it in such works as Victor
Pasmore's *Relief Construction in White, Black
and Indian Red* (1962), or Kenneth Martin's
curved *Oscillation* (1962), both in the Tate
Gallery, London. The children could be asked
to draw the Kenneth Martin as accurately as
they can, after doing some rough sketches of
the form in their sketch-books. They could try
constructing their own curved forms from
rolls of paper or card, stuck together.

With the Victor Pasmore, which is made up
of pure, geometric forms, the children could
work out how many times the smaller oblong
fits into the bigger shape, and, using the same
proportions, draw out a plan for a bas-relief
construction, using boxes cut to different
depths, and stuck on to a card background.

Machines

Children of all ages enjoy drawing and
designing machines; their imagination can be
stimulated by looking at the way others have
approached this area. In the bicycle project in
Chapter 5, the Futurists were discussed, and
any book on their work is worth looking
through, when the children are working on an
art activity based on machinery. Before
drawing details of a machine, the children
could be shown *Machine* (1916) by Morton L.
Schamberg or Francis Picabia's *Child
Carburetor* (1915-18).

Other twentieth century artists have taken
the aesthetic of the machine as their
philosophy, and drawn on the forms of
machinery in their work. One of these was
Fernand Leger (1881-1955), a French painter
who used tubular shapes in his paintings. He
was called 'a Tubist' for a time. His paintings
have the flat, polished surface of a well-oiled
machine, and his people have the puppet-like
limbs and heads of robots. Leger painted in
black, white and the primary colours. He
painted a picture of a building site in 1950,
called *The Great Constructors*, which shows
men working up in the girders during the
construction of a building. This could be used
as a discussion point during an activity on
houses or building materials.

Much of the sculpture of this century has
inevitably been influenced by the metallic
manmade objects that surround us. Rudolf
Belling's *Head* (1923) is made from a bell and
assorted highly polished metals. It bears a
symbolic resemblance to a head.

Robots

Most children enjoy building robots, and
many recent figurative sculptures are robotic
in effect. In Lynn Chadwick's *The Watchers*
(1960), three sinister and anonymous shapes,
with box-like heads, stand on machine-sharp
metal spikes. Eva Renee Nele's *The Couple*
(1961) are more machines than people, and
look as though they were assembled from old
car parts. A machine and robot-orientated
sculptor is Eduardo Paolozzi (1924-) who
designed the murals for London's Tottenham

Court Road Underground station. His sculptures of the 1960s were made up of casts of pieces of machinery, colourfully painted.

The art historian Herbert Read (1989) says of Paolozzi's work, it 'is as if the mechanical computer has finally achieved a soul, and with that apotheosis ceased to function as a machine'. Apart from their aesthetic value, these sculptures are amusing and colourful, with strange and evocative titles, and most children find this work to their liking. *Japanese War God* (1958) is made from scrap metal, whereas *The City of the Circle and the Square* (1963) is made from wood and metal, painted in bright primary colours, and resembling an escapee from a highbrow fun-fair! Paolozzi's *Twin Towers of the Sphinx* (in the Whitworth Art Gallery, Manchester) is a sculpture that would give children ideas for ways of using boxes. Point out the pattern and texture on the sculptures – although they are made of what used to be unconventional materials, such as recycled metal and machine parts, the placing of these elements is far from arbitrary. The various small shapes produce a rhythmic pattern that enhances the whole sculpture.

The children could be allowed to make their own robots after looking at examples of such sculptures. Before the children start work, paint the boxes with white emulsion to obliterate lettering and logos.

What you need

A variety of boxes, sketch-books, pencils, paints, brushes, silver foil, PVA adhesive, spreaders, scissors, egg boxes, squeezy bottles, string, electric circuit (with batteries and small bulbs).

What to do

This could form part of a science topic on electricity in which the children learn to construct a simple electric circuit.

Discuss the role of robots in our society, and ask the children to work in pairs or small groups to design a humanoid-type robot that could help around the home. Tell them that it must light up when it is working, so that people know when it is active. They should also consider some of the following questions:
• Would it work at night? Or would it be put away in a cupboard?
• Would it have to look pleasant (people might not like to have it round them if it didn't)?
• Would it have wheels or feet?
• Would it have a face?
• Where would it store its tools – sweepers, dusters, etc?
• How many arms would it have?
• Where would its lights go?

Ask the children to draw their ideas in their sketch-books, then proceed to build their models out of the boxes, either painting them or covering them with silver foil. Show the children how to put the electric circuit into the model (see Figure 2), and tell them to make the robot as decorative as they can. Explain that it should be a friendly robot.

When they have finished, discuss their models. Ask them to write their robots' life stories, from the time they came off the production line to the time they went back to the factory for a first service.

Draw their attention to the Paolozzi robot and god figures, and point out the way he used box-like shapes and discarded material.
Art: AT1, AT2; Science: AT3, AT4;
Technology: AT1, AT2, AT3, AT4

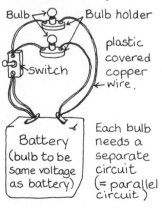
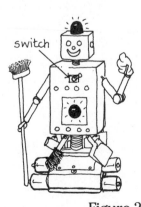

Bulb
Bulb holder
plastic covered copper wire.
switch
switch
Battery (bulb to be same voltage as battery)
Each bulb needs a separate circuit (= parallel circuit)
Figure 2

Landscape paintings

Often, children's paintings and drawings of landscape improve dramatically when they have studied the way artists painted similar subjects. A group of junior children in an inner London primary school studied *The Haywain* (1821) by John Constable as part of a project on farming methods in the past, which arose after a school trip to the West Country, where the children visited a farming museum. While there, they took photographs and made drawings of old barns and cottages, which were later drawn out as plans, and built into models.

The finished models were then drawn. During the course of this project, the children painted their own version of *The Haywain*, matching the colours in the painting, and finding out about Constable's work on clouds and how he saw the sky as 'the key to nature'. They were shown how the composition of the painting developed and changed over a period of time.

Later, in January, the children were taken to a local park, after it had snowed, and did some rapid sketching. Back in the classroom, each child painted a different view of the park. Each showed an awareness of colour, composition and shape that indicated the influence of the Constable study, and the fact that the school made regular use of the local art gallery and its education staff. All the paintings were well observed; it was possible to recognise the different types of tree from the paintings, even though the drawing skills varied.

This analysis of an artist's work in a similar subject matter could lead indirectly to an urban or rural study. There are many artists who have used landscapes as a subject for paintings. Select one whose work relates to the subject being considered. For example, Monet would be a good choice for studying the methods of painting water, Corot and Constable for the tones of light and dark, and Turner for drama and atmospherics. More recent works by L.S. Lowry, Patrick Caulfield, Tom Phillips and, to some extent, David Hockney could be used by the children to to help them examine the modern urban and suburban environments.

View through a window

There are two good ways of using a viewfinder to concentrate children's attention on a specific aspect of a view. Attach a large viewfinder to a pointed stick, and push this into the ground, so that the children only have a limited view of what is in front of them. Alternatively, fix a smaller viewfinder to a window. Some school windows have transoms or subdivisions; these can also be used as viewfinders, with the children each being assigned a different view to paint. The final works could then be assembled to form a long mural.

Some time before beginning practical work, display a selection of artists' paintings that are relevant to the locality of the subject matter. Discuss the work with the children, and, if possible, arrange with a local art gallery for their education staff to show the children a selection of appropriate paintings. Let the children make colour studies and paint their own version of a picture that they have seen.

What you need

Viewfinders, a range of pencils, rulers, sketchbooks, paints, brushes, palettes, wax crayons, pens, ink, paper.

What to do

As a preliminary exercise, let the children make a series of tone studies, reflecting contrasting weather conditions, for example a dark, overcast day and a light, sunny day. If the children need some revision of this, refer back to Chapter 1 for ways of discovering tone with pencils. Some sketches and detailed studies could be carried out using pen and ink. This is a good way of recording impressions, and often captures a feeling of spontaneity and movement, as it cannot be rubbed out. Tell the children to draw on top of the first sketch, if they feel dissatisfied.

Before the children start their paintings, give them a small piece of the painting paper, and let them practise making a tonal palette, using shades of black and white. Ask them:
• How many shades of grey can you make from mixing black and white?
• How can you make dark areas have lighter highlights?
This exercise will familiarise them with the medium, as well as drawing their attention to tone. (Look at Constable's use of light and dark in his paintings.)

When they start the paintings, tell the children to paint lightly in the outlines of the darkest tones that they can see, followed by the outlines of the lightest tones. When these are in place, allow them to start to shade in the middle tones and to build up the rest of the picture in this way.

When the view is assembled, let the children compare and contrast their efforts, learning from each other in the process. The work could be displayed with the tonal palette.

Art: AT1, AT2; English: AT; Science: AT2, AT3; Technology: AT1

Transforming still life into landscapes

Giorgio Morandi (1890-1964) used still-life compositions of everyday objects, such as bottles and jars, to suggest monumental forms of architecture and garden landscapes. In the following activity, the children could use a still-life study as a starting point for a landscape or an abstract painting.

What you need

A selection of still-life objects (bowls, fruit, grasses, dried flowers), a light-coloured background, paints and painting equipment, charcoal, white chalk, cloths, A2 sugar paper, viewing windows, A4 drawing paper, reading-lamp (optional), sketch-books.

What to do

Arrange the still life against the light background, and place the reading-lamp in a position so that the shadows are clearly defined and interesting. Draw the children's attention to the fact that the lightest areas are those where the light falls, and the darkest, where the light is blocked. Tell them to use the charcoal and white chalk to draw the still life, reminding them to mark in the proportions first. Tell them not to turn over and start again if they make any mistakes, but to use the cloths to remove most of any incorrectly drawn lines; the marks that remain can be used to form a tone in the finished drawing.

When the drawings are finished, ask the children to use the viewing windows to look closely at the shapes and patterns in their pictures. Do the shapes remind them of anything? Do any of them resemble landscapes? Ask the children to try several thumbnail sketches in their sketch-books. When they have found a part that they like, let them draw it on the A4 paper, leaving a margin all round to allow for mounting. Suggest that they try to imagine walking among the shapes that they are painting. This should help to stimulate their imagination, and help them realise that everyday objects can be transformed into abstracts or other scenes.
Art: AT1, AT2

Abstract painting

Children are often asked to draw trees. Y5 and Y6 children would find it interesting to see the *Tree* series by Piet Mondrian (1872-1944), painted between 1909 and 1919. In this series the tree dissolves gradually into abstraction and spirituality. Through a series of studies, Mondrian develops the image of a tree into a pattern of vertical and horizontal lines. These images resemble present-day computer graphics and children usually respond to them readily. They are reproduced in *The Twentieth Century* by Rosemary Lambert (CUP).

Abstract with chairs

The following activity suggests how children could make a similar series, based on the spaces between chairs.

What you need

Chairs, A2 sugar paper, soft pencils, tracing paper, white cartridge paper.

What to do

Group the chairs together in an interesting arrangement, then tell the children to draw them in outline only. Place the tracing paper over their drawings, and tell them to trace the spaces between the chairs, and then transfer them to the cartridge paper. Encourage them to repeat the process on the same piece of paper, to make a pattern from the shapes between the chairs.

Follow-up

The shapes could be coloured, or inked-in as a linear design; a print, such as a linocut or monoprint could be developed from them.
Art: AT1, AT2

Perspective

By Y5 and Y6, children like to find out how to make buildings and scenes look as though they are disappearing towards the horizon. This can easily be achieved by using single-point perspective. The most well-known example of this is the way that lines appear to meet in the far distance (Figure 3).

Figure 3

Older juniors tend to be very concerned that their drawings should look real. In our society, concepts of reality in art are heavily influenced by the western European art tradition, and by the photographic images that surround us on billboards, television and in magazines and newspapers. The camera takes a full-frontal image seen from a single viewpoint. In fact, this conveys less information than a ground-plan, but this itself reflects a way of recording reality that accords with the western European Renaissance tradition. Indeed, as the interest in creating the illusion of three dimensions on a flat surface became intense, artists used mechanical methods similar to a camera, to study the effects of perspective. The camera obscura was probably used by Vermeer, and Joshua Reynolds' portable version still survives in the Science Museum, London. It works by projecting an image on to paper through a lens or hole into a darkened box or room, the image being whatever the lens sees. It produces an inverted image which painters would draw round to get an outline. A mirror could be used to turn the image the right way up. It was this device that led Fox Talbot to invent the first working camera. It is still possible to see Samuel van Hoogstraten's perspective box at the National Gallery, London.

This enthusiasm for making 'a window on to nature' reigned supreme in western art until the mid-nineteenth century. The camera image not only reflected the cultural values of the time, but provided a way of preserving that image and, as such, was enthusiastically embraced by artists like Manet.

Before they start to experiment with drawing in perspective, discuss the meaning of some of the terms that the children will use.
• Horizon line: this lies at the same level as the observer's eyes. There are two easy rules to remember: firstly, all lines beneath the horizon line (eye-level) will rise up towards it; secondly, all lines above the horizon line will come down towards it (Figure 4).

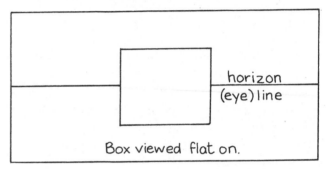

Figure 4

• Vanishing point: this lies on the horizon line. It marks the point where parallel lines going away from the viewer appear to meet on the horizon. There can be several vanishing points at different places along the horizon line (Figure 5).

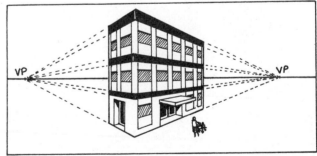

Figure 5

• Vertical lines: upright lines, usually at a right angle to the horizon line.

Single- or double-point perspective is a useful tool for creating the illusion of depth, but it is a mathematical exercise, and should not constrain children by being too rigidly adhered to.

Let the children try some set exercises and then apply it to their drawings and paintings more freely. In technical perspective drawing, it is not what is seen that is being drawn, but rather the impression of depth.

Drawing boxes

This activity suggests an exercise in simple perspective.

What you need

A box for each child, sharp HB pencils, rulers, A4 drawing paper, rubbers, a picture showing distinct use of perspective, such as Raphael's *Betrothal of the Virgin* (1504).

What to do

Show the children the picture, and discuss the way that the lines recede to the horizon. Explain that the horizon line is always at eye-level; even if you are lying down or up in an aeroplane, it moves around with you. Demonstrate the way to draw a box that is below the eye-level.

Using the rulers, tell the children to draw a similar box, lightly marking in the lines of the two vanishing points. Remind them that the nearest side of the box will look biggest. Ask

them to shade the box to make it look more solid. Repeat the exercise with a box above the eye-level. Explain that whether the top or the bottom is visible depends on where you stand when looking at an object.

Art: AT1, AT2; Mathematics: AT1, AT4

Draw a house

As a development from this, draw a box on a board or flip chart, showing the horizon line and the vanishing points. Ask the children how they can turn a box into a house. Point out that all parallel lines meet at a vanishing point. Ask them whether the roof ridge would be parallel with the walls.

Let them try drawing a house for themselves. Correct the work, and encourage them to grasp the basic principles of perspective.

Scale

Altering the scale to which objects are drawn can change the appearance and meaning of the object. The painter Paul Nash (1889-1946) frequently used this approach in his work. In his paintings *Flight of the Magnolia* (1944) and *Eclipse of the Sunflower* (1945), he uses giant flowers as clouds or suns wheeling through the sky. He employs the same distortion of scale when photographing or painting dead trees. *Monster Field* (1939) is a good example.

The children could try out this effect by altering the background scale of an observed drawing of twigs or driftwood.

Conclusion

These are just a few ways of introducing children to artists' work. Art is an area that can reward and add interest to life in a manner unique to each person. Some knowledge and experience of looking at artists' work can be educational to the children, not only immediately, but later in life. It leads to a wider appreciation, not only of art and beauty, but of nature, and the many wonders of form and colour that surround us.

Chapter 8
Cross-curricular projects (Key Stage 2)

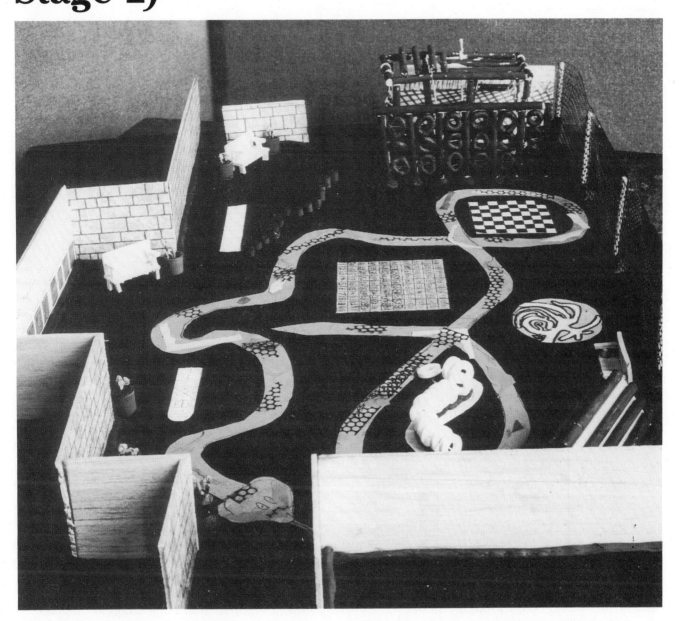

The integrated day is at the centre of much of the teaching in primary schools. As a foundation subject in the National Curriculum, art should be taught on occasions as a separate subject, but it also has a role either as a support subject or as a means of introduction to cross-curricular activities. The connections between art and the core areas are close, in both the sciences and the humanities, as art is concerned with the nature of materials, and with light and colour, as well as with the imagination. Moreover, looking at the way other artists have painted and sculpted involves consideration of history and geography, as the children investigate the backgrounds both of the people who produced the works and of their subject matter.

In this chapter, we indicate some ways in which these connections between art and other areas can be made at the junior level of the primary school.

Using the local environment

Improve the school playground

SCIENCE

Weeds/plants found
Conditions for new plant
growth
Effects of weather on
materials
Composition of walls/
strength of bonds

ART

Planning design
Drawing/sketching ideas
Building models
Using appropriate tools
and materials

MATHS

Measuring
Area
Scale work
Estimating costs

IMPROVE THE SCHOOL PLAYGROUND

GEOGRAPHY

Map-making – routes
through the playground
Uses of clay and its
origins

HISTORY

The school history
Games of the past
What was here before?
Reminiscences about
schooldays
Meanings of past nursery
rhymes (eg 'Ring-a-Roses')
Try copperplate writing
What children wore

TECHNOLOGY

Design and make models
Investigate the qualities of
materials
Planning designs

LANGUAGE

Technical language
relating to buildings
Group discussions
Nursery rhymes (past
and present)

PE

Play a game of old times

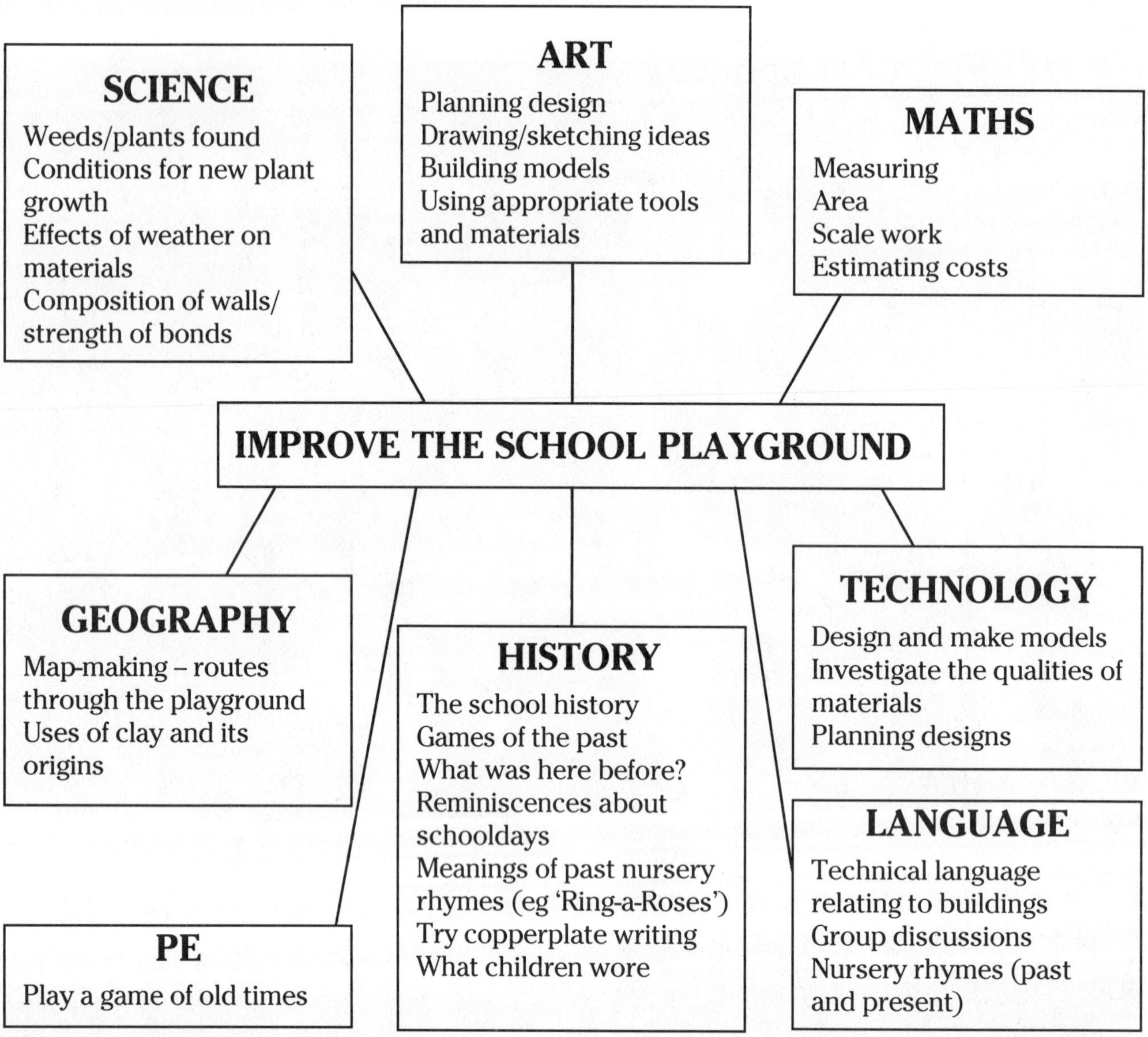

Figure 1

This topic would cover most areas of the curriculum (Figure 1), and could also provide activity suggestions for use by teachers, children and interested parents. Children often have ideas for improving their playground. When students have been invited into schools to carry out this type of project, the children have generally been very practical in their responses.

Such a project should start with a discussion about what changes the children would like to see in their playground. This could develop into making suggestions for improving the outside surroundings of the school. In inner city areas, these often include turning small areas of waste ground into gardens, sometimes with a pond. If the pond is a reasonable size, threatened species such as toads can be introduced. In one season the pond can become a useful resource for art and science, providing opportunities for studying form, movement and colour in art, and observation of the seasonal changes and animal behaviour in science.

Many school playgrounds have tarmac surfaces and children often come up with ingenious suggestions for improving these areas. Wooden tables with draughts and chess games sunk into the tops, barrel gardens to grow herbs, mosaics to divide games from quiet areas, tree stumps to make jungle paths and old car tyres to form a crawl-through snake have all been suggested at various times.

Once the ideas have been discussed, tell the children to write them down. The practical aspects of each suggestion then need to be discussed. Safety, expense, difficulties of construction, pathways for the free movement of people from building to building, access for mothers with push-chairs and suitability to the school's style of architecture should all be considered.

When the more extreme or unsuitable ideas have been weeded out, take a vote to discover which are the most popular suggestions. Divide the class into groups of six to eight children, and make each group responsible for planning and modelling designs for one particular area of the playground, enlarging and refining the suggestions that have already been put forward.

Art: AT1, AT2; Mathematics: AT1, AT2, AT4; Technology: AT1, AT2, AT3, AT4; Geography: AT1, AT5; Science: AT1, AT3; English: AT1, AT2, AT3

Make a scale plan of the playground

This activity supports mathematics and map-making skills, as well as enhancing work on shape and the understanding of space in art, and draughtsmanship and planning in technology.

What you need

Writing paper, pencils, surveyors' tape measure, coloured pencils, coloured adhesive paper, small-scale graph paper, rulers.

What to do

Agree a simple scale with the children. This could be one square of graph paper for every 30cm of playground. The chosen scale will depend on the size of the area to be planned. Tell the children to measure the length and width of the playground, and write the measurements down beside a small outline plan. Ask them to agree on a range of symbols that they can all understand to indicate doors and windows.

Let the children work in their groups, measuring and making notes of any special features of their area of the playground. When the measurements and drawings are complete, discuss their accuracy, and send

the children out to check again if there is any uncertainty. The plan of the playground can then be drawn up to scale, using the graph paper. Ask each group to work on their own separate sheet, and to leave a border round the plan so that they can be assembled later to form a plan of the whole playground.

Lay the various parts of the plan out and discuss the groups' ideas. The children might suggest that they would like more places to sit, in which case you should remind them of possible problems. What materials could be used that would not be vandalised? Remind them of the effects of weathering, and the limitations of cost. Children in one school suggested logs for sitting on; another group of children thought large pieces of artificial rock could combine climbing and sitting areas. Breeze-blocks and bricks are other materials that could be used to make relatively vandal-proof and weather-proof seats. Ask the children:

• Would they want the seats to be decorated, and if so, how? (Paint wears off, but mosaics can be effective on the backs and sides.)
• Should there be other types of seating for parents, who may have to wait while collecting their children from school? If the adult seating is already adequate, the children could consider if any improvements could be made to its position.

Draw the children's attention to the various ways the playground is used. For example, perhaps some areas have to be kept free for people to play ball games. Ask the children:
• Should an area be kept as a separate games area?
• How should it be marked out?
• Should there be a different area for other, quieter games?

Nearly all children like to see some flowers or shrubs in a school playground, even if they are only in a small area. The children could research into quick-growing summer climbers, such as nasturtiums, to cover unsightly fencing.

Once all the changes have been agreed on, ask each group to work out the flat ground shape of the seating and other additional features in their area of the playground, using the same scale as in the plan. Let them cut the

shapes from coloured paper, so that they can be clearly seen when they are placed on the plan. Then, as a class, assemble the whole plan, including the shapes of any seats, tubs, ponds and games.

It should then be possible to see if the changes would make the playground overcrowded or too sparse. Again, ask the children to discuss the arrangements, and make any agreed changes to the plan.
Art: AT2; Mathematics: AT1, AT2; Technology: AT1, AT2, AT4; Geography: AT1, AT5; Science: AT3

A model of the new playground

Once agreement is reached on the layout and contents of the improved playground, the model-making can start.

In this activity, the children use art and design skills to support a thoughtful consideration of their immediate environment. Technology, science and mathematics are involved in this activity: technology in aspects of model-making; mathematics in measuring and working to scale in two and three dimensions; science in the discoveries the children will make about the behaviour of materials. The purpose of this activity is practical and connects theory with the children's own environment. The group and class work needed to ensure the success of the activity encourages teamwork and co-operation, which are important skills for this age group as they near adolescence.

What you need

Baseboards for the models (hardboard is cheap and can be cut into sections to fit the plan areas; thick card can also work well as a baseboard), plaster, PVA adhesive, Cernit, soft wire, tissue-paper, small sponges, paint and painting equipment, craft knives, balsa-wood, balsa cement, scissors, small-scale graph paper, pencils, rulers, adhesive pads, non-fungicidal wallpaper paste or paper paste, newspaper, chicken wire, cardboard, Mod-Roc, string, Polo mints, matchsticks, forks, stick-on mosaic pieces, Plasticine, sequin waste, silver spray paint, staple gun, self-hardening clay.

What to do

Start by suggesting that each group should cover their baseboard with the right type of material and colour for the background.
• For a black tarmac playground, paint the board a dark grey-black.
• Grass can be suggested by a layer of plaster, given texture with the forks before it is totally dry, and then painted green.
• For a raised area or pond, make the basic curves in chicken wire, then cover it with newspaper to soften the shape, and coat it with plaster or Mod-Roc.

Once this is done, put the base to one side and allow it to dry, while the children start to measure and make the small models. Stress that these should be kept to scale, although some children might find this quite difficult when they are working on small details, such as chair legs and play structures. For items such as seats or slides, tell the children to start by drawing a pattern to scale (see page 86), using the small-scale graph paper. Ask them to cut their patterns out in separate sections, and attach them to the balsa-wood with adhesive pads. They should then draw round the outline, before they start to cut the wood with craft knives or a junior hacksaw.

Trees and shrubs can be modelled in several ways, after preliminary studies of their leaves, bark and shape have been made. Allow the children to choose whether to construct the main shapes from Plasticine, or from wire covered with tissue-paper or plaster. Let them add foliage using crumpled tissue-paper or small pieces of sponge, Cernit or Plasticine. These materials can also be used to add berries or flowers to the foliage.

Logs and posts can be made from balsa-wood or, more economically, from rolled-up paper. If the children are going to use paper, ask them to brush the side that is to be rolled up with non-fungicidal wallpaper paste or paper paste, before rolling them up into long lengths, then help them to cut them up into appropriate sizes and paint them. Ask the

children if the log would be the same colour all over. Remind them that the ends of the log are inside the tree. Ask them to think whether the sides and ends should be in different colours.

Ask the children for suggestions of ways to make fencing and walls. Remind them that the fences have to stand up. Give them a selection of materials to work with. They may suggest their own solutions to problems that they come across; if not, here are a few possibilities.
• Wooden overlap fences can be made from strips of card, supported at intervals by balsa-wood pieces for the fence posts. Help the children to make holes in the plaster base at corresponding intervals and fill them with adhesive before inserting the fence posts. If the holes get too large, help the children to fill round the balsa fence post with newspaper, plaster or Plasticine, pushed in with a pencil.
• Picket fences can be made from matchsticks, and joined together with fine wire.
• Link fences can be made from a strip of silver sequin waste, or by netting string together, spraying it silver, and stapling it to balsa-wood posts.
• Brick walls can be made either from self-hardening clay, or by pasting paper decorated with a brick pattern on to card. Let the children print brick patterns on paper, using the end and side of a small oblong piece of balsa to represent the headers and stretchers of the brick.

Ask the children to make patterns and games on the ground from strips of paper, fixed in position on the baseboard with PVA adhesive. Plant containers and swings made from old car tyres can be modelled in Plasticine. If the scale is right, Polo mints painted black can also be used.

When the models are finished, ask the children to discuss the effectiveness of their designs and to estimate the cost of materials and labour. They could also investigate the skills that would be needed to implement the improvements. Children are often surprised at the amount labour adds to the cost of any work, and at the range of craft skills needed to carry out the designs. This investigation would increase their knowledge of the skills employed by the country's workforce.

Follow-up

The finished models could be displayed with photographs of the present playground, taken by the children, and accompanied by written descriptions of the methods they used to make the models and the estimates of cost. The models could be drawn from different angles and viewpoints, and could form the basis for a painting of children playing in the redesigned playground.
Art: AT1, AT2; Technology: AT2, AT3; Mathematics: AT1, AT2; Science AT2

Using local shops

This cross-curricular activity is also based both on the local environment and on investigating industrial methods. It is suitable for use with children in Y4 and Y6. Its cross-curricular applications are shown in Figure 2.

Most shopping areas are a productive source for a variety of art activities, ranging from linocut to three-dimensional work. Before the activity, arrange for the children to visit a selection of local shops. Speak to the owners or managers in advance and explain that the visit will be brief, and that the children will be looking at a number of local shops to find out about different methods of organisation, the range of products on sale and their source of supply.

A questionnaire for the children to fill in will need to be devised. It should take into account the variety of shops the children are going to visit. Some of the following questions could be included:
• How many people work in the shop?
• What do they do?
• What does the shop sell?
• How are goods stored?
• How are they transported?
You could also take photographs of the shop facades for use in art work back in the classroom, and as a reference when the children research the dates of the buildings.

If enough extra help is available from interested parents, it would be useful for the class to be divided into groups, each of which could visit a different shop and then compare their findings back in the classroom. If this is not possible, make sure the children visit at least two different types of shop – a greengrocer's and a general store, for example. A visit to a supermarket would be enlightening for the children, but many of these very large shops only allow group visits from secondary-school children.

Once the visit or visits have been arranged, prepare the children for the work by discussing the source of the goods they are going to see, and the different methods by which they are produced and marketed. A visit to a bakery or greengrocer's shop, for example, could involve investigation into this country's farming methods, contrasting them with the methods employed in other areas of the world, such as Europe and Asia. Eating habits of the people in the various countries could be compared, and the benefits and disadvantages of the different diets and climates considered. The children could write an account of a day in the life of a farmer from one of the countries they have studied, and paint a picture of his farm, including the plants he grows and the animals he keeps.

The children could also look at the way farming has been depicted in the past, as well as today. John Constable's *The Haywain* (1820) in the National Gallery, London, shows a horse and cart crossing a ford. At Hatfield House, Hertfordshire, the four Sheldon tapestries of the seasons show farming and husbandry methods in the seventeenth century. These could be compared to the methods used today. Millet's drawings of peasants show not only the clothes, but give us an idea of just how hard their lives must have been. *The Celebrated Bull, Alexander*

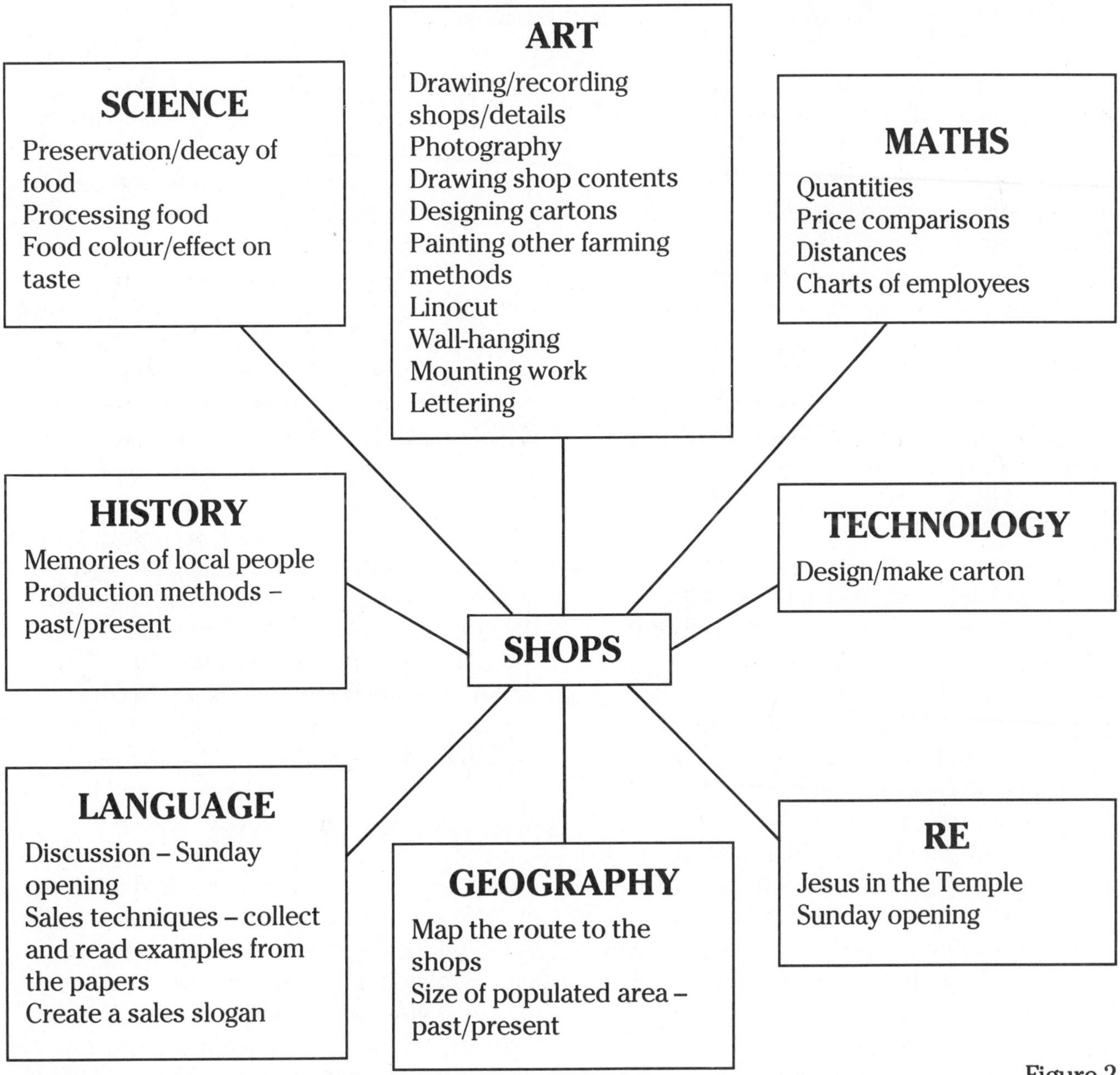

SCIENCE
Preservation/decay of food
Processing food
Food colour/effect on taste

ART
Drawing/recording shops/details
Photography
Drawing shop contents
Designing cartons
Painting other farming methods
Linocut
Wall-hanging
Mounting work
Lettering

MATHS
Quantities
Price comparisons
Distances
Charts of employees

HISTORY
Memories of local people
Production methods – past/present

SHOPS

TECHNOLOGY
Design/make carton

LANGUAGE
Discussion – Sunday opening
Sales techniques – collect and read examples from the papers
Create a sales slogan

GEOGRAPHY
Map the route to the shops
Size of populated area – past/present

RE
Jesus in the Temple
Sunday opening

Figure 2

(1816), in the Tate Gallery, London, by Benjamin Marshall could be compared with a recent photograph of a prizewinner at a county show. More recently, Bill Brandt's photograph *Saving Britain's Plum Crop* (September, 1942) and the Ministry of Information photograph of *The Sower* (1945) give a vivid impression of the changes that have taken place in farming methods in the post-war period. Pictures like these could be discussed and compared. Explain how they all reveal aspects of rural life still to be found in parts of Europe. The advantages and problems of mass farming production could be discussed.

Once the preparatory work has been completed, take the children to visit the shops. Encourage them to ask appropriate questions so that their questionnaires can be filled in. During the visit, try to arrange for the children to take back some samples of the goods on sale, so that they can display and draw them in class. Let each child take one selected photograph of the visit.

A rough ground-plan of the layout of a shop could be drawn, and some of the advertising lettering sketched, to make a note of the different typefaces. Ask the children to make drawings of the shop facade in their sketchbooks.

Drawings in pastel or pen and ink could be made to record the different produce. (This could later be used as a basis for designing new packaging for various processed foods, such as cereals.)

Once the children have completed their visit, the results of the questionnaire should be analysed back in the classroom.

Display the photographs and drawings that the children made of the shops and details of the facades, and discuss their appearance and architectural style. The details of the architecture can be turned into patterns, or the buildings used as a basis for a linocut or group work such as a mural or a wall-hanging. Linocut patterns could be used as the basis for the cover of a class book about the shop project, containing drawings, maps, descriptions and accounts of the origins of the goods on sale. The books could go into the school library for all to use.

Art: AT1, AT2; History: AT3; Technology: AT2, AT3, AT4; Geography: AT1, AT2, AT3, AT4, AT5; Science: AT2

Shop front print

Taking the drawings as a basis, and using the photographs as reference, the children could make a linocut of the shop front, and print it in several colours. The prints would make excellent illustrations for a class book, and the careful thought and adaptations necessary to the process would develop the children's knowledge of the disciplines and skills needed to produce a successful prints.

The children could be shown linocuts by artists who worked in this medium, such as Edward Bawden or Pablo Picasso, whose prints are illustrated in many books about linoprinting.

Explain to the children that extreme care should be taken when making linocuts. Have some sticking plasters to hand in case of accidents.

What you need

Lino and lino printing equipment (see Chapter 9, page 147), cloths, felt-tipped pens, pencils, a selection of photographs of buildings, old newspapers, newsprint, cartridge or other better-quality paper.

What to do

Tell the children to refer back to their sketches and to choose a shop-front to draw. Ask them not to put in too many details. Remind them that the drawing will be reversed when it is printed, so if they want to put in the name or number of the shop, it will have to be in mirror writing.

Give each child a 4cm square piece of lino and allow them to practise the linocut technique (see page 147) so that they can discover what sort of marks the various tools make in the material. Show them how to use the lino tools. Demonstrate the way to hold the lino block, with one hand positioned *behind* the direction in which they are cutting, so that if the tool slips, it will not injure their fingers. Tell them to make an outline of the design first with the V-shaped cutting tool, and then to cut the lino away. Point out that there is no need to cut through to the hessian on the back of the lino; it is characteristic of the method to retain some of the texture made by the cutting tools in the lino. Also the lino block tends to fall apart if it is cut too deeply. Encourage them to use a variety of different thicknesses of line and texture. (Some school prints are weedy specimens that do not exploit the potential of the medium!) Tell them to use the newsprint to make a print of the marks they have cut out. Comment on the way that the cut-out shapes remain white in the final print. Explain that this is because the lino that is left uncut is the part that prints. In other words, a line cut into the block will not print on the paper. Tell the children that to print a black line, the lino on either side of the line has to be cut away. (This can be difficult if the tools are not razor sharp, as lino has a tendency to crumble.)

After the children have experimented with their small lino blocks, tell them to go over the lines of their drawings with black felt-tipped pens to make a linocut design. Explain that some areas of the drawing can be black and solid, representing the area that will print as a block of colour; others can be textured, using some of the marks found when the children experimented with their trial piece of lino. Some areas can remain white; these are the areas that will eventually be cut away.

Remind the children of the basic shapes of the buildings – straight walls and simple geometric forms. Using the photographs, draw the children's attention to the textures that can be found on buildings. Ask them:
• How are you going to show these textures?
• How are you going to distinguish between transparent and opaque materials? The bricks are easy, but how could glass be shown?

Encourage them to try out different effects again, using small blocks of lino.

After the children have completed their rough designs, let them transfer them straight to the block using the felt-tipped pens, and start cutting. Explain that it is important to keep the block very clean when printing, as each speck of dirt prints like a tiny star. While this can look attractive in the right place, it is usually disappointing for the children.

Let the children test-print their blocks on the newsprint, before making a final print on the better-quality paper. The prints can be window-mounted; this would be a good opportunity for the children to make their own mounts, as the prints are fairly small.

If the children get on well with the medium, it should be possible to make a two-colour linocut. This method is described in Chapter 9, page 147.
Art: AT1, AT2; Technology: AT2, AT3

A wall-hanging of the shops

Although this is a group project, it involves the children working individually. The whole wall-hanging is constructed out of the various parts made by the children.

What you need

Pictures of famous wall-hangings (such as the Overlord Embroidery in Portsmouth), background material (such as hessian or linen, either in a natural tone or a limited selection of colours), felts, a selection of fabric scraps (assorted colours and patterns), wool thread, soft or stranded embroidery cotton, knitting and/or rug wool, large crewel needles, pins, scissors, transparent fabric adhesive, sewing thread, tracing paper, carbon paper, sketch-books, sewing machine (optional), sequins, beads, buttons, acetate, pipe cleaners, dowel rod, tassels or fringes.

What to do

Explain to the children that they are each going to appliqué and embroider a square that will form part of a wall-hanging, based on the shops they have seen in their study of the local environment. Show them pictures of wall-hangings that depict places and events. The Bayeux Tapestry is the most famous example, but there is also the Battle embroidery in Hastings Museum, which is more recent. There are five panels executed by Beryl Dean in 1974 in St George's Chapel, Windsor, and another example entitled *Minerva* (1964) by Stephen Lee, which can be found in the boardroom of the Joint Matriculation Board, Manchester.

Discuss the design and the presentation with the children. For example, if they visited a baker's and a greengrocer's shop, ask them:
• Are the contents of the shop going to form part of the hanging, as well as the shop-fronts? How can we arrange this?
• Are the fruit and cakes to alternate with the shop-fronts, or should they form a border between the shops?
• Are any people going to be included? If so, will they be the customers or staff, or both?
• What about scale? (If the fruit and cakes were worked to the right scale, they would be very small, and would not be seen.) How can this be resolved?

Tell the children to try out some roughs in their sketch-books, then lay out the roughs and, using a board or flip chart, discuss the suggestions with the children and decide on a layout. Once the layout has been determined, work can start on the individual panels. Agree on a size for the panels, then ask the children to draw the size of the squares on to paper, and try a few designs. Ask the children each to choose the one they like best. As a whole class, arrange the designs into a satisfactory layout, then choose colours for the finished wall-hanging. Two sets of contrasting primary colours could be used, alternating squares of red and yellow with green and blue. Another

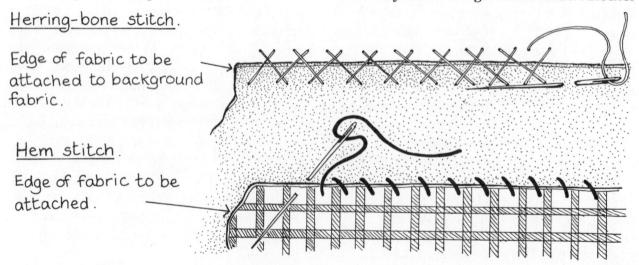

Herring-bone stitch.

Edge of fabric to be attached to background fabric.

Hem stitch.

Edge of fabric to be attached.

Figure 3

approach would be for the colours to harmonise, in which case various shades of one colour could be used. Alternatively, the whole panel could be worked in shades of black, grey and white, to make a tone study.

Demonstrate to the children how to stick fabric on to a background, showing them that they only need to apply adhesive to the edges. Point out that gluing does not work well with fabric that is too fine or frayed.

Tell the children to mark the basic outlines on to the background fabric using carbon paper then to trace the largest shapes and cut them out. Help the children to pin the paper shapes to the pieces of fabric they have chosen to use, and cut them out. These can then be stuck or sewn to the background fabric. If the fabric pieces are to be sewn on, show the children how to use herring-bone or hemstich (see Figure 3). These are less obtrusive than the unattractive blanket stitch. If a sewing-machine is available, the pieces can be zigzagged down after tacking. Extra patterns and textures can be added, using simple stitches such as cross stitch, couching, running and dot stitch (Figure 4). Sequins, beads and buttons enhance the work, and shadows and windows can be suggested by using layers of net or cutting holes in acetate and sewing it to the fabric. Let the children make figures from pipe-cleaners, dressed and attached to the background. If Velcro is used, the figures can be moved about on the picture.

When the children have finished their squares, place them all together, and ask them if they think any more details need to be added. Discuss the finishing process. The squares will have to be machined together, which should probably be carried out by the teacher. The panel could be finished by sewing or sticking cord or strips of fabric in a contrasting colour, around the edge of each square, covering the machining. To hang the panel, add a fold of fabric at the top, and thread a dowel rod through it. The bottom can be left plain, or decorated with tassels, fringes or loops.

Follow-up

The hanging could form a background to an assembly presentation, telling the rest of the school about the shop visits. This should include the linocut and a description of the results of the children's investigations, supported by maps and paintings.

A similar approach could be used if local houses were chosen as a subject. The children could find out who used to live in the houses, interview some of the present inhabitants and take photographs and make sketches of the residents. The people and the houses could then be used as a basis for a linocut.

Art: AT1, AT2; Technology: AT1, AT2, AT3, AT4; Science: AT3; Mathematics: AT1

Cross stitch

Can also provide decorative texture using different threads.

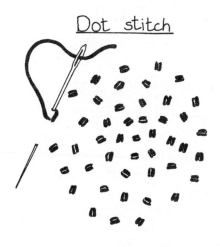

Dot stitch

Random texture stitch. Twice into the same place in any direction.

Figure 4

Light

In investigations into light, science and art are closely linked, as light and its effects are important in both areas. The following work is concerned with light, shadows and reflections. Cross-curricular applications are shown in Figure 5.

It is assumed that the class has already investigated the growth of seeds (such as beans), drawing, measuring and recording their progress, and that the children will record by drawing as well as writing when they set up an electric circuit.

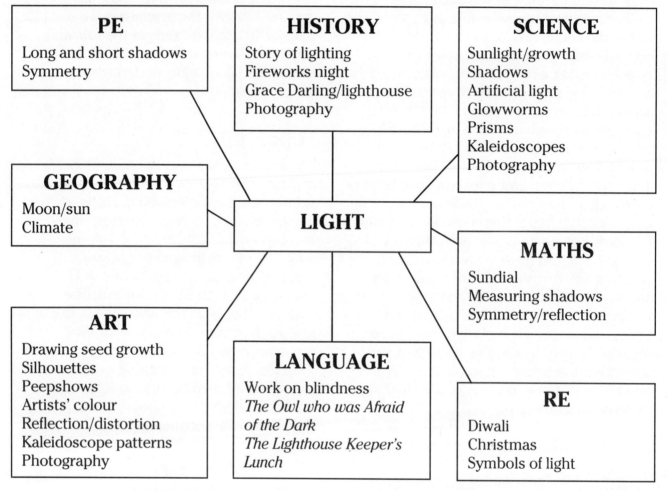

PE
Long and short shadows
Symmetry

HISTORY
Story of lighting
Fireworks night
Grace Darling/lighthouse
Photography

SCIENCE
Sunlight/growth
Shadows
Artificial light
Glowworms
Prisms
Kaleidoscopes
Photography

GEOGRAPHY
Moon/sun
Climate

LIGHT

MATHS
Sundial
Measuring shadows
Symmetry/reflection

ART
Drawing seed growth
Silhouettes
Peepshows
Artists' colour
Reflection/distortion
Kaleidoscope patterns
Photography

LANGUAGE
Work on blindness
The Owl who was Afraid of the Dark
The Lighthouse Keeper's Lunch

RE
Diwali
Christmas
Symbols of light

Figure 5

Make a peep-show

This activity could develop from investigations into the history of lighting. A visit to a museum exhibition about the history of lighting would support areas both in science and art.

Light filtered through coloured paper or acetate can produce quite magical effects, and is easily achieved in Y4, Y5 and Y6. The history of home and street lighting would make an ideal subject for a shoebox peep-show. If possible, let the children see an example of a peep-show before the activity.

They can be bought, but it would be useful for the teacher to make one if it is a new activity. Make sure that you choose a different subject area from that which the children will use.

What you need

Old shoeboxes, rulers, cartridge paper or thin card, scraps of wallpaper, paint, brushes, scissors, craft knives, paints and painting equipment, felt-tipped pens, pencils, double-sided adhesive tape, acetate, reference books on past and present lighting and costume, compasses, sketch-books, computer.

What to do

Ask the children to work in pairs and to decide on a type of street or home lighting which they would like to show, and tell them to look up appropriate references to help them with costume, furniture, lamps, etc. Any relevant information should be noted down in their sketch-books.

Give each pair a shoebox. Explain that they will have to cut a hole in the front, about 3cm in diameter. It needs to be 4.5cm from the base of the box, otherwise too much of the floor of the box will be seen when the hole is peeped through.

Explain to the children how a peep-show works. Tell them how the objects and people nearest to the viewer are only slightly larger than those furthest away and that the placing is crucial. The objects and people have to be staggered, otherwise they will hide each other, and each successive scene needs to be slightly higher up from the floor, as they progress towards the back of the box. Take the lid off the demonstration peep-show, and let the children see how it works.

Tell them that the first step is to paint and decorate the insides of their boxes so that they resemble a street or a room. If they have decided to depict a room, let them decorate the sides of the box with wallpaper, and paint in the fireplace or radiators, along with some

items of furniture, such as a Welsh dresser or a sideboard. If they choose to make a street scene, let them paint the sky at night and a row of houses.

Remind the children that they are portraying lighting effects from different periods, and ask them to think about the colours they need to use when they are painting. For example, if they are making a rush-lit cottage interior, it will be very dark; if it is a robot-inhabited car factory, it could also be dark, as robots do not need light to function.

The next step is to paint the end of the box. If they are depicting a room in a house, ask them if they are going to have a view through the window. If so, they can use the black felt-tipped pens to draw a silhouette of small trees, the back of the neighbouring house or a view of the countryside. If they have decided to make a street scene, suggest that they could draw a road junction, a railway station, gasometers or a motorway in the distance silhouetted against a night sky. Explain that any details can start roughly a quarter of the way up the back of the box, as most of it will be concealed.

Once this is done, the children can decide where the other parts of the peep-show are going. Tell them to cut the thin card or cartridge paper to the size of the box, leaving an overlap of 2cm on either side. Let them

illustrate this first card with drawings of appropriate subjects – streetlights, people and traffic, or gaslamps, people in costume and furniture. Make sure that they leave the middle of the card bare, as it will need to be cut out to make the scene at the back of the box visible.

Explain that the drawing should be on a small scale. The figures in the centre should be no larger than 5cm and the street and house furniture at the sides should be in proportion to them. Remind the children to keep the large objects at the sides, and point out that the people and objects must be standing on a carpet, road or pavement. Remind the children who are designing a room that they need to paint or draw in the central light. Ask all of them how they are going to make the lights look as though they are shining. Discuss with the children the various effects that come from different sources of light – gas, torches, sodium lights and strip lights, for example.

When they have finished, let them cut out the centre of the card, and place it in the shoebox. Show them how to attach it to the sides of the box with double-sided sticky tape, making sure that the tape cannot be seen through the peep-hole.

The children can then construct another layer of objects to fit into the shoebox in the same way, making sure they can see them clearly through the peep-hole. When they have completed the interior, help them to cut several slits, about 2cm wide, across the top of the box, checking the effect through the peep-hole. Encourage them to try different colours of acetate and tissue over the slits, to get the right colour effect for the sort of lighting they are using.

Get the children to decorate the front of the box with an appropriate scene or pattern, such as an Arts and Crafts movement tile. Overlay this with an equally appropriate title, such as 'A Victorian Sitting Room', using lettering generated on the computer. The computer could also be used to design wallpaper to cover the sides of the box.
Art: AT1, AT2; Science: AT1, AT4; History: AT3; Technology: AT2, AT3, AT4; English: AT1, AT3

Portrait silhouettes

This activity introduces children to another aspect of light – shadows.

What you need

Examples of portrait silhouettes, A2 white paper, A4 black paper, paper adhesive, scissors or craft knives, pencils, chair, overhead or ordinary projector, adhesive pads, tracing paper, paint, brushes, felt-tipped pens, a class photograph.

What to do

Show the children some examples of portrait silhouettes, and explain that they were widely used in the last century, as photography was still unusual. Sit each child in turn on the chair, and project the shadow of the child's profile on to a sheet of paper attached to the wall with adhesive pads. Tell the child to sit very still, and get another child to draw the projected outline.

This can then be traced on to the black paper and carefully cut out. This is best done with a knife, but scissors can be used if necessary. Let the children stick their silhouettes on to white paper and devise a decorative border, or frame them in coloured window mounts of their own choosing. All the silhouettes could be mounted together to form a group picture and displayed next to a class photograph.
Art: AT1, AT2; Science: AT4

Reflections in a spoon

This activity further investigates light through the study of reflections. This would form part of an investigation into reflection and refraction.

What you need

A4 white paper, soft pencils, polished spoons, mirrors.

What to do

Give the children a spoon and a mirror each, and tell them to compare the reflections that they can see. Ask them to look at themselves in the mirror, then in the convex side of the spoon. How has their appearance changed, and why? Repeat the process with the concave side of the spoon.

Ask them to try to draw the two images in detail, using pencil, and to employ both line and tone to suggest the curve of the spoon. Go round the class as they work, reminding them to ensure that proportions and detail are well observed. The drawings could be used as illustrations to written work on the science theme.

Follow-up

This activity could be enhanced by a look at Flemish art; the artists in the fifteenth and sixteenth centuries often used mirror reflections in their paintings. In *Banker and his Wife* (1514) by Quentin Massys, the distorted image of a room is reflected in a mirror at the front of the painting. This device is also employed by Petrus Christus in *St Eligius in his Shop* (1449), and by Jan van Eyck in *Giovanni Arnolfini and his Wife* (1434). These paintings are widely reproduced in books on Renaissance art. Ask the children why, apart from the novelty value (mirrors were not all that common at that time), should mirrors be used in these paintings? They may suggest that it adds a different view and a greater depth to the picture. Other activities that could be related to light could include studies based on prismatic colour. The children could look again at painters who used pure colours, such as Seurat and the Impressionists. They could also be introduced to Morris Louis (1912-62), an American Colour Field painter and Jules Olitski (1922-), who sprayed his works with great sweeps of colour that flow down and across the canvas.

The children could draw the images they have seen through looking into a kaleidoscope, and paint an imaginative composition of what it would be like to live in a world made up of shattered and curved reflections. This could be preceded by a study of the distorted image created when an object such as a biro or pencil, is stood in a glass of water. Tell the children that the 'reflection world' would be full of the distortions they have drawn, as if they were inside a kaleidoscope. Paper-backed foil and reflective paper could be used in the pictures.
Art: AT1, AT2; Science: AT1, AT4; History: AT3

Using stories

Many cross-curricular themes begin with stories, and these can stimulate the imagination of the child in a remarkable way. There are various ways in which to use the pictures that the story draws in the mind. The children could paint a straightforward illustration. Alternatively they could choose a character from the story, and work alone or in groups to explore various ways of portrayal, using a variety of media. The latter approach is described in the following activities.

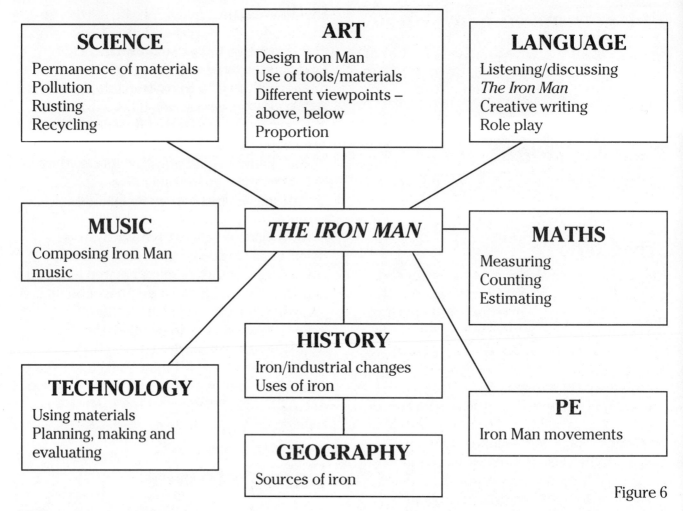

Figure 6

The Iron Man

The story of *The Iron Man* by Ted Hughes deals with waste, and this in itself could be the basis for art work. The children could investigate recycling, and the use of cans and disposable materials for printing and model-making. Reading the story could lead to an integrated arts event for assembly in which the children could tell their version of the story, and compose a tinny, rhythmic accompaniment, using such items as dustbin lids, bells and cymbals to simulate the sound of the Iron Man's steps. The class could be divided into groups – the music-makers, the story-tellers and the model-builders. A large model figure could also be made that would move and eventually collapse. Figure 6 suggests cross-curricular ideas.

What you need

A selection of various sizes of tin can (with holes pierced in one end, and the other end removed), strong string, scissors, thin garden canes, boxes of various sizes, foil, sketchbooks, clothes-line.

What to do

Tell the children to make a design for an Iron Man made from cans and boxes. Remind them of the story, and ask them to think about how big they want him to be. Explain that the model will be hung up and used during the assembly, and that while some of the class tell the story, others will move his arms and legs by manipulating garden canes tied to the model at the elbows, wrists, knees and ankles.

Let the children discuss their ideas for designs, and select the one that they agree is the most interesting. The construction of the model could be very simple by threading string through the tins and boxes to make mobile arms and legs, and then decorating it with foil and small boxes. (Once, during a rather elaborate production, a group of

Follow-up

The children could make drawings of the model, using large sheets of sugar paper and charcoal. When the figure is cut down and lies collapsed on the floor, they could draw it again, using either white pastels or chalk on black paper.

The natural world

All the previous cross-curricular activities have been linked with the man-made environment or the imagination, but it is also important to raise children's awareness of the natural world. The following series of activities would be possible even in an inner city school, provided there was a park nearby.

Cross-curricular applications are given in the topic web overleaf (Figure 7).

The hedgerow

The common hedgerow is often passed by without a glance, but there is an enormous wealth of history and nature to be observed in even the lowliest example.

As an introduction to the subject, the children could discuss the way people marked the boundaries of their land in past times. They could talk about the ancient divisions of land, in particular, the strip system. Examples of this system can still be seen at Farthing Downs in Croydon, Surrey. This could make an interesting school visit and sketching expedition.

The planted hedgerows came later in our agricultural system, and the children could be told how to measure the age of a hedgerow through a plant count. If there is an example of an old hedgerow near the school, take the children out to count the plant varieties and draw them. They could take a good reference book to help with identification. Before going out, show the children pictures of the poisonous plants that they might find, and tell them to make a note of their location, but on no account to touch them. These include ivy, yew, deadly nightshade, the spindle bush,

children who did not want to perform with the others used this method to build a model that stretched from floor to ceiling. When it was due to 'die' at the end of the performance, the string on which it was suspended was cut, and it fell to the floor with a dramatic clatter, breaking the strings in places, and disintegrating completely.)

The Iron Man should be suspended from a clothes-line or girder during construction, and later moved to the room where the school assembly is to take place. The sticks can be attached to the string at the elbows and wrists, at a point between two tins. These can then be operated to raise and wave the arms and legs.

Art: AT1; Technology: AT2, AT3

HEDGEROWS

SCIENCE
Growth
Local habitats
Poisons in nature
Conservation
Soil

LANGUAGE
Records and descriptions
Imaginative writing
Legends

HISTORY
Boundaries
Changes in land use

ART
Drawing plants, insects,
birds, animals
Models of insects
Hedgerow batik
Imaginary creatures

TECHNOLOGY
Using materials
Design/make a litter bin

GEOGRAPHY
Map of hedges
Land structure
Collections of stones, etc

Figure 7

foxglove, buttercup and some types of cow parsley, among many others.

What you need

Sketch-books, ballpoint pens, pencils, clipboards, reference books on plants and wildlife.

What to do

Tell the children to choose a plant in the hedgerow and to draw it. Encourage them to look closely at details, such as the number and the position of the thorns on a branch of hawthorn. Remind them to look at the plant carefully before they start drawing. They should be aware of the shapes of the leaves, the way they join the stems and the patterns made by the veins.

When they are drawing twigs and branches, tell them to look at the differences in width between the bottom and the top, and to notice the type of mark or pattern on the bark. After the children have drawn the hedgerow plants, they could look for and record the insect, bird and animal life that they might find there. They are almost certain to find hedge sparrows and such common

creatures as spiders. They could be noted down, and then looked up in reference books back in class, and enlarged drawings made. The children could research the wildlife that lives in or around hedgerows and waste ground, and then make large models of creatures such as ants, mistle thrushes and beetles.

Art: AT1, AT2; History: AT3; Science: AT1, AT2; Geography: AT5

132

Make a model ants' nest

What you need

Papier mâché (see Chapter 9, page 144) wire, paints, palettes, brushes, wire cutters, reference books, sketch-books, newspapers, Mod-Roc or clay, twigs and leaves, cardboard tubes, scissors, Cernit.

What to do

Talk to the children about the complex structure of the ants' nest, and tell them about the many different kinds of ant. (Some grow fungi for food, and some sew leaves together by holding their larvae to the edge of the leaf.) Encourage the children to research into the tunnel and brood chamber of a particular type of ant, and let them make drawings in their sketch-books.

Tell the children to make a cross-section of the nest as a background for model ants. This could be made from newspapers covered in Mod-Roc or from clay. Real twigs and leaves could be incorporated into the model.

The children could then be allowed to make model ants. The queen ant could be made from cardboard tubes cut and flattened to form her large thorax. She could then be surrounded by eggs made from Cernit.

To make a worker ant, help the children to cut and bend wire to form an armature, and make legs from wire that is strong enough to bear the weight of the body. Help them to make the ant's six legs out of three pieces of wire, and put them to one side. Let them make the body out of three wire cages – one (the smallest) for the head, should be a flattened circle, the second, a slightly elongated and narrow square for the upper abdomen, and the third, a longer oblong, for the lower abdomen. Help the children to wire the legs to the body parts, and join the three pieces together. Remind the children that the front legs join on to the upper abdomen, but that the position of the lower legs depends on the type of ant; they will need to look at the reference books for this. Once the wire structure is in place, the model can be built up and moulded from papier mâché.

1. Wood ant : Worker has no wings.

Bend the wire frame into shape, curling the ends round the sections to join them together.

Wrap the frame with Mod-Roc and bend legs to hold up the body.

2. Winged male.

Wings can be made of fine wire. Wrap the body and paint it black.

When the models are dry, ask the children to paint them and put them around the ants' nest.

Art: AT1; Science: AT2

Follow-up

This model could form the beginning of a progressive series of art explorations based on the hedgerow. The children could make large drawings of the sticks and pebbles they have collected, and see if the change of scale makes the subjects assume a different character.

To stimulate their imaginations the children could be shown the work of such artists as Graham Sutherland, whose paintings of thorns and trees, such as *Thorns* (1945), in the National Museum of Wales, Cardiff, seem rightful heirs of the 'pathetic fallacy', exemplified by Max Ernst's *Joy of Living* (1936). (The term 'pathetic fallacy' was used by the Victorian critic John Ruskin to describe the attribution of human feelings to non-human subjects.) Another good example for discussion would be Johann Christian Dahl's *Birch Tree in a Storm* (1849).

Twigs could be used, together with clay and Plasticine to construct an imaginary creature that lives secretly in the hedge; it could be a friend or familiar of the legendary woodland spirit the Green Man. Read the children some of the legends of early, wooded England, such as Herne the Hunter, who is closely identified with the Green Man. They could look for pictures and sculptures of him on pub signs and in older churches. There are examples of the Green Man in Exeter Cathedral and on the choir stalls at Winchester Cathedral.

Finally, the children could make a batik based on the leaves and shapes of the undergrowth they have sketched and observed in the hedgerow. The finished cloth could be used as a scarf, a cushion cover or as part of an outfit for a toy.

Hedgerow batik

What you need

Batik equipment (see Chapter 9, page 140) fabric, green, yellow and blue cold-water dyes, examples of batik, iron, newspaper.

What to do

Show the children pictures and examples of batik from Java. Explain that the word 'batik' means wax writing, and that the craft is thought to have originated in India, where it is still widely used. If possible, ask a local practitioner of the craft to come into the school and give a demonstration.

Tell the children to draw a picture of the leaves and plants directly on to the cloth using the hot wax. (This technique is described in detail on page 140.) Check that the wax is transparent on both sides of the fabric, otherwise the dye will seep through and the picture will be lost. Encourage the children to draw overlapping leaf shapes, and lines for grass and twigs. Tell them not to worry about the odd blob or smudge of wax, as it adds to the quality of the picture, and can suggest blossom, insects and falling leaves.

When the children have finished applying the first layer of the batik, it can be dyed, rinsed and dried. Do not remove the wax; the children can apply another layer over the top

of the old one, and the cloth can be redyed in a different colour. After this, iron off the wax, remembering to protect the iron and ironing board with newspaper, and each side of the cloth with a layer of newsprint. When most of the wax has been ironed off, wash and dry the cloth. The last layer of wax can be spread across the cloth and the cloth crumpled to give the fine network of lines so characteristic of batik, before dipping again into a final dye bath. Tell the children to iron and wash the cloth, as before. The picture should then be complete.

Each child could be asked to describe to the class what his picture is about and the children could compare the effects of the batik with a painting or a linocut.
Art: AT1, AT2; Science: AT1, AT3; Technology: AT1, AT2, AT3, AT4; History: AT3; Geography: AT1, AT2; English: AT1

Conclusion

The activities in this chapter have encouraged the children to look closely at their environment, and at the way artists have used it in their work. The art work has been related to other areas of the curriculum. The children have explored their own imaginations, as well as trying new, more advanced techniques. They should feel confident and able to express themselves individually in their art work, as well as contributing co-operatively to whole-class activities.

134

Chapter 9
Art techniques, materials and tools

The first look at an art supplier's list can be alarming as there is a vast range of tools and materials available to choose from. This chapter suggests some of the basic materials and tools needed in art; there are also some suggestions for ways of using them. Instructions are also provided for the care and maintenance of the materials and tools.

Drawing tools

Pencils

The most common drawing tool is a pencil. The graphite pencil is graded from H to B, indicating the softness, range of tone and blackness of the mark that the pencil will make. The H range includes the greyest and hardest pencils; the B range contains the softer and blacker drawing pencils. The higher the number beside the B, the softer and blacker will be the line or tone made by the pencil – thus a 6B is darker than a 2B. The HB pencil is the writing pencil, and is useful for drawing maps, details, plans and small patterns. There are also available thick soft pencils, such as the Berol Alphex, that are suitable for children. The Berol Alphex is a large-diameter pencil, with a soft lead that lets children make a black line without the need for too much pressure.

Line and tone in drawing are not limited to pencils alone, and children should learn when to discard the pencil and use alternative tools such as wax crayons to create thick mottled line and rich texture.

Wax crayons

Wax crayons are available in two sizes. Generally the larger size is more useful with reception and Y1 and Y2 children. Wax crayons are useful for making rubbings and for colouring patterns. They can also be used in layers, which can be scratched or scraped away to reveal the colours underneath.

Charcoal

Charcoal can be used for larger-scale drawings; it is made from willow twigs, and comes in a range of sizes. The children will find it interesting to note how the joints of the twigs are still visible in the charcoal stick. Explain that charcoal is made by baking the twigs slowly in an oven. (This could be demonstrated by letting the children take some burnt twigs from a dead bonfire and use them for drawing.)

Charcoal can be broken into smaller pieces, and the side of the stick used for creating areas of tone, as opposed to the line produced by the tip of the charcoal twig. Mistakes can be wiped away with a cloth and, although this leaves a shadow of the previous line, can add depth and life to a drawing.

Chalk

Chalks are a limited drawing medium, although they can be used effectively on coloured or black paper. White chalk is useful for highlighting charcoal drawings. Coloured chalks are made in pallid pastel shades, and it is hard to mix the colours effectively.

Charcoal, wax crayon and chalk are better than pencil as a preliminary to painting, in all except the smallest-scale work. Their use precludes the drawing of any fine details that can inhibit the free use of the brush when the paint is applied.

Other drawing media

Ballpoint, felt-tipped and fibre-tipped pens are all suitable for drawing small pictures, for pattern-making and for planning work.

Ink is a lovely medium for drawing, and can be diluted with water and used as water-colour. It is transparent, and can produce areas of rich colour in small-scale work, such as illuminated letters or inset pictures to illustrate stories.

Using colour

Buying paints can be an expensive and limiting activity if the wrong colours are ordered. Many of the prettiest looking colours do not mix well together, and this can restrict the children's activities in mixing and matching. There are just three primary colours from which all others can be mixed, at least in theory. As school paints are inexpensive and therefore not made from pure pigment, this does not work in practice, but it is true that most colours can be mixed from the following colours:
• lemon yellow;
• yellow ochre;
• scarlet red;
• crimson red;
• Prussian blue;
• ultramarine or brilliant blue.
Black and white will also be needed, and it is advisable to order more white than black. It is a good idea to keep shade cards in the classroom so that the children can check colours against them.

Black and white can be mixed together to make greys, or used singly, but their main role is to create tone. Black makes colours darker, creating the mossier, earthy tones and deeper colours; white, mixed with a colour, produces pastel shades such as sky blue and

strawberry pink. (Why they are given these evocative names is hard to know, as the colour often bears no resemblance to the description. Flesh pink, for example, is a most unfortunate name!) Children as young as four years old can be encouraged to mix and colour-match plants, skin, etc, to make a wide range of colours. They will gradually become aware of the inaccuracy of many of these names.

There is no need to buy any greens as this is the easiest colour to mix, and the range of greens that can be made from yellows, blues and blacks is extensive. For example, lemon yellow and ultramarine (brilliant) blue make a clear green; yellow ochre (dark) with blue make a light mossy green; black and yellow ochre produce a khaki shade.

Other simple colour mixes are:
• scarlet red and yellow – orange;
• crimson red and ultramarine blue – purple;
• scarlet red and blue – brown.

Types of paint

There are three basic types of school paint that can be used for art work:
• powder paints;
• ready-mixed paints, such as tubes of poster paint or tempera;
• block paints.
There are other paints for special purposes, such as finger paints, luminous paints, or water-colour, but these are self-explanatory.

Powder paint is cheap, water-soluble and dries a much paler shade than wet colour, losing its depth of tone in the process. This is because it contains large quantities of chalk,

and rather small quantities of pigment. This accounts for its low cost. The effect of powder paint can be improved by adding small amounts of PVA adhesive, washing-up liquid or wallpaper paste (non-fungicidal!) to the mixed paint. It is useful, in that it lasts for years, and children enjoy mixing it. Powder paint has to be mixed like cocoa, adding a little water at a time, otherwise the powder runs around the water in small furry balls.

Similar, but generally more satisfactory are the ready-mixed paints, which are only slightly more expensive than powder paints, but come ready to use. They contain less chalk, so the colours are better. They also can be thickened with PVA adhesive, washing-up liquid or wallpaper paste.

Colour block paints are suitable for finer work, but are no use for larger paintings. Their chief advantage is that they are very clean. The more expensive water-colour tubes are far more satisfactory for finer work undertaken by Y3, Y4, Y5 and Y6 children.

Ideally, a school should have a selection of different types of paint in the stock cupboard.

Brushes

It is important to provide a variety of brushes for the children to use from the earliest years. Children need to be taught to use both large and small brushes so that they can put in details, such as nostrils and the stamens of flowers, with some degree of accuracy, and without frustration. For example, it is impossible to paint a detail with a number seven nylon oil brush, unless the scale is large – A2 at least.

Useful sizes for small soft brushes are round-ended size eight and size ten. These are suitable for adding fine detail to large work, and for colour-matching or small studies, using thin paint. In the large range there are brushes of various shapes, and for infants there are especially strong round-ended brushes that stand up to hard wear. These come in packs of ten, and are medium or large. Both sizes are needed.

Caring for brushes

There are a few rules that, if followed, will lengthen the life and maintain the condition of school brushes considerably.

Brushes should always be stored with the bristles upwards. They should be cleaned after use, and never left to dry with paint of any type still on them. Cold water is best for washing brushes, as hot water unglues the bristles from the handle. This will also happen if the brushes are left in water pots. This will result in a neat oblong of bristles floating on the top of the water, and someone holding an empty metal holder at the end of the wooden handle! Leaving the brushes in water will also make the bristles bend at right angles to the handle, or spray out in a star shape. This is not conducive to careful work.

Caring for brushes will become a habit if the children are taught to do so from the nursery or reception age.

Painting equipment

There should be a good supply of palettes and mixing plates in the classroom – these can also be used for rolling out printing ink. Non-spill water pots are useful with the younger age-group, and children need to be advised to change the paint water frequently, or they will end up mixing brown shades with all their colours. A good supply of paint cloths is also useful, both for wiping up spillage and blots, and for drying brushes after they have been in the water. The rag should always be wiped down the brush towards the tip, so that the point is not damaged.

Paper

The best paper for general art work is cartridge paper, but this is relatively expensive. Art room paper is less pricey. Newsprint or kitchen paper is the cheapest, but is rather too much like blotting paper for painting purposes; it is, however, useful for printing and drawing. Sugar paper is an excellent painting surface, and is suitable for use with charcoal and felt-tipped pen, but it is unsuitable for colour-matching as the shades of the paper alter the paint colour. Every stock cupboard needs several rolls of mural or frieze paper, preferably in different colours.

There should also be available a selection of coloured tissue-paper, gummed paper, foil and a roll or two of corrugated card. These are useful resources for collage, decorating models and for backing displays.

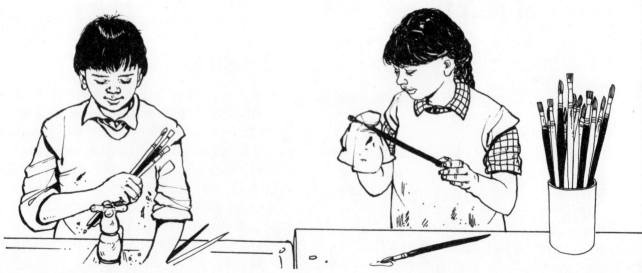

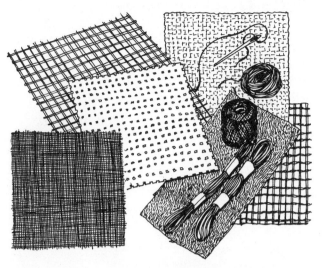

Fabric and thread

Embroidery

The type of embroidery fabric most often found in school is an open coarse-weave fabric, which is ideal for the early years and for counted thread work, but rather too limited for use with any other thread activities. A better basic material is hessian, which is strong and has a loose weave, making it easy to pass a blunt needle back and forth. There should also be a selection of cotton fabrics, and a scrap bag or box, with pieces of plain and patterned dress fabric, velvet, silk, satin, nylon, net, etc. These can be stuck and sewn to the hessian background. In addition, the bead box and the button box are a never-ending source of delight to children, and their contents can be sorted into many different categories – colour, shape, size, etc.

For the early years, tapestry needles, which are blunt with big eyes, are the best. For older children, chenille needles, which come in varying sizes, but which have large eyes and points, are preferable to the ordinary sewing needles.

The basic threads for embroidery are soft cotton, a solid thread with no sheen, and stranded cotton, a silky thread that can be split up (however, this is best used with the older age-group). All forms of knitting yarn can be used, and string, feathers, twigs and raffia can be stitched to fabric with couching. Tacking thread is also useful.

Weaving

Weaving is basically is making a piece of cloth out of two lengths of yarn. One yarn is fixed (the 'warp'), and the other yarn (the 'weft') threaded through it from side to side.

Looms

The warp can be held in place by a variety of methods, but probably the easiest for school use are weaving card looms, which can be bought from art educational suppliers, and are available in oblong or circular shapes. If these are too expensive, it is possible to cut slots into either end of a piece of stiff card to make a weaving card (see page 25), or to push pins into a cork tile to hold the warp thread. A larger loom can be made using a picture frame with nails hammered in across the top and bottom at 2cm intervals. The warp is then threaded round the nails.

On a small loom or weaving card, the weft thread can be passed over and under the warp thread using plastic bodkins; these are obtainable from an art educational supplier. It is also possible to make a shuttle to hold the weft thread by cutting V-shaped notches in either end of a strip of stiff card (Figure 1). Most small weavings can be made using a bodkin, or by threading coarse weft material, such as twigs, through the warp with the fingers.

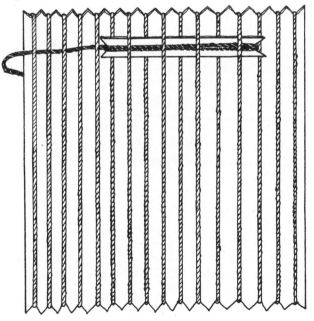

Figure 1

Weaving materials

Knitting yarn can be used for weaving, provided the warp thread is a firm one. Spools of warp thread are available from art educational suppliers, but a firm string works well for wall-hangings. In addition to wools and weaving threads, many other materials can be incorporated into a weaving – dustbin and garden bags, cut into strips; newspaper; twigs; raffia; old tights; strips of carpet; plastic-covered wire; vegetable bags. In fact, any type of material that can be threaded in and out and has a pleasing colour and texture can be used.

When the weaving is finished, it can be lifted off the weaving frame and window-mounted. Alternatively, pass a dowel rod through the top and bottom loops, or just use the dowelling at the top, and hang bunches of wool or tassels from the bottom loops.

Tie and dye

The principle behind tie and dye techniques is simple – the dye does not go where the cloth is tied or bunched together. The resulting patterns are only obtainable using this technique. They are widely used in areas of India and Africa to make patterns on cloth.

There are a variety of methods to stop the dye from reaching certain areas of the cloth.
• The cloth can be pleated and tied with string, cotton or rubber bands.
• It can be pinned with wooden clothes-pegs.
• Objects such as pebbles, marbles or nuts can be tied into the cloth, in either a planned or random pattern.
• The cloth itself can be knotted, although it is difficult to do this tightly enough.

More detailed ideas for using tie and dye are given on page 23, but the basic method is as follows.

What you need

Rubber gloves, tongs or wooden spoons, cold-water dyes, bowls, cloth for dyeing, elastic bands, clothes-pegs or string to tie the cloth, pebbles, marbles, nuts, etc to tie into the cloth, spin-drier, iron.

What to do

Wash the cloth if it contains dressing or starch, then mix the dye according to the instructions on the container. Tie the cloth and wet the bundle before placing it in the dye bath. The cloth can be dyed more than one colour, by taking off all or some of the ties and then retying. If more than one colour is being used, use the palest dyes first.

After dyeing, rinse the bundle until the water runs clear before untying it. Spin, and iron the cloth while it is still damp, otherwise it is hard to get rid of the creases.

Batik

Batik is similar in principle to tie and dye in that the cloth is made resistant to the dye. However, in batik, hot wax is used to make the resist. The best results are produced when a fine cloth of natural fibres is used; the wax does not take well on synthetic fabric. Cotton is suitable, or linen. Silk is the best fabric to use, but this is extravagant for beginners of any age. Ideas for using batik are given on page 134, but the basic method is as follows.

What you need

Wax (This can be paraffin wax, melted candles, beeswax or batik wax. The latter is available from art educational suppliers, the others from hardware stores or chemists. A wax substitute that does not require heat is available from suppliers; it is useful for beginners), a double saucepan or an old tin placed inside a saucepan containing about 2cm of water, a gas cooker or electric hotplate, a batik wax pot (These are quite expensive. A discarded and cleaned baked bean tin will do just as well, and is more economical.), brushes (the *tjanting* – the traditional Javanese batik tool is very difficult to use but it may interest the children to see one), sticks or candles to drip wax on to the cloth, newspapers (these are useful as padding to raise the fabric away from the work surface; alternatively, the cloth can be pinned across an old picture frame), pins, an iron, brown paper or newsprint, cold-water dyes, bowls, detergent, a metal spatula or palette-knife.

What to do

Prepare the cloth by stretching it and pinning it either over a layer of newspapers or over a picture frame. Warm the wax in the 'double saucepan' and brush or drip it on to the cloth. Make sure that the wax is kept warm so that it penetrates the fabric, otherwise the dye will seep underneath. It is easy to see whether the wax is soaking into the fabric, as the parts it covers will be translucent (like cooked bacon fat) when held up to the light. If the wax has not soaked into the fabric, coat both sides with wax.

After waxing the material, mix the cold-water dye, and soak the waxed cloth in it; the longer it is left in the dye, the darker the colour will be. When the cloth has been soaked, rinse it thoroughly, and leave it to dry.

To remove the wax, first scrape as much as possible from the cloth on to a newspaper, using the knife. This will only remove the top layer, so the material will need to be ironed to melt out the remaining wax. Put brown paper or newsprint either side of the cloth, with newspaper underneath to protect the ironing board, and iron over it with a hot iron. When the brown paper or newsprint becomes saturated with wax, replace it with fresh sheets of paper. The cloth will be stiff after ironing, and will need washing in hot or boiling water, with plenty of detergent, to remove the last of the wax. (This makes it essential to use a dye-fix, otherwise the colours will run.) The wax can be retrieved from the water, and reused; it floats on top of the bowl and is easy to scoop up.

Paraffin wax should be used to create the cracking pattern that makes traditional batik so attractive. The cloth is coated with wax, and then crumpled up in the hand before submerging it in the dye bath.

Three-dimensional materials

Clay

Clay is a deeply satisfying modelling medium, provided it is kept in good condition. It needs to be stored in a bin with a fitted lid, such as a dustbin. It is supplied in plastic bags, and these should remain unopened until the clay is put in the bin. In case the bin is not airtight, place a sheet of polythene over the clay, so that it does not dry out. If a kiln is available, keep clay that has been used in a separate bin, as any impurities in the clay that is to be fired can cause work to break in the kiln.

Ideas for working with clay are given on pages 27 and 84, but the basic technique for modelling with clay is as follows.

What you need

Polythene bags, boards or sheets of plastic, hessian or sacking, fine wire, small pieces of wood or buttons, sponges, modelling tools, lolly sticks, old cutlery, sieves, clay, rolling pins.

What to do

Use a length of fine wire, or fishing-line, with the ends twisted round small pieces of wood

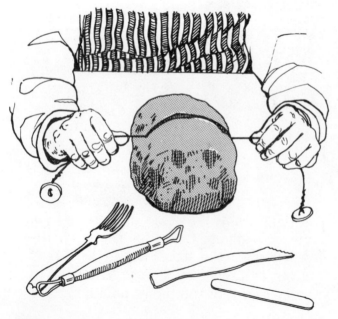

or threaded through buttons, to cut the clay into manageable pieces for the children to use. This can also be used to slide under models or tiles that get stuck to the work surface. This should only be used by the teacher.

Boards, or a sheet of plastic, make the best work surfaces for the children to use, although a formica-topped table is satisfactory. Boards or sheets of plastic have the advantage that the whole model can be moved to the storage area. Place pieces of hessian or sacking under the clay to prevent it sticking to the work surface when it is rolled out. Let the children use rolling-pins to roll out clay to make tiles or slab pots.

Texture can be achieved in several ways. Large and small sponges are useful for smoothing the surface of the clay. Old cutlery – forks, spoons and blunt knives – can be used to make patterns in the clay. A tea strainer and a kitchen sieve can be used to make hair, fur and other fine textures by pushing clay through them. The resulting tiny coils are much loved by children, and can also be used to make appealing plants to decorate model buildings or castle walls. However, younger children are best left to discover the qualities of clay by using their fingers as modelling tools.

While work is in progress, it requires careful storage, as it must not be allowed to dry out. Store the work in polythene bags between sessions to keep it damp. After it is finished, the model needs to be dried slowly, away from central heating or direct heat, as this causes cracking and disintegration.

The best way to join or stick clay together is with slip. Basically, this is a combination of clay and water mixed to the consistency of single cream. It is preferable to do this by mechanical means using a blunger but it can be done by hand if necessary. Slip should be sieved before use, and should be applied sparingly, never on any clay that is not 'green', that is to say damp. An alternative method is to use water to join the clay together.

There are various types of clay available. Red terracotta and grey general purpose clay are the most widely used in schools.

Self-hardening and low-firing clays

As well as the usual potters' clay, there are self-hardening clays available that can be fired in a domestic oven, for example, 'Back Ton' oven clay, which can be ordered together with specially formulated glazes that also fire in a domestic oven.

Dough

Other types of modelling materials are available, for example dough, which can be made at home. Dough is a cheap and readily available material for use in the classroom. It is easy to use, and is a suitable material for introducing young children to the malleable qualities of materials. It cannot be hardened permanently, but it can be baked very slowly in an oven, and painted when cool. As young children tend to lose interest in their own products after a short time, the relative impermanence of the material is not important. Dough is not as firm or as mouldable as clay, and can only be used to make simple shapes. It can be coloured, using food dyes. Ideas for using dough are given on page 31, but the basic recipe is as follows.

What you need

450g plain flour, 225g salt, 4 tablespoons of oil, 850ml water, 8 teaspoons of cream of tartar, food colouring (optional), saucepan, cooker.

What to do

Place all the ingredients in a large saucepan. Heat gently, stirring all the time, until the mixture thickens. Turn the mixture out on the table, and knead the dough when it is cool.

Dough will last up to four weeks if it is kept in an airtight container.

Plasticine

Another material frequently used in school is Plasticine. Unlike clay, Plasticine is generally built up into a form, piece by piece. It is suited to small, detailed modelling. For example, it is useful for making flowers and small bushes that are part of a large-scale model.

When Plasticine is old, it becomes quite hard, and often the colours mix so that a grey tone spreads throughout the material. If it is too hard to model easily, soften it up by placing it on a radiator or in a very low oven.

NESplast and Cernit are also available for use in modelling, and have their uses for small-scale work. The colours are pretty, but both are relatively expensive.

Mod-Roc

Mod-Roc is plaster-impregnated bandage, and is an effective modelling medium for the older age groups, from Y3 and Y4 upwards. It is supplied in bags in wide strips that can be cut, passed through water and wound round a base. The surface can then be smoothed with a damp sponge, or roughened, as desired. Mod-Roc dries rapidly, and can then be painted. For a base, use a wire or chicken-wire armature, covered with newspaper. Alternatively, for younger children working on a small scale, newspaper moulded to a rough shape can be covered with Mod-Roc.

Plaster of Paris

Plaster of Paris has been widely used since Egyptian times as a wall surface, and for modelling. The ceilings of houses were decorated with plaster moulding; this was widespread in Victorian England. In East Anglia, a type of Plaster of Paris relief modelling called pargetting is still used on the outside of houses.

For school use, dental or potters' plaster are suitable for making casts, or for carving. Plaster 'goes off' (sets) rapidly, and attracts moisture. It must be stored away from all sources of damp; a damp wall will ruin plaster in no time at all. To mix plaster, add one part of plaster to two or three parts of water. Sprinkle the plaster on the water, and carry on doing so until it reaches the surface. Let it settle for a minute, then stir it gently with the hand, trying not to make bubbles. Do this quickly, as it sets very rapidly. As soon as it becomes smooth and runny, pour it into the

mould. The plaster will thicken as it sets; it also becomes warm.

Never pour plaster down a sink; it will totally block the drain. Even the remnants round the side of the bowl will set, if washed down a drain. Plaster cannot be made liquid again; once set, it is there for ever. Wait for it to set, and then put it in the dustbin.

Plaster for carving

This activity is suitable for Y3 to Y5. As plaster is a soft medium, it is a good material for children to use for carving. To prepare the plaster, find some small cardboard boxes, reinforce the bases and any side seams with brown sticky tape, remove the tops and pour in the mixed plaster. Leave the plaster to set overnight, then tear off the box, and the plaster is ready to be carved.

Using plaster for modelling

Y5 and Y6 children can be allowed to make sculptures with plaster, by applying it to an armature, either with a spatula or by hand. The armature can be made from wire, twigs, or chicken-wire, attached to a board, or stuck into Plasticine.

Other uses for plaster

A plaster block can be cast, left to set and then incised (scratched) to make a block for printing. Alternatively, the incised lines can be filled with coloured Plasticine.

144

Papier mâché

There are two types of papier mâché. One is made from layers or strips of pasted paper, and the other type is pulped. Use layered papier mâché when covering a base to make a model or a mask and pulp type for modelling details.

What you need

Bowl, non-fungicidal wallpaper paste or flour and water paste with salt added, paper towels, newspapers, tissue paper (optional), paint, varnish.

Layered method

Mix the wallpaper paste in the bowl, then tear the newspaper into strips and lay them in the bowl to soak. When they are thoroughly soaked, place them on the surface that is to be covered, and press them down. Cover the whole surface. Let each layer dry slightly before the next one is added. Repeat this process up to six times.

Use tissue-paper or coloured paper towels on the last layer to give colour and a smooth texture to the surface. Alternatively, once dry, the papier mâché can be painted and varnished.

Pulp method

Tear the newspaper into small pieces and soak them for a day in a bucket of water. Shred and pulp the paper thoroughly, squeeze out the mash and put it in a bowl.

Mix the wallpaper paste, and add it to the bowl containing the pulped mash. The pulp should be easily malleable, not too rigid or too runny. The pulp can then be used for modelling. Add plaster to the pulp for a firmer consistency. The pulp does not keep, so use it within twelve hours or cover it with plastic or cling film.

Paper-making

This is a rewarding area for children, and makes them aware of recycling. Ideas for paper-making activities are described on page 78, but the basic technique is as follows.

What you need

A wooden frame covered with fine mesh, such as fine curtain netting (wet the netting before putting it on the frame or it will sag when the wet paper pulp is put on it), a second wooden frame of the same size (Together these form the 'mould' and the 'deckle'. The mould can be used alone – this may be easier for the children, but runs the risk of the pulp running over the edge), a deep washing-up bowl (large enough for the mould to fit into), a liquidiser, a wooden spoon, a sponge, a good supply of all-purpose cloths, a bucket, paper to recycle (brown paper bags, newspapers, envelopes, computer paper, wrapping paper), water, measuring jug, newspapers for draining the paper before drying.

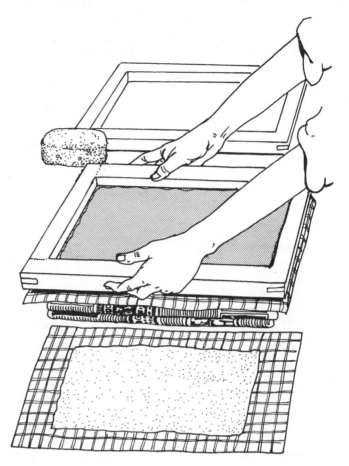

Figure 3

What to do

Tear the paper into small pieces, and put it in a bucket filled with water. Stir the paper and leave it to soak. Strain off a small cupful of the wet paper and put it into the liquidiser, then add approximately three-quarters of a litre of water. Liquidise the pulp for 15 seconds; if the machine labours, switch it off, remove some of the pulp and add more water. Take care not to liquidise the pulp for too long, otherwise the paper fibres will be destroyed, and the finished paper will fall apart.

Pour the pulp into the washing-up bowl and pass the mould and deckle through the pulp, net-side upwards (Figure 2). Drain the mould on a pad of newspaper. Place a wet, all-purpose cloth on a board or pad of newspapers and lay the mould on it, pulp-side downwards. Sponge the net to remove surplus water. Carefully peel the layer of cloth and pulp away from the mould (Figure 3). The cloths and the pulp can then be stacked. Remove the paper from the all-purpose cloths and hang it up to dry while it is still damp, but not quite dry.

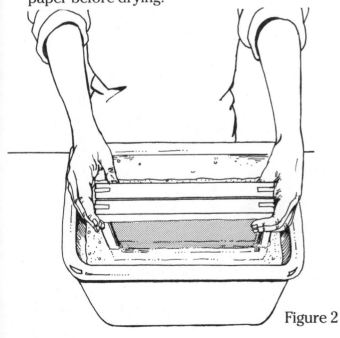

Figure 2

145

Graphic techniques

Print-making

There are three basic ways of printing an image:
- stamp printing;
- roller printing;
- screen printing.

There are, of course, subdivisions within these areas. Many of the materials, tools and equipment cover more than one method.

What you need

Rollers, water-based printing ink, inking trays, sponges or cloths, a supply of old newspapers, cloths, newsprint or printing paper. (Easiprint is a useful addition for making impress prints and is available from educational suppliers.)

Stamp printing

The basic technique for stamp printing is simple. The object to be printed is held in the hand, and pressed, firstly on a paint or ink-impregnated surface, and then on to a printing surface, which has previously been placed on a newspaper.

Cloths soaked in paint can serve as pads for the younger age-group. Place the soaked cloths in polythene trays or shallow tins.

Roller printing

The term 'roller printing' covers several areas – monoprints, Plasticine prints, string prints, plaster prints, card prints, balsa-wood prints, linocuts, texture prints and roller prints.

Monoprints

To make monoprints, additional equipment will be required, namely an A4 Perspex sheet or a table, pencils and brushes. One method of producing a monoprint is described in Chapter 3. Older children could be allowed to roll out the ink, as described on page 50, lay the paper on top, and draw the image on the back, using a pencil or the wrong end of a brush. Alternatively they could be allowed to use their fingers which would add a smudgy texture and could be used as part of the design. Explain to the children that they should not accidentally handle the paper while it is on top of the ink. Explain that when they lift the paper off, a reverse image should have been produced.

Plasticine, plaster, Easiprint or card print

Plasticine can be rolled or pressed out, and objects such as cotton reels or buttons used to impress shapes into it, or lines can be scratched into it. Plaster can be incised in a similar way once it has set, as can Easiprint which can also be impressed. Printing blocks can also be built up from layers of card. In all

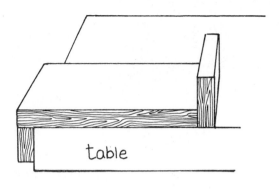

side view of bench-hook

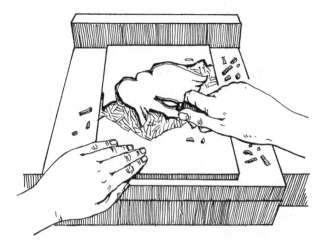

Hold lino with hand behind
the cutting tool.

Figure 4

these prints, the technique is the same. The only additional equipment required is an old dessert spoon. The print surface is rolled up with the ink, and the paper to be printed laid on top, rolled with a clean roller, and, for a good finish, burnished with the back of a spoon.

Linocuts

The linocut technique is suitable for use with Y4 to Y6 children.

Lino printing can be a sophisticated way of building up an image. It is not as easy to work successfully in lino as people think. The tools have to be very sharp, or the edge of the cut becomes crumbly and ugly. Safety precautions are therefore very important. For example, have a supply of sticking plasters available and, if possible, use soft-cork lino which is relatively easy to cut. This does harden as it gets older, but can be softened by warming on a radiator or in a cool oven. Easiprint can also be used for cutting, but is not so effective.

Additional pieces of equipment necessary are lino tools. These are available in boxes, containing a handle and up to ten cutters of varying shapes; alternatively, the nibs and handles can be bought separately. In some ways, this is the best way to buy, as it is only essential to have three basic tools – a knife-blade cutter, a V-shaped cutter and a gouge.

It is important to insist that the children hold the lino behind the cutting hand, and cut in the opposite direction, preferably using a bench-hook (Figure 4). Although the cuts from a lino tool are rarely serious, they can become infected, and are quite painful. Tell the children to draw a design on the lino, then to cut round their picture, using the V-shaped cutter, and scoop the lino out with the gouge. There is no need to dig too deeply. Before using the linocut to print, take a rubbing from the block, to see if more lino needs to be cut away. When it is finished, print the block several times to see the effects of different colours and papers.

Two-coloured linocut

Cut the first block as described above, and make an initial set of prints, using different colours. Clean the block, then cut more of the design away, and make a print on top of the first prints, carefully lining up the block with the top edges of the first print. This process can be repeated several times using a selection of different colours. The first colour will remain where the block is cut away, and will be overprinted to make another colour where the first and second print coincide. If this is done in several colours, each print will look different.

Screen printing

Silk-screen printing is basically a way of using a stencil to transfer a design. Colour is then pushed through the screen, to print round the stencil. The screen can then be reused.

The children may be interested to learn that this method was used by the Crusaders to print the red cross on their tunics. They used tar or pitch to paint out a resist area round the shape of the cross on a fine cloth screen. The red was then forced through the mesh with a coarse brush. This in itself could form part of a history project.

The simplest method of using a screen-print technique with Y3 to Y6 children is to cut shapes out of newsprint and place them on the printing table. They will stick to the screen after the first pull of printing ink has been taken, forming an indirect stencil. It is also possible to use a wax crayon or candle to draw an image on the mesh of the screen, thus making a direct stencil. However, bear in mind that it is difficult to get the screen clean afterwards, and requires the use of white spirit.

There are various other methods of making stencils, but they are complicated, and not always totally successful with this age-group.

The screen

The screen is an open frame, big enough for the squeegee to fit into, and covered in organdie. Ideally, use the best type of cotton or dressmaker's organdie, which has 60 threads per inch. A cheaper but effective material is Terylene gauze, with 28 threads per centimetre. The mesh needs to be stretched tightly across the screen, initially using drawing-pins to position it on the straight grain of the fabric. Start pinning at the centre of each edge of the screen and work out to the corners. When the material is in position, staple it firmly to the sides, remove the drawing pins and trim away any surplus fabric with scissors. To stop the printing ink leaking between the screen and the mesh, use 5cm wide brown gummed tape to seal the underside and the edge of the screen. Start with the underside and seal all four edges of the frame, including the wood. Reverse the screen and seal the inside, again including the wood; fold the tape in half, and put the folded edge along the inside of the frame, overlapping the wood and the organdie to form a seal.

Screens can also be bought, either ready to assemble, or ready-made, from an educational art suppliers.

The squeegee

The squeegee should fit into the screen with a space either side. The squeegee consists of a synthetic polyurethane blade set into a handle; they are usually 10, 14 or 18 inches wide. The squeegee is pulled along the screen to force the ink through the mesh. For school use, it is possible to make a primitive and temporary squeegee from a thick strip of folded card. However, this will need replacing after every session, is not very efficient and can only be used for one colour. As squeegees are not very expensive, and last for years if they are washed thoroughly after use, it is better to have a supply of them in the school resources.

The printing process

This is a relatively easy process. Put the paper into position, and draw a cross to mark the location of each corner of the screen to ensure that the print is in the right place. Put the screen down on the paper, lining up the crosses. Pour the printing ink evenly across one end of the screen. Standing at the opposite end, pull the squeegee evenly towards you. Lift the screen away from the print, tilting it up slightly to prevent the spare ink from running. Lift the print, and hang it up to dry. The spare ink and the squeegee can be reused for the next print. Although printing is an easy process, a practice print is useful, both for the children and for the teacher.

Cleaning the squeegee and screen

To clean the squeegee after use, hold it up and scrape off all the extra ink, using a piece of scrap card, allowing it to drip into the end of the screen with the other surplus ink. This can be scooped out with a spatula or blunt knife and put into a screw-top jar for later use.

Rest the screen on a bed of newspapers and wipe it clean with dry rags. Peel off the stencil, then wash the screen under the cold tap, until it is clean. The cleaning must be thorough or the holes in the mesh block up, and the ink will not print through.

Printing inks

For school use, a ready-mixed, water-based printing ink is best. There are various types available from the art educational suppliers' catalogues. The best type can be fixed on to the cloth by ironing on the reverse side for about three minutes. Order the primary colours and black and white, as other colours can be mixed from these.

The print surface

This can be any table covered with a smooth layer of newspapers. A better surface can be obtained by covering the table with two layers of old blanket or foam rubber taped to the sides with masking tape. Cover this with a plastic sheet, also taped to the sides of the table with masking tape.

Using the computer

Computer graphics packages are now widely used in schools and, although they do not replace observed drawing and imaginative work in two- and three-dimensional materials, they do allow the children to familiarise themselves with industrial and commercial design methods. Their main advantages are that they can reproduce and vary shapes and colours quickly, and that work can be stored on disk, as well as printed. Mistakes can be easily rectified and several versions can be produced.

At present, computer graphics programs come in the form of drawing or desktop publishing packages. There are programs available that combine both facilities.

Drawing programs

Drawing programs usually let the operator draw shapes and fill them in with textures and colours. These shapes can be enlarged, reduced, repeated and reversed as the operator wishes. The line can be varied, using the different sizes of 'brush' available in the program.

Desktop publishing

Desktop publishing packages offer a choice of lettering (font), placing of text and drawing facilities that the operator chooses from a menu bar that appears when the relevant button is pressed on the keyboard or the mouse activated. A mouse is an external device that is plugged into the computer. It enables the user to communicate with the computer without typing in information on the keyboard. A touch pad can also be used to operate a program.

At first, teacher support will be needed to help the children operate the programs, but they will soon become adept in their use. All children will enjoy using the keyboard and moving the mouse about to produce shapes. These shapes are limited to some extent, as the computer works visually on a series of small squares, called pixels. As a result, curves can often assume a rather stepped

shape. The speed with which the shapes appear and can be changed is very satisfying, as is the facility to enlarge, reverse and repeat. Colourways can also be tried and varied, although the printout can be rather disappointing. Filling the design shapes with textures and colours stimulates the children's imagination, as well as ensuring a degree of success.

The turtle

A menu-driven graphics package that can be operated without the user having any relevant skills is the computer-controlled floor turtle. Young children from reception and Y1 can learn to press the relevant keys so that the turtle moves backwards and forwards, and turns at different angles. The turtle toy often has a pen attached to it that leaves a trail. It is operated by a *Logo* program that can be used to draw shapes. These can be combined to create houses, blocks of flats and vehicles. Although these are based on simple geometric shapes, they can be used in conjunction with maths and art to reinforce children's learning.

Conclusion

It is impossible to cover every method of making art, and this chapter has merely outlined the foundation techniques, tools and materials for use in the primary school. There are many books dealing with each area individually, and these should be used for further exploration of methods and approaches.

Chapter 10
The school environment and display

An important part of art in a school includes making the whole school an attractive and aesthetically pleasing environment. Children learn through the senses; sight and touch are important as a part of their general education. The impression made by a school starts as soon as a visitor enters the playground. A bleak unadorned expanse of tarmac creates a depressing effect, especially on a grey wintry day. This can be lifted by the sight of some evergreens in pots, a series of games and structures for the children to use and welcoming notices on the doors, painted neatly and decoratively on wood, or professionally printed.

Once inside the school, the interest and pride taken by the staff in their children's work and development is reflected in the quality of the displays, the tidiness and health of any plants or pets and the labelling and notices that direct people, not only to the secretary and headteacher's office, but also to other places of interest to visitors and children, such as the parents' room or library. One school even has its own museum, which is left open for visitors to look at. Such notices displayed around the school might well reflect a multicultural intake, and be written in a number of community languages.

The classroom

Classroom organisation is an important part of a pleasing environment. There should be, to use the old cliché, 'a place for everything, and everything in its place'. This requires clear labelling, so that the children know where to look for things and where to return them after use. Clearing up should be organised so that the sink is not full of half-washed paint pots, and brushes are not stored covered in coagulated paint. A clear, uncluttered definition of activity areas is desirable, together with a representative display of the children's work.

The teacher's own pride in the school and the class is conveyed to the children by a well-organised classroom. Untidy, messy rooms give out a negative message, whereas pleasant working surroundings encourage a constructive response from the children.

The displays throughout the school should be changed frequently, so that the children do not see them as a permanent part of the wall, but find them a source of interest and stimulation, rousing their curiosity. Some of the corridor or hall displays should contain objects that the children can touch, examine and read.

In the classroom, the displays should give the children an opportunity to see the work of their peers. There should be resources tables with two- and three-dimensional objects and books related to a current topic or theme.

Often, magnifying glasses, microscopes and mirrors can be included to help close observation of details and to encourage the children to investigate the effect of reflections and symmetry. A good lighting arrangement will enhance the display and, at the same time, arouse the children's interest. Spotlights are best, but an ordinary reading-lamp works well. Even very ordinary objects can be transformed by clever lighting, and this is one way of varying the effect of a display.

Choosing a background

When choosing the background paper for a display, remember that the contents should be enhanced by the background colour, not overpowered by it, so use bright colours with caution. When planning the display, make sure that any written sections are low enough for the children to read in comfort.

Colour

Background colours, as well as being complementary to the work on view, can be arranged in a variety of ways. One colour could be used over the whole display area. Alternatively colours could be arranged in vertical or, more rarely, horizontal stripes to draw the viewer's attention to different aspects of the theme. Another option would be to arrange colours to form a chequerboard pattern, or any other appropriate shape. For example, work for a geography project could be displayed on a cut-out shape of a particular country. Remember that shapes can be drawn and then enlarged for tracing, using the overhead projector.

Fabric

Fabric drapes also make a good background to a display. These are effective for exhibiting puppets and collections of craft objects or natural forms, but do not enhance mounted drawings or paintings. The background should be considered in relation to the content of the display, not only in terms of colour, but also as a way of emphasising the character of the items on show.

There are various ways of arranging the fabric drapes. Material can be pleated and pinned so that it hangs down one side of the display, spreading out on the table below. This arrangement could be particularly effective for a display of craft items, such as spinning wheels and distaffs, which show the way cloth is made. Alternatively, material can be pleated and attached to a pre-cut piece of thin card, measured to the required size, so that the fabric hangs either to one side, or right across the back of the display area.

Corrugated card

Another useful material for display is corrugated card. If it is supported on one side, it can be used as a divider; doubled, it can form bays for quiet areas, or partitions for specialist sections, such as a mathematics area. It should be attached to the side of a table with tacks or staples to make it secure. Drawings and light objects can be displayed on corrugated card using dressmakers' pins. To preserve the card for future use, slide the pins down the flutes on the card, without piercing it through if possible. Corrugated card can be used flat as a backing on display boards, but this is quite extravagant – brown wrapping paper on a board is cheaper and is equally effective.

Other materials

Sugar paper, frieze paper, wrapping paper or cover paper make good backing for displays. Garden trellis fixed to one side of a table is a useful way of adding a see-through display area to a classroom.

Many three-dimensional forms are best displayed on a flat surface, which can be made more interesting by raising it in places. This can be done by covering boxes or breeze-blocks with the same paper that has been used to cover the table. Any items that should not be touched can be placed on the raised areas.

Shells and pottery can be effectively displayed on silver sand or wood shavings. However, this is not practical if the display is going to be handled; in this case, make sure

the paper or cloth on which the objects are displayed is firmly fixed to the table to prevent the whole display becoming too untidy. Be prepared to tidy it up frequently – if this is done often, it will only take a few minutes.

Labelling the display

Lettering is an essential part of all displays, and should be used in a variety of different sizes. The title should be large and clearly legible from a distance. Individual captions should be smaller, according to the age of the children. Children should be introduced to a variety of different forms of lettering, ranging from the basic sanserif school lettering to joined-up letters and gothic script. The computer is a useful tool; using it, the children can discover different typefaces or fonts and make their own labels.

Many schools keep a supply of templates of different-sized letters and various typefaces for the staff to use. This resource is difficult to gather together initially, but saves endless time in the long run. Templates of various types and sizes are available from educational suppliers, and these should be part of the school's stock. Letters taken from newspaper headlines can be enlarged on a photocopier, traced on to sugar paper or thin card, cut out and made into templates.

Handwritten lettering

Most displays are labelled with handwritten lettering; this can be drawn or traced, and then inked or brushed in. It is essential, unless the teacher is a skilled calligrapher, that guidelines are measured and lightly marked in above and below the letters to keep the line even throughout. Spacing also has to be considered. There are three simple rules of spacing.
• Upright letters, such as the 'm' and the 'n', need more space between them.
• Less space is required between an upright letter, such as an 'l', and a curved letter, such as an 'o'.
• Two curved letters, such as 'o' and 'c', should be the closest together.

The principle behind spacing letters is to maintain a uniform style throughout the word, so that it does not disintegrate, but reads smoothly with no sudden breaks or unevenness of tone. To achieve this needs practice, but it soon becomes second nature. The rules of spacing are based on the simple idea of considering the amount of background space behind each word.

Stencil and Letraset

Another way of producing lettering is to use either a stencil or Letraset. Neither is as easy as it seems. The stencils have annoying little gaps, and a tendency to smudge. To avoid this, lift the stencil straight up into the air when taking it off the paper.

Letraset is expensive, and needs practice when transferring it on to paper, especially if the letters are on a large scale. Often parts of letters remain attached to the backing sheet, especially if it is old, or has got warm. It is easier to learn to write notices and captions, even though this takes practice. Learning to use the appropriate computer package to create professional labels and headings is the quickest method.

Mounting the work

Work for display can be mounted in a variety of ways. Children's work should not be cut out before mounting, unless the children are told in advance that this is part of the design. To do so might denigrate their decision to place their work in a specific place on the sheet of paper.

Make sure that the children are given neatly trimmed paper to start with, varying the shape and size to suit the subject. This need not apply only to art, but to all areas of the curriculum.

Double mounts

Both written and pictorial work can be double-mounted. Ensure that the first mount contrasts in tone with the work. Then attach the work to the mount with small pieces of masking tape, spots of Blu-Tack or adhesive pads. Double-sided adhesive tape is useful for mounting work.

The second mount should be wider than the first, and can be attached directly to the display board, using dressmakers' pins inserted with a pin push. Take care not to push them in too far, some of the pin needs to be left sticking out, otherwise extracting them could prove to be a difficult and time-consuming task. Attaching the second mount with pins means it can be reused. It can be made from coloured, black, white, patterned or textured paper or manila. Black, white and coloured cardboard make pleasing mounts. Mounting board is hard to cut, and very expensive, but is the best choice for work that is going on public display, or being entered for an exhibition.

Single mounts

Single mounts should be made from plain coloured paper, card or manila. A black or coloured thin line ruled round the mount, about 1cm from the edge of the work, can look very effective. However, the classical mounts of black or white card are best left plain and unadorned.

All outer mounts should be of equal width on either side, and should be larger at the bottom than the top. This counteracts the optical illusion that the work is falling off the paper.

Cutting a window mount

For special occasions, window mounts are the most professional way of presenting work. These can be cut from manila or paper.

What you need

Card (manila or other), a cutting board, Stanley knife (or equivalent), a steel rule, pencil, measure, notepad.

What to do

Measure the work that is to be mounted, leaving a border of at least 1cm round the edge, so that the work can be attached to the back of the mount. Decide on the size of the outer edges of the mount, then measure and mark them on the card.

Using the knife and the steel rule, cut the mount out on the cutting board. When cutting there is no need to press hard with the knife; several light strokes down the side of a firmly held ruler are more effective than one hard cut. Hold the ruler tightly pressed down on the line; run the knife lightly along the line; if necessary, do this several times.

On the back of the mounting card, measure and mark the proportions of the inner mount. When the four corners are marked, using the ruler as a guide, make a nick in each corner. This stops the blade slipping and scoring the card and it also shows where to cut when the card is turned face upwards. Turn the card over, and cut out the window. Always cut card or thick paper from the side which will be visible, as it helps to prevent a furry edge. Make sure the window is free from the surround, and let it drop out. Tag the four corners of the work with masking tape, turn the mount over, and, holding two opposite corners, place the work into the mount. Press the masking tape down, turn over the mount and check that it is correctly positioned. If it is, reverse the mount, and fasten the picture firmly in place with a strip of masking tape round the edges. It is best to use masking tape, as it peels off easily, and, if used with care, the window mount can be reused.

If several mounts are to be cut, ensure that there is a good supply of fresh blades, as paper and card blunt sharp edges surprisingly quickly.

Arranging the display

Two-dimensional work should be arranged so that there is some continuity of line. Either line up the vertical and horizontal edges of the work, or arrange it as if it were hanging from a line stretched across a little way from the top of the display board. The work can also be arranged using one or more central focal points. This is a good way to group and sequence work.

Many people think that the more there is in a display, the more interesting it becomes. This is not true. Try to plan the display before putting it up, making sure that each item is clearly visible, and that the whole effect is uncluttered. Never overlap work. When planning the display, think of the sequence of the work, and which pieces of work need to be the focus of attention. Make a small drawing of the way the display may be arranged. This will provide a starting point, but do not be afraid to change the plan when the display starts to go up; it rarely works out perfectly as planned, and some adjustments are usually needed.

Get the children involved in putting up the display; they can help with the measuring and check that lines are straight. They can also learn to mount their work, even in Y1. Discuss

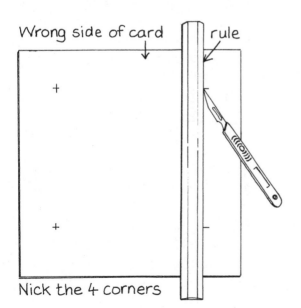

Wrong side of card   rule

Nick the 4 corners

the displays with them; find out if they like having their work on show, and ask them which pieces they would like displayed. It can be as embarrassing for a child as it is for an adult, if a piece of work they know is not their best is stuck up for all to see. Children seem to have little say in the way their work is treated, and this cannot be a good idea – it is their work after all.

Captions should be kept simple, so that they have an immediate impact, and inform the viewer of the area of investigation that is the basis of the display. The smaller headings can enlarge on this, and give details of the work and theme.

If you should have to tidy work up before mounting it, avoid using pinking shears to neaten the edges; they are a lazy and ugly way to present anything other than fabric, which is what they were intended for. Nobody uses pinking shears on a Turner or Picasso drawing! If a child's work has become ragged, torn or crumpled, iron it (unless it is in wax crayon), trim the sides as closely as possible to the original edge, and then mount it. A neat, well-selected and correctly cut mount can transform a piece of work, and create a feeling of achievement and pride.

Adhesive tape and drawing-pins should be invisible if they are used. A strip of tape across a corner of a mount is unattractive. Moreover, it is not the best way to put work up, as it has a tendency to peel off. Blu-Tack works well on most surfaces, but remember, the smallest amount possible works better than a large blob. Double-sided adhesive pads also work well and, for large permanent notices, foam pads are useful. A few display tools make life much easier.

• A steel rule is essential for cutting straight lines. A wooden rule is rarely accurate, and it is easy to slice into it when using a sharp knife.

• A good supply of pencils and pens should be available. The H and HB pencils give a fine crisp line. Do not press too hard, otherwise the paper will be scored; cultivate a delicate touch.

• Metal or tape measures can be used to measure spacing, but the metal measure is more accurate because of its rigidity.

• A plumb-line should be used to assess the straightness of edges.

• Dressmakers' pins (lilliputians) are small pins, which do little damage to the display boards, and are less likely to snag fingers.

Other display tools include:

• A cutting knife;
• A cutting board;
• A pin push;
• Double-sided adhesive tape;
• Masking tape;
• Blu-Tack;
• Double-sided adhesive pads;
• Scissors;
• Staple gun and staples;
• A staple remover.

Conclusion

As a final note on display, the school should include examples of artists' work that are relevant to the theme of the children's projects. Use frames that can be unclipped easily so that the pictures can be changed. There are many reasonably priced frames available, and art educational suppliers advertise both ready-cut mounts and frame kits.

In today's competitive system, it is even more important that the environment of a school should appear welcoming and visually attractive. Remember, display includes the whole environment of the school. There should be a general aura of efficient thoughtful organisation and planning, as well as wall displays. It is time-consuming, admittedly, but it is also rewarding.

Chapter 11
Assessment and record-keeping

In the National Curriculum Council's *Non-Statutory Guidance* of 1992, there is substantial advice on planning both a school policy for art (F1) and several suggested methods for planning sequential schemes of work in art (D2, D5 and D6). There is less information on assessment at the end of the fourteen Key Stages in Key Stage 1 and Key Stage 2. A further SEAC document for assessment is promised by Council, who state, 'Assessment should... be simple for teachers.' A set of criteria are put forward as a model on which to base assessment. These are that at Key Stage 1, for Attainment Target 1, pupils should demonstrate that they can:

• start to look closely at the natural and made world and to record what they see; be confident in using their memories and imaginations in developing their ideas for art;
• be willing to explore the use of a variety of materials, tools and resources for practical work;
• understand that art has its own language, lines, shapes, colours, etc, and show some awareness of this in their work;
• control tools safely, organise and care for materials and equipment; develop the practice of planning their work; try out ideas beforehand; be prepared to change parts if needed.

For Attainment Target 2, pupils should demonstrate that they can:
• look closely at artefacts and objects (including their own work) and talk about them with others;
• start to understand that ideas and feelings can be expressed and communicated through art;
• understand that there are connections between their own and others' work, and the work of artists past and present.

At Key Stage 2, for Attainment Target 1 pupils should demonstrate that they can:
• select aspects of the natural world and record what they see, imagine and feel;
• take some responsibility for gathering information in support of their work and be discriminating in using it;
• be selective in their choice and application of materials to suit the task;
• develop confidence, control and understanding in using different materials and techniques;
• experiment with the elements of art and begin to use more formal ways to communicate ideas and feeling, eg. scale, distortion;
• be able to visualise ideas, discuss them with others and modify them with justification.

For Attainment Target 2, pupils should demonstrate that they can:
• discuss the different purposes of art and describe how artists have represented their ideas, making use of an art vocabulary;
• recognise and discuss the work of a number of artists, representing different styles and periods, and understand something of the times in which their work was made and how their work influenced others;
• apply what they have learned from other artists' work in an imaginative way to inform their own.

To fulfil these criteria, thorough record-keeping will be required, so that the children's progress throughout their primary and early secondary years will be recorded and followed by successive teachers. Although the Council states, 'Record-keeping should be kept to a minimum and should be sufficient to track curriculum progress, and support the annual report to parents,' the criteria suggest that the minimum requirement of the teacher will be individual record sheets for each child, and a record of work, either by photographs, photocopies, folders of work or a mixture of all three. The record sheets could be tick charts, supplemented by further written comment if notable successes occur, or if evidence of a lack of understanding, skills, or failure in aesthetic response in a particular area is evident. There should be suggestions of strategies for further development when needed. The proportion of weighting between Attainment Target 1 and Attainment Target 2 is clearly stated by Council – two to one in favour of Attainment Target 1 (*Non-Statutory Guidance*, B1.2). Therefore the emphasis is on practical art work. Council stresses that the teaching of historical and cultural awareness in art should be pluralistic in approach, and should include art from various cultures, both western and non-western; it should not be divorced from personal and practical experience on the part of the child (B1, B2); the Council states, 'although the programmes of study have been set out in relation to each attainment target, there is no implication that teaching activities or learning opportunities should be designed to address them separately' (*Art in the National Curriculum*, NCC 1992).

What then does the teacher need to do, to find out if the children have fulfilled the end of key stage statements?

Key Stage 1

Attainment Target 1

At Key Stage 1, Attainment Target 1, the first End of Key Stage Statement requires the children to have demonstrated that they can 'represent in visual form what they observe, remember and imagine'. If a collection of the children's work has been accumulated in an individual folder, this should present no problems, provided the three areas of observed drawing, remembered visual form and work from the imagination are covered.

158

Possibly, the area that is least used in school is visual memory. This can be encouraged by a modification of the method of teaching art used by Robert Catterson-Smith (1853-1938), a famous art educator who developed a system of 'shut-eye' drawing. In this, an object is displayed, and the artist draws the shape in the air using the fingers; this is repeated with the eyes shut. The object is looked at again and drawn on paper, with closed eyes. Young children's visual memory could be developed in a similar way, by placing an object in front of the children, and asking them to trace its shape in the air with their fingers after feeling and discussing it. This would then be repeated, with their eyes closed. The object could then be removed and the children could be asked to draw it from memory. They could then compare their drawing with the object, to see how accurate their visual memory was. As well as teaching the children to notice line, shape and texture, this should help the teacher to assess children's ability to draw from memory.

The development of memory through observation followed by drawing gives the children a visual vocabulary of the elements of art – shape, line, colour form, space, texture – which they can use when creating a picture or three-dimensional form from their imagination. Let us take as an example a theme suggested by the Council in the *Non-Statutory Guidance* (1992), that of a jungle. A child who has had experience of observed drawings of a selection of plants over a period of time would be able to produce far more imaginative and varied foliage for jungle plants than a child who has had to rely on imagination unsupported by observation. An additional stimulus for the child would be a study of appropriate paintings, such as those by Rousseau, to encourage a sense of composition and colour, as well as sparking the imagination. The composition that resulted from this type of input should enable the teacher to assess the children's progress at Attainment Target 1, and of Key Stage Statement (a) and Attainment Target 2, End of Key Stage Statement (c).

The End of Key Stage Statement (b) requires the children 'to select from a range of items they have collected and use them as a basis for their work'. Again, this should be relatively easy to assess while work is taking place in the classroom on a theme such as mini-beasts or making greetings cards. Assess the children by the amount of enthusiasm and understanding they show in gathering together and arranging collections of objects, in making suggestions and in talking about the process and results with their peers. Take note of the children's use of appropriate words to describe the colours, textures, shape, etc, of the collection, as this would contribute to their capacity at End of Key Stage Statement (d) for Attainment Target 1. The level and involvement in the discussion must be sensitively handled by the teacher, as there are many factors to take into account, such as gender and ethnicity, as well as the child's own personality. In some Eastern cultures, for example, girls of any age are reluctant to express an individual view in front of boys, so it is obviously difficult to discover their thoughts. Some children become shy when they are emotionally involved in an activity, and are unable to express themselves, especially in the early years. This is where the teacher's knowledge and understanding of children is invaluable.

The End of Key Stage Statement (c) requires the children to 'work practically and imaginatively with a variety of materials and methods exploring the elements of art'. To understand what this means, ask yourself the following questions:
• Have the children mixed colours?
• Have they used pencils, crayons, coloured pencils, charcoal and felt-tipped pens?
• Have they handled clay and dough?
If the answer is yes each time, then they have used a variety of tools and materials.

How confidently can the children select a specific tool for art work, without being told which one to select? They should all be able

to do this, within a limited range, by the age of seven, provided they have been able to experiment and discover the way the tools and materials can be successfully used. Again, ask yourself the following questions:
• Have the children colour-matched objects from nature and the man-made world?
• Have they rubbed surfaces to discover texture?
• Have they made patterns?
• Have they made models?
• Have they used some of their observed drawings to form patterns or designs?
• Have they painted and modelled from their imagination?
If they have, then the second part of the End of Key Stage Statement has been fulfilled.

The final End of Key Stage Statement (d) asks that the children 'implement simple changes in their work in the light of progress made'. The changes and discussion could be observed and noted in a group or class project, or it could be done through individual work. For this to be successful, the teacher's individual powers of observation and encouragement are important. The children need to be taught to consider the development of their drawings and patterns, and to learn the appropriate vocabulary of art to discuss their ideas. Careful record-keeping will be needed to enable the child's individual profile to develop in their progress through school.

The stage of development that children have reached will affect their capacity to

reach successfully the final end of key stage statement of Key Stage 1. However, it is worth remembering that with encouragement, the right stimulation and programmes of work, children can advance rapidly through the stages of art development. The National Curriculum advocates a more sequential thinking and considered approach to the art curriculum in primary schools, from both teachers and children.

Attainment Target 2

This new approach is clear when the second attainment target at Key Stage 1 is studied. After reading through this, look at paragraph 3.21 of the Council's report. 'Council consider that the working group's proposals pay insufficient attention to the study of art history. In order, therefore, to ensure that 1) the practical work of all pupils is rooted in an informed understanding of our artistic heritage and 2) pupils who do not have a practical aptitude for art have a proper opportunity to develop their appreciation of art, Council recommends that the PoS should be strengthened to include references to the study of art from a variety of periods and cultures.'

This statement needs to be put in the context of a previous statement (3.15), where the Council states, 'this is not to say that the two ATs should not be linked: knowledge, for example, should not be taught in a vacuum'. In other words, the teacher is not required to teach primary children the history of art, except where it relates to practical experience.

In the End of Key Stage Statement (a) at Key Stage 1, Attainment Target 2, the children are required to 'recognise different kinds of art', both in their own environment and historically.

The teacher would need to ensure that the children not only realised that art existed within galleries and museums, and in a historical context, but also that art is part of everyday living. The teacher will have to establish a criteria that is appropriate to the children in the class to enable her to judge whether the children recognise different kinds of art, both in their home, their environment, and in the context of museums and galleries. This criteria should be mutually agreed by the school staff.

The children could be asked to talk about art in the locality, if they had made a local study, and their understanding could be gauged from this, and from accompanying drawings; a similar approach could be taken with a class discussion on clothes, mugs, book illustrations, for example, and the teacher could assess the children by their observation and ability to appreciate the differences and similarities in the subjects, using appropriate art terms, such as colour, shape, etc. Again, observations would need to be recorded by the teacher.

The children could be assisted to fulfil the End of Key Stages (a) and (b) for Attainment Target 2 by visits to local museums or galleries, where the education staff could introduce the children to art work related to a theme taking place in the classroom. The visits would need to be followed up with both practical work and discussion back in the classroom, to make sure that the children have understood what was experienced on the visit. This again relies to a great extent on the teacher's understanding and knowledge of the children.

The End of Key Stage Statement (b) requires that the children be able to 'identify some of the ways in which art has changed, distinguishing between work in the past and present'. This again demands a structured input from the teacher for the children to be able to fulfil the requirements. The themes of their work in art must relate to a study of the way artists from different periods and cultures have approached similar themes. The children must be able to talk about the differences between the examples. One suggestion is that they study the different ways plants and animals are portrayed in the carvings of medieval artists, and in the work of Rousseau and Elisabeth Frink. The children could also look at the way trees were drawn in medieval books, and compare them with the paintings of Gainsborough, Monet and Van Gogh. Pictures of house interiors could be compared, selected from different periods in art and history, such as an interior by the Dutch genre painter, Jan Vermeer (1632-75), a domestic scene by Pierre Bonnard (1867-1947), and a recent interior by Patrick Caulfield (1936-). These could be closely studied, and the different artists' approach to the subject matter and the elements of art could be discussed by the group. The teacher could note the various responses and understanding shown by the children. To discover how much the children understand of the differences in art styles, ask them to arrange a series of pictures in chronological order, or to describe a scene in a particular picture and to indicate whether it was made in this country, or far away. The children could point out the colour range used, and note the use of line and brush strokes.

The End of Key Stage Statement (c) asks that the children 'begin to make connections between their own work and that of other artists'. Their ability to do this would be reflected in the way they interpreted artists' work. Practically, they could paint their own version of a picture, or make their own three-dimensional version of a model. Alternatively, they could compare their own use of colour, texture, etc, with that used by the artists.

Key Stage 2

Attainment Target 1

At all key stages of the art curriculum, the attainment targets are the same, but the end of key stage statements vary slightly, in ways that are clearly indicated in the programmes of work and are explained more fully in the *Non-Statutory Guidance*. In Attainment Target 1, the End of Key Stage Statement indicates that, by this stage, children should 'communicate ideas and feelings in visual form based on what they observe, remember and imagine'.

The similarity to the statement in Key Stage 1 is marked, but the inclusion of the reference to communicating ideas and feelings indicates an expectation of a more developed grasp of the visual language of art.

This is spelled out further in the programmes of study and the examples. By this age, it is expected that the children will be able to draw successfully from different angles and viewpoints, thus beginning to learn the simplest rules of perspective. They should be able to draw and record reflections

Scene from the school playground, by a ten-year-old

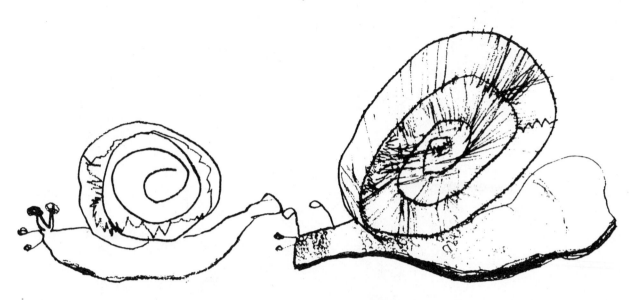

Observed drawing of a snail, by a Reception child

and shadows, use a sketch-book, work with a draw/paint system on a computer and make models that produce images – a diorama is given as an example, but a pinhole camera would be a valid alternative. To assess the children's ability to fulfil the End of Key Stage Statement, the teacher could look through each child's sketch-book and folder of work.

An important pointer to the more mature approach expected from each child is indicated in the word 'select' used in PoS(i) for Key Stage 2, where the pupil should 'select and record images'. This implies a conscious selection of shapes, lines, colours or forms by the pupil from the subject matter that is being drawn. The teacher should note the degree of independence in the child's choice, although constructive discussion with their peers should not be regarded as disadvantageous.

Emphasis is laid on the sequential development of work in the End of Key Stage Statement (b), in which the children are required to 'develop an idea or theme for their work, drawing on visual and other sources, and discuss their methods'. An obvious way of discovering the child's ability to form sequences in their work is to include the making of a storyboard in their programme of study. However, the child's sketch-book can also indicate the ability to form a sequence of ideas. The drawings and colour sketches reveal the progressive

development of an idea, from the first drawings of source materials to the final works, which could be a linocut or a card print, for example.

During this process, the children will have fulfilled not only the second End of Key Stage Statement, but also part of the third, where they must demonstrate that they can 'experiment with and apply their knowledge of the elements of art, choosing appropriate media'. The prints should include work in texture, shape, colour and line, as well as the appropriate use of materials.

In the Programme of Study the work is expected to be both expressive and experimental; to include various qualities of line (thick, thin, solid, broken, etc) tone (a range of lights to darks), and to use a range of colour mixes derived from the primary colours, including variations of one colour. The children's abilities in these areas could be observed and recorded by the teacher over a period of time, supported by work in their folders and sketch-books.

Some children's work will develop slowly, however much stimulus and encouragement they are given. They will continue to lack the confidence to widen their range of expression and use of media. The teacher needs to think of strategies to enable these children to experiment. For example, a timid, tidy child could be encouraged to work on a larger

scale, using charcoal, or in a different medium such as clay. By contrast, a disorganised, careless worker would benefit from small scale work, such as using a fine soft brush and watercolour paints to match the details of a flower, or picture containing fine detail, such as a Beatrix Potter scene.

These exercises would not alter the character of the children's work, but would present them with a challenge requiring thought; a similar approach works effectively with the gifted child, and helps them all to fulfil the End of Key Stage Statement (c) for Attainment Target 1 for Key Stage 2 children especially if accompanied by a discussion of their work with others.

The fourth and final End of Key Stage Statement would also have been fulfilled, if the children had changed and developed the design of the prints, and experimented with the effects of various colours and overprinting. They would have had to 'modify their work in the light of its development and their original intentions'.

The teacher could assess the children's grasp of colour by setting a painting exercise. Their colour sense should have developed by this stage and age, and there ought to be evidence of the ability to distinguish a variety of subtle shades within one colour. It is no longer enough to know that red is red, as the children did at Key Stage 1, but they should be able to perceive, colour-match and talk about shades of colour. For example, they ought to be able to distinguish the various shades of red in the autumn leaves of a Virginia Creeper, or between the various greens in a landscape or in a potted plant. They should also be able to explain the basis from which they achieve the right colour mixes and matches.

Attainment Target 2

Attainment Target 2, Knowledge and Understanding, requires 'the development of visual literacy and knowledge and understanding of art, craft and design including the history of art, our diverse cultural heritage and a variety of other artistic traditions, together with the ability to make practical connections between this and the pupils' own work.

The End of Key Stage Statement (a) requires the children to be able to 'identify different kinds of art and their purposes', which links closely with the End of Key Stage Statement (b), that children will 'begin to identify the characteristics of art in a variety of genres from different periods, cultures and traditions, showing some knowledge of the related historical background'.

Both these End of Key Stage Statements present a knotty problem for teachers, already under stress from the wide range of new tasks imposed by the National Curriculum. The two requirements assume that the teacher already has a working knowledge of the history of art, or has the time to learn. We have suggested a basic book, which is easy to read, and is a standard for many first-year art students. Teachers may also find it interesting. *The Story of Art* by E.H. Gombrich covers western art from prehistoric to modern times. If teachers feel unsure in this area, this book would be an invaluable addition to the staff room bookshelf.

The understanding of the various art styles and movements could arise from a study based on a gallery visit, or a school outing to a place of interest, where the children could have firsthand experience of art, with specialist support. Their written accounts of the visit, together with the accompanying art work that emerged after the visit, should give a good indication of the level of their comprehension.

Another approach would be for the teacher to include art as part of a historical study. For example, if the teacher and the class are working on a theme of exploration and explorers (History KS2), which includes the Aztecs, they could compare the treatment of the human figure by the Aztecs with the way it was portrayed by the Greeks and Henry Moore. They all used stone, but the society and the resulting changes in art approach could be discussed, using appropriate art terms, such as form, space, curve, line, and the children asked to draw their own version of the sculptures in an appropriate historical setting, or model their own sculpture against a painted historical scene, which should give some indication of the children's understanding.

The areas of art covered by the school would need planning, to prevent repetition and ensure some continuity of the areas of art and art history covered.

The final End of Key Stage Statement 'make imaginative use in their own work of a developing knowledge of the work of other artists' would have to be assessed over a period of time, so that the children not only have the opportunity to study closely and analyse the methods and style of artists, but also have the opportunity to try out and develop what they have seen. The effect of their studies, and its application and development in their own work should be apparent in their folders, and could be noted by the teacher at the end of each term.

Conclusion

All the End of Key Stage Statements can be assessed primarily through each child's folder and sketch-book. These should show that both observed drawing and sequential work has developed, and that the children can use various artists' approaches and techniques to improve their own individual visual language of art. The children's ability to describe the processes they have used, their reaction to other artists' work and their understanding of its historical context can be structured into the everyday working of the curriculum.

Provided the new approach suggested in the National Curriculum for Art is not regarded as a burden, it should give both teachers and children knowledge that can broaden and deepen the enjoyment to be found in viewing, as well as making art.

Appendix 1

Using a sketch-book

In *Art for ages 5 to 14*, the programmes of study for Key Stage 2 include the use of a sketch-book to 'record observations and ideas'. A sketch-book is the traditional means whereby an artist, craftsman or designer jots down drawings, notes and pictures as a reminder, or as a source of ideas for future development. Not all the ideas will be developed, but they none the less serve as a valuable resource.

There are many examples of notable artists' sketch-books to be found in museums and galleries. The Victoria and Albert Museum has a collection of John Constable's exquisite, tiny sketch-books that reflect his interest in the sky. The most remarkable sketch-books of all belonged to Leonardo da Vinci, and have been a source of awe and delight for generations. There are many published versions of Leonardo's sketches, and they include not only sketches of people, plants and weather conditions, but also anatomical studies and doodles of plans for tanks and war defences. They reveal a remarkable breadth of knowledge, imagination and skill.

The role of the sketch-book

The role of the sketch-book is to provide a sequential development of ideas. Source material, thumbnail sketches and colourways, the recording of places and people of interest, the occasional note, the odd memento or photograph, doodles and dream sketches should all form part of a sketch-book. Unfortunately, the very name, 'sketch-book', suggests to many people that it should only be used for pencil drawings, with a single sketch on each sheet. Some inexperienced students become agitated when told their sketch-books are too tidy, that the drawings in them do not indicate a thoughtful approach to colour, line, texture or shape, or that they reveal a disjointed approach and a lack of continuity. It is hard to persuade them that the point of having a sketch-book is to record ideas and to draw items that could stimulate future work and development, or that are relevant to their current project.

A visual and written record

In the context of the primary school, what should we expect to see in a child's sketch-book? It will, of course, vary from child to child, but basically, the sketch-book should form a visual and written record. It should reflect the child's own interests, and include drawings made during school investigations or visits, magazine clips, dried plants and records of experiments with tools and techniques. It should be a well-used, personal notebook, mainly visual in its imagery, that reveals the breadth and depth of the child's thinking and imagination.

Children can be taught to turn naturally to their sketch-books whenever they begin a new topic. To illustrate the way the sketch-book can be used, suppose a group of children were taken on a visit to the Tower of London, arranged as part of a history investigation of the Tudor dynasty. The children could use their sketch-books to draw any details of the journey that they found interesting, such as the coach, the pattern of the material on the seats, their friends looking out of the window or the driver.

The children could supplement their drawings with notes, and record the colours they see, using felt-tipped pens or coloured pencils. They could jot down words to describe the way they felt about scenes and people they passed on the journey.

The drawings could be made in ballpoint or felt-tipped pen, coloured or pastel pencils. However, the children should also be encouraged to draw in other media, and not just in pencil. Indeed, pencil can be inhibiting, leading to endless rubbing out, with poor results, or no results at all. Children should be taught to draw over mistakes, and to improve the drawing, using the first attempt to show them where they went wrong. Point out to the children that the drawings in a sketch-book are only a beginning; they should lead to further work, and are not finished drawings in themselves. Sometimes sketch-book drawings turn out so well that they can be presented as finished work, but this is not their prime purpose.

To return to the example of the visit to the Tower of London, the children could be asked to make a quick sketch of the Beefeaters, the ravens or the White Tower, using black felt-tipped pens. They could also be asked to make small sketches of details beside their main drawings; for example, they could study the insignia and decoration on the Beefeaters' tunics, the beaks and eyes of the ravens or the stone pattern on the White Tower. Inside the Tower, they could record details of decorations from a gun or a suit of armour, labelling the drawings with notes of the materials and colours that were used.

The children may like to put a leaf from the grounds in their book, to be fastened in later. They may like to draw a map of part of their route round the Tower. They could also include postcards to supplement their drawings. Photographs could be stuck into the sketch-books, and used as reference later on. There are many possibilities.

Back at school, the children could use their drawings, postcards and photographs as a basis for scene illustrating an incident in Tudor history, such as the young Elizabeth arriving at the Tower, via Traitors' Gate.

In the classroom, the sketch-book can form a useful personal record, gathering together the preliminary drawings that often go unrecorded in the individual child's profile. Again, as an example, if the children were investigating growth as part of a science project, drawings of a seedling's development could be made in their sketch-books. The series of drawings that resulted from this record would reveal the individual child's accuracy of observation and level of drawing skills, together with any progress that had been made in the positioning of the drawing on the paper and the appropriate use of space.

What sketch-book to use?

There are many types of sketch-books on the market; all are quite expensive. With the younger juniors, it is probably better for them to be allowed to make their own sketch-books (see Figure 1).

A sewn book should last longer than a stapled one, and will not prick the children's fingers. Although cheap notebooks are available, the paper is usually of very poor

A. 3 point for smallish books.

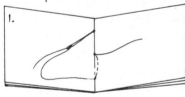

Mark centre of spine first. Measure one hole above and one below. Open book. Push needle and thread through centre to outside. Bring back through lower hole. Make one big stitch over centre and take down through upper hole. Pull tight.

Bring up through centre again, but on opposite side of big stitch from first end of thread.

Pull tight and tie ends firmly over big stitch, using a reef knot. Cut off surplus.

B. 5 point for big books.

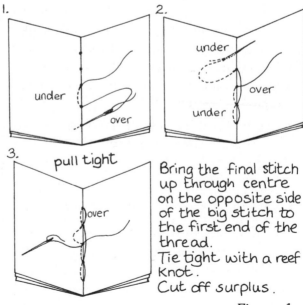

Bring the final stitch up through centre on the opposite side of the big stitch to the first end of the thread.
Tie tight with a reef knot.
Cut off surplus.

Figure 1

169

quality, limiting the children's choice of drawing tools. Letting the children make their own sketch-books ensures that they have available cartridge or art paper for drawing, and possibly some sheets of coloured sugar paper at the front and back, both for the occasional charcoal drawing and for sticking in newspaper cuttings or mementos.

The cover of the sketch-book would be best made from manila. Unlike a commercial sketch-book, it will not have a stiff back cover, so each child will need either a clipboard or a piece of cardboard to rest on when drawing. If a cardboard support is used, clips will be needed to keep the sketch-book stable while the children are drawing.

If school funds will allow the purchase of commercial sketch-books, A4 is a useful all-purpose size. They contain sheets of cartridge paper held together with a spiral binding and supported on a chipboard back. These would be excellent both for drawings made outside the classroom, and for trying rough sketches of ideas in class.

Ingres pads

There are other uses for a sketch-book and different types of pads are produced for these purposes. The range includes Ingres pads, named after the painter Jean Auguste Dominique Ingres (1780-1867), which come in two or more tints, and contain a thicker, textured paper. This paper's rough surface is suitable for pastel and charcoal drawings and it gives interesting effects with soft pencils. It would be stimulating for the children to use the sheets from an Ingres pad for an occasional pastel drawing, as the effect is much more satisfying than working on cartridge paper. The children could compare

the differences of colour and line between a picture drawn on the Ingres paper and one executed on cartridge or sugar paper.

Cotman water-colour pads

Another type of sketch-book that is available is the Cotman water-colour pad. This is named after the English water-colourist who specialised in landscapes, John Sell Cotman (1782-1842). Again, the paper is thicker than that in a normal sketch-book and, as the name indicates, suited to water-colour. It has a slight texture, and is much less inclined to wrinkle under the impact of the water in the paint. The children would find painting water-colour washes on this paper a rewarding experience; they could devise a landscape or urban scene based on examples of Cotman's work.

Layout pads

Finally, there are layout pads. These are inexpensive, and made from very thin, almost transparent paper. They are used to trace in any alterations or new elements to an existing design or picture, and are widely used by graphic artists. Their use in primary school is limited, but they could be helpful in planning a group project, such as a series of scenes for a puppet play.

The children's sketch-books should be helpful in the assessment of a child, provided the teacher recognises that a well-thumbed, smudgy book, full of information and ideas, however unfinished they may be, is worth more than a neat, efficiently executed, unrelated set of one-off drawings, dutifully carried out. A sketch-book is a personal visual diary.

Appendix 2

Dictionary of art definitions

Altamira

A site of Palaeolithic cave paintings in northern Spain, discovered accidentally by the young daughter of an antiquarian in 1879. At first labelled as fakes, the discovery of other cave paintings forced people to acknowledge that primitive man had portrayed animals with amazing realism. They were painted in about 12,000 BC, and show horses, bison, aurochs (wild ox) and boar, among other animals. The painters used earth colours – black, yellow ochre, dark red, browns and dull purple.

Appliqué

In embroidery, the sewing or sticking of pieces of fabric on to a background material to form a pattern or picture.

Armature

A framework on which clay or plaster or Mod-Roc is built up to make a three-dimensional figure.

Bayeux Tapestry

In fact, this is an embroidery not a tapestry (stitched not woven), quite crude in technique compared to the work of the Embroiderers' Guild of the day. Probably worked by Norman ladies, it shows the events in English history from the accession of Edward the Confessor to the death of Harold by the Normans in the Battle of Hastings. It is full of lively detail, and the borders contain pictures of both Aesop's Fables and casualties from the battle scenes. Very popular with children, it is 227 feet long and 20 inches wide, worked in coloured wools on linen. There is a painted replica of the Bayeux Tapestry on display in the Victoria and Albert Museum in London.

Bestiary

A medieval manuscript depicting animals or fabulous beasts. Favourite picture-books in their day, they influenced the way animals were drawn, and the decoration of architecture, furniture, embroideries and tapestries.

Blunger

A revolving machine used by a potter to mix clay and water to produce slip.

Book of Hours

A medieval prayer-book used in private contemplation, containing prayers for hours, days of the week or the seasons. The books were beautifully illustrated, at first by hand. The best known example is *Très Riches Heures du Duc de Berry*. After the fifteenth century, the books were printed from woodblocks.

Brueghel or Bruegel (c. 1525-69)

Known as Brueghel the Elder, born in the Netherlands. Painted landscapes or genre paintings. One of his most celebrated is *Hunters in the Snow*; he also painted peasants and illustrations of proverbs. One of his most famous proverb paintings is *The Blind Leading the Blind*. His *Peasants' Wedding* and *Children's Games* are of interest to most children.

Cartoon

A full-size drawing made to transfer a design to a painting or tapestry. The drawings had holes pricked round the lines, and chalk or charcoal was rubbed through the holes to transfer the design to the canvas. Leonardo da Vinci's cartoon for *The Virgin and Child with St Anne* (1510-12) is in the National Gallery in London, and Raphael's full-colour cartoons for tapestries can be seen in the Victoria and Albert Museum in London. This method is still used to transfer large embroidery designs to fabric.

Cassatt, Mary (1844-1926)

American painter and film maker, who lived in Paris and worked with the Impressionist painters. She painted realistic scenes of contemporary life.

Classical

A term used to describe art that is either Greek or Roman, or influenced by Greek or Roman art in style. The Parthenon in Athens is the apex of classical Greek architecture, and the Parthenon frieze in the British Museum exemplifies classical Greek sculpture.

Rather confusingly, classical can also mean the opposite of Romanticism. David and Ingres were classical painters; they emphasised the importance of line as opposed to colour, and were more restrained in their subject matter.

Colour field painting

This type of work developed in America in the late 1940s and 50s. Colour is the dominant feature in the paintings. Among its best-known exponents are Helen Frankenthaler, Morris Louis and Mark Rothko.

Composition

The arrangement of colour, shape, line etc, in a picture, design or three-dimensional work. One of the main rules of composition is to consider the effect of the spaces left round the main shapes – all parts of the picture are of equal importance. Compositions can be balanced by repetition of shape, with small variations in scale, by using a limited range of colour or texture.

Cubism

A movement in painting that altered people's perception of space in art, by abandoning traditional methods of modelling and perspective, and portraying things as they are known from several simultaneous points of view. This approach to painting was influenced by African sculpture and by the later paintings of Cezanne. The first Cubists were Pablo Picasso and Georges Braque (1882-1963).

Elements of art

A phrase much used in the National Curriculum for Art, it refers to the language of art. These are line, shape, tone, space, composition and colour.

Epstein, Sir Jacob (1880-1959)

Sculptor of Jewish origin born in America, who worked in Britain. A remarkable sculptor who, due to anti-semitic prejudice and his bold modern treatment of the figure, was not acknowledged as a major artist until late in life. His public sculptures on buildings, influenced by ethnic art (Aztec, African) were often hacked about, or had to have adjustments made to their anatomy. At one point his large stone carving of *Adam* was exhibited in a funfair at Blackpool. His portrait busts, by contrast, were very popular, resembling Rodin's work in technique. His *St Michael and the Devil* at Coventry Cathedral and *Rock Drill* in the Tate Gallery, London, are two of his most well known works.

Expressionism

The rejection of traditional naturalism in favour of the distortion and exaggeration of form and colour to express feeling. Expressionism was the main movement in German painting between 1905 and 1930. Vincent Van Gogh was a forerunner of Expressionism. Famous Expressionist artists include Franz Marc in Germany, while in France, Matisse and the Fauves (literally, 'wild beasts') formed the French equivalent of the movement.

Fauvism

Painting that uses colour to express emotion rather than objective reality. André Derain, for example, painted *The Pool of London* (1906) in pinks, reds and shades of blue and mauve. The Fauves worked in the first years of the twentieth century, and finally freed painting from pictorial representation. They have clear affinities with the German Expressionists. The main painters were Matisse, Derain, Rouault, Braque and Dufy.

Folk art

Objects and decoration made for daily use by craftsmen, employing traditional techniques and forms. Usually the objects are handmade rather than mass-produced. Examples are corn dollies, lace, barge painting, Yugoslav embroidery and Peruvian weavings.

Frink, Dame Elisabeth (1930-)

British sculptor, working mainly in bronze. Her favourite subjects include horses and riders, rather savage birds and huge heads wearing goggles.

Futurism

Italian movement, active from 1909-14, that glorified the beauty of speed and the machine. The main exponents were Umberto Boccioni, Giacomo Balla, Gino Severini and Luigi Russolo.

Genre

A term applied to paintings about everyday life, usually domestic. This style was particularly prevalent in seventeenth-century Dutch art.

Giacometti, Alberto (1901-66)

A Swiss sculptor who worked mainly in Paris. His most famous works are of very elongated isolated figures. He used the space between his shapes to animate the sculptures, which, although so elongated, have a powerful and often moving presence.

Gogh, Vincent Van (1853-90)

Dutch Post-Impressionist painter, who used swirling brush strokes and thick paint to express his violently contrasting emotions. He was a friend of Paul Gauguin, at least until they lived together in Arles, France. They squabbled, and Van Gogh cut of his ear, presenting it to a prostitute. It is hardly surprising that poor Vincent was not a commercial success, and he ended up in a mental hospital, where he committed suicide. He is now extremely well known, and his paintings sell for millions of pounds.

Hard edge painting

A form of abstract painting in which the artist uses flat colour and crisp edges. Two well-known painters who work in this style are Ellsworth Kelly and Kenneth Noland.

Hepworth, Dame Barbara (1903-71)

An English sculptor who lived and worked in St Ives, she was a major figure in the rise of abstract art in Britain and a friend of Henry Moore. Unlike Moore, her work is abstract, very elegant and concerned with the relationship of the inside to the outside of her holed geometric shapes which were often connected by threaded string. She usually worked directly into wood or stone, using the quality of the stone, or the grain of the wood, to enhance the form of the work. She described carving as 'an extension of the telluric forces which shape a landscape', thus declaring her affinity to the Romantic movement.

Hiroshige, Ando (1797-1858)

A Japanese printmaker, who was a part of the dominant movement in Japanese art of the seventeenth to nineteenth centuries known as *Ukiyo-e*. This means 'pictures of the floating world', an elegant term to describe the transience of their subject matter, which was drawn from everyday life – country scenes, bath house girls, theatre scenes, actors, flowers. Two other well known printmakers were Katsushiko Hokusai (1760-1849) and Kitagawa Utamaro (1753-1806). They had a great influence on the French Impressionists who loved their flat colour and decorative composition.

Impressionism

An art movement that began in France in the 1860s, when a group of young artists started to investigate the effects of light on colour. They used brightly-coloured dabs of paint on a white ground to capture the changing effects of light. They were among the first painters to work in the open air in front of their subject. The movement was a rebellion against the heroic emotionalism of the Romantic painters. The Impressionists believed in objectivity in painting, and that the artist should paint the contemporary scene. This approach was considered scandalous at the time; railway stations were not suitable subjects for art – they did not ennoble the human soul. The influence of Impressionism on younger artists was enormous. They were gradually accepted by the public and are now extremely popular. The best known artists in this movement include Monet, whose water lily paintings are one of life's great experiences, Pissarro, Renoir and Sisley.

Line

These can be dark, light, thick, thin, curved, straight, broken, solid, jagged, long, sensitive, powerful, etc. Lines create form and shape, both inside as well as round the edge of a shape. They can be expressive, creating mood in a drawing or painting.

Lowry, Laurence Stephen (1887-1976)

Lowry lived in Salford or Manchester all his life, working as a rent collector. He painted after finishing work, drawing scenes of the industrial north with which he was so familiar. Although at first sight his work can appear childlike, he was a skilled draughtsman, having studied at art schools for twenty years on and off. He is either loved or hated by those who study his work, but it does give a good historical picture of industrial life in the earlier years of this century.

Michelangelo Buonarroti (1475-1564)

With Raphael and Leonardo da Vinci, Michelangelo is one of the great figures of the Renaissance. He was a painter, poet, sculptor, architect and draughtsman. He was a nobleman's son, and faced considerable opposition when he wanted to become an artist's apprentice.

In 1503-4 he carved *David*, a figure influenced by Hellenic work being excavated at that time in Rome. Look at this amazing and tender figure, and remember Michelangelo was only in his mid-thirties when he finished it. What an achievement!

Among his work, the most famous is the Sistine Chapel ceiling, which he tackled with reluctance, being forced into it by Pope Julius, who promised that Michelangelo could complete his tomb, a huge sculptural project, if he finished the ceiling first.

Michelangelo nevertheless produced a wonder of the world, of which Sir Kenneth Clark wrote, 'an image of divine perfection'. It took Michelangelo four years to complete, in uncomfortable conditions.

Mirò, Joan (1893-1938)

Spanish Surrealist painter, graphic artist and designer of theatre costumes. Mirò's work is abstract, drawn from his subconscious, usually playful in character, although it became darker in mood during the Spanish civil war. His colours are rich and glowing.

Moore, Henry (1898-1986)

English sculptor and draughtsman, acknowledged as one of the greatest sculptors of the twentieth century. He believed in truth to materials, a philosophy exemplified in his large carved figures of women that combine the sensuous curves of the female figure with the monolithic quality of the stone from which they were carved.

Morisot, Berthe (1841-95)

A French Impressionist who painted delicate domestic scenes in oils and watercolour. She married to Monet's younger brother, Eugene.

Morris, William (1834-96)

Influential English designer, painter, poet and social reformer. Morris was a Pre-Raphaelite and rejected the industrial revolution.

In 1861 he founded Morris & Co, together with Philip Webb, Rossetti, Burne-Jones, Ford Madox Brown and others. The Firm, as it was known, produced furniture, ceramics, carpets, embroidery and stained glass. The intention was to improve English design, and follow the example of the medieval guilds in involving the designer in the whole process, unlike the method used with mass production. His own most successful designs were those for wallpaper and materials, usually based on plants. They are still produced today.

Unfortunately, due to the rejection of machine methods, the excellent craft work produced by Morris and his followers in the Arts and Crafts Movement was extremely expensive, and could only be bought by the wealthy. This ran counter to Morris' socialism. Morris was involved in the founding of working men's colleges, and the society that later became the National Trust.

Morris' ideas were adopted by the founders

of the Deutsche Werkbunde, a design school in Germany, and were adapted to the needs of industry. This developed into the Bauhaus School of Design at Weimar, which believed, as did Morris, in truth to materials. However, the Bauhaus was worldwide in its influence, being the foundation of the European modern movement in design and architecture.

Neo-Impressionists

A group of painters who were as interested in the effects of light on colour as the Impressionists, but who believed that in the pursuit of painting the passing moment, the Impressionists had forfeited solidity of form. The Neo-Impressionists used paint in a controlled, planned and scientific way, placing dots of pure colour side by side, so that from a distance they each enhanced the other. The greatest painter of this movement was Georges Seurat (1859-91).

O'Keeffe, Georgia (1887-1986)

American painter, a founder of Modernism in the United States, who painted strong and rhythmic close-ups of floral and plant form, and townscapes of New York. She later painted scenes of the world seen from aeroplanes.

Palmer, Samuel (1805-1881)

Lyrical English landscape painter who worked in Shoreham in Kent. Palmer was influenced by William Blake, a visionary artist who saw angels in the trees at Peckham Rye and believed he dined with Isaiah.

Palmer was the leading member of a group called the Ancients, whose work imbued the landscapes they painted with pastoral romanticism. His work can be seen in the Tate Gallery, British Museum and Victoria and Albert Museum in London, The Ashmolean Museum in Oxford and the Fitzwilliam in Cambridge.

Samuel Palmer became widely known to the general public in recent years when Tom Keating's forgeries came to light.

Perspective

A way of making a flat surface look three-dimensional. The technique was developed in Italy in the fifteenth century. Scientific perspective was the basis of all European painting until late in the nineteenth century.

Picasso, Pablo (1881-1973)

The most famous painter of the twentieth century, who participated in most of the major art movements of his lifetime, working in many media, including graphics, ceramics and sculpture. A genius in art, he is impossible to describe in a few sentences.

Pop art

An art that was at its peak between 1950 and 1970. The artists in the movement used the products of a consumer society as the basis for their work – television, comics, advertising, etc. They also employed commercial methods of production, such as the silk screen. In this country, the leading figures were Richard Hamilton, David Hockney and Peter Blake, while in America, Andy Warhol, Roy Lichtenstein, Jasper Johns and Robert Rauschenberg were the movement's chief exponents. Pop was important, because it reintroduced figurative work to an art scene that had become dominated by abstraction. It reflected the structural changes in society at the time, and was the first movement to take mass culture seriously, drawing attention to new themes and subject matter for both art and intellectual consideration.

Quattrocento

Fifteenth century Italian art.

Renaissance

Literally 'rebirth', this refers to the revival of interest in classical Greek and Roman art that took place in Italy between the fourteenth and sixteenth centuries. This revival influenced architecture and painting, and meant the end of the Gothic style. Its influence eventually spread to all parts of Europe, and produced such great artists as Leonardo da Vinci, Michelangelo, Raphael, Titian, Botticelli, Correggio and Piero della Francesca. Examples of their work can be seen in the National Gallery in London and in the National Gallery of Scotland in Edinburgh. It was only at the end of the nineteenth century that painters developed a new approach.

Romanticism

A movement of the late eighteenth and early nineteenth century that is difficult to define. The artists of this movement believed in the power of the emotions, often laced with a touch of terror or horror. This reflected the philosophical approach of the time that reacted against the over-simplified rationalism of the previous century. The painters were involved in the mortality of humanity, man at the mercy of nature, the ruins of past grandeur and were in revolt against the conservative approach of the traditional classicists. Some famous painters associated with the movement are Turner in England, Delacroix and Géricault in France and Friedrich in Germany. In a way, Romanticism has never died; the spirit of the movement lives on in the experimental work being done today by Land artists such as Richard Long.

Rousseau, Henri (1844-1910)

A French amateur or 'Sunday' painter, sometimes called *le Douanier,* whose dream world was based on visits to the zoo and to the *Jardin des Plantes* in Paris. His paintings are the most famous naive works, and are both strange and decorative. For example, *The Dream* shows a woman lying on a settee in the middle of a jungle. His paintings of foliage and flowers are detailed and beautifully coloured. Some of his work reveals a sense of fun – *The Football Match* for example.

Rousseau was a source of amusement to fellow artists, such as Picasso, but he himself knew his work was good; he stated that he and Picasso were the only great artists left. Unfortunately, he died in great poverty, and his pictures were only acknowledged as masterpieces after his death.

Shape

This can be made or natural, large or small, symmetrical or asymmetrical, two- or three-dimensional, solid or transparent, textured or smooth.

Space

The depth of an object, as opposed to a flat two-dimensional picture. An illusion of space on flat surfaces can be made by using perspective; it can also be created with colour.

Stubbs, George (1724-1806)

The greatest English horse painter, whose work reflects his knowledge of the horse's anatomy. He was widely commissioned to paint not only the horses, but also the owners and grooms.

Surrealism

Much influenced by the work of Freud, this movement is concerned with the subconscious and dreams. Originally conceived as a revolution in life as well as art, it started in Germany, but spread across Europe, and to America, taking many forms. The best known Surrealist artists are Salvador Dali, Max Ernst, Joan Mirò and René Magritte.

Tone

Gradations of dark and light which can be used to create shape and form. Black and white mix to make many grey tones; colours also have tones – a range of light to dark blues, for example.

Valadon, Suzanne (1865-1938)

A French painter, who worked as a model for Degas and Renoir. She painted still lifes, portraits and figures, using flat colour and strong contours. Her son was the painter Maurice Utrillo.

This is a purely introductory list of definitions; art is a study of endlessly rich rewards for those who choose to look and read further, not only for what they discover about art, but for what art tells us about the human condition and our perception of the world.

Appendix 3

A brief history of paint, painting, tools and materials

Prehistoric man

Early man painted pictures of the animals he hunted, deep in the caves where he lived. He used colours found in the earth or from his fires. These included browny-reds, ochre yellows, browns, and black and white. The latter were made from soot or chalk, mixed with animal fat.

Cavemen probably made brushes from twigs, animal hair set in a quill, and sticks. They also would have used dry moss to apply colour, and it is possible that they used their fingers and hands as well. This is still the way colour is applied to walls in parts of India and Africa. It is a method of application that has been adopted by David Tremlett, a modern conceptual artist (that is, he is more interested in the idea than the product).

The ancient Egyptians

The colour range available for the artist to use expanded as humans learned more sophisticated ways of using tools. The ancient Egyptians crushed minerals to make powdered pigments, such as cinnabar (vermilion) from mercury and sulphur, and green from malachite. They synthetically produced Egyptian Blue, a 'frit' or glass colour which could be used in glazes on ceramics.

The Egyptians used a range of reed brushes, made by crushing one end of a reed, splitting the fibres, and binding the brush with twine at the point where the reed was split. They also used twigs to draw and paint with. These brushes would have been made for use by scribes to decorate books and draw hieroglyphics on papyrus paper, as well

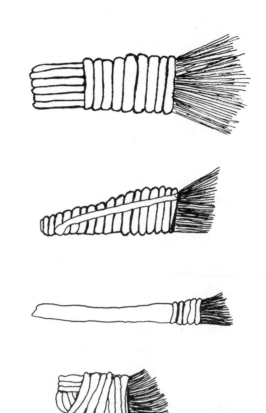

Egyptian brushes

as by artists for wall paintings on plaster. Examples of brushes have been found in tombs.

The Greeks

The Greeks added purple extracted from whelks, and green, derived from verdigris, to the colours available. We know little of the drawing tools they used as none have survived.

The Romans

The Romans used pigments mixed with wax, a technique known as 'encaustic painting'. For this technique, the palette has to be kept hot, and often the wax surface can be reworked using a heated metal tool to pass over the surface. The wax and pigment mix was applied to a wooden board. Encaustic painting was widely used until the Middle Ages.

Jasper Johns (1930-), an American pop artist, used this technique for some of his paintings of the American flag. In encaustic work, the colours do not change or fade, as the wax and pigment interact (provided the work is not exposed to the glare of the sun!).

The Middle Ages

In the thirteenth and fourteenth centuries, there was an expansion of the range of colours available for art work. Lapis lazuli was ground to make ultramarine, raw and burnt umber were produced from earth, the raw umbers from the Cyprus, north Italian and German clays, each of which varied slightly in tone. The earth was roasted to produce burnt umber. Lead-tin yellow was manufactured for glass making, and a greater range of colours were produced from berries and plants.

Animal hair brushes were widely used. Stiff brushes were made from hogs' hair; this was softened by using the brushes in large clumps as house decorators' brushes, to apply whitewash to walls. The clumps were then untied, divided into various sizes, and a stick was inserted into the top of the bristles. The bristles were then bound to the stick, to form a brush. Brushes were made this way until the nineteenth century.

Soft brushes were made with miniver hair inserted into a quill; the bird from which the quill came determined the size of the brush a vulture's quill was a large brush, a dove quill relatively small. A stick was put into the other end of the quill to make the handle. Quill pens were used for graphics.

Charcoal had long been known, and was made at this time by tying willow twigs in bundles, sealing them in a terracotta pot, and leaving them in a baker's oven overnight. It was used to rough in compositions, which were then gone over with pen or brush.

Fifteenth to nineteenth centuries

Silver point was widely used for drawing at this time. Pencils as we know them were crude until the end of the seventeenth century, being made from graphite sawn into thin shapes, with two pieces of wood glued either side. The wood would then have been rounded off by hand. It was not until the nineteenth century that pencils were produced by modern methods. Silver-point consisted of a needle of silver inserted into a stick. When used on prepared paper, it leaves a mark. Leonardo Da Vinci frequently used it when drawing.

The range of colours went on extending during this time, particularly in the nineteenth century, with the introduction of chemical dyes. Familiar names begin to appear, such as lemon yellow (1809), cobalt yellow (1848), alizarin crimson, which was first extracted from madder in 1826. Ultramarine was artificially manufactured in 1822, from kaolin, soda ash, etc, instead of lapis lazuli. After 1751, lead was no longer the only base for white with the introduction of zinc white, although it is still used in artists' colours today, in flake white. It is never used in school paints because of its toxic nature.

In the 1850's dyes from coal tars were produced; many early coal tar based colours faded and turned black, with dire results for such painters as Delacroix.

Delacroix was one of the great colourists of the nineteenth century, but this is not always evident in his pictures when we look at them today, due to the chemical changes that have taken place in the colours. Nevertheless, without the vast expansion of colours available to the artist at this time, the Impressionists would have found it difficult to put into practice their ideas of painting local colour and the way it is affected by light.

Another advance in artists' tools in the nineteenth century was the invention and manufacture of the metal ferrule for holding bristles in a brush. This meant that brushes could be flat as well as round.

Twentieth century

In this century, a vast range of new materials and tools is on the market, too numerous to mention. Although our paints are no longer, or rarely, pure pigment, and may mix less well, there are advantages. We no longer have to force-feed cows with mango leaves, and use their urine as a basis for yellow, or grind down the remains of mummies to get shades of brown. Probably the biggest development in paint so far this century has been the arrival of acrylics, which can be used as oils, gouache or watercolour.

Among tools, the most exciting newcomer is the graphics pack on the computer, which is still in its infancy. Recent advances have been rapid and extensive; it is likely that everyone will be able to design, paint and print in colour on their own home computer in the near future.

Some people see this as the death of the more traditional forms of art. As this demise has been predicted since the invention of photography, and since any method of making art depends on the imagination and dedication of the artist to produce a personal statement, as opposed to a stereotyped image, it seems unlikely that traditional art will die. Information technology will change, but this is part of the normal cycle of art history.

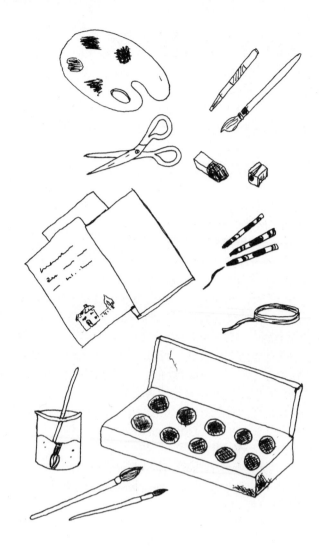

Appendix 4

Safety in the classroom

Although accidents are unusual in art lessons, teachers should ensure that they organise materials and tools as safely as possible. Give the children clear instructions about safe ways to use tools. Demonstrate safe methods of use. The children will take more notice of rules if they know why the rules are there.

When materials are not in use, store them safely away from the children. Do not allow anything to be placed in the mouth, nose or ears. Try to ensure that supervision is adequate, and that children using scissors or cutting tools can be easily seen by the teacher, or helper.

This probably sounds an alarming list, but accidents are rare; let us make sure they become rarer!

Fire risks

Keep work and storage areas uncluttered, and clear of debris, to minimise any fire risk. Fire is a potential hazard if you are working with paper, card, fabrics, wood, acetate, string or rope.

Fumes

As well as being flammable, some materials give off toxic fumes; these include polythene, polystyrene and flexible plastics.

Cuts

Remember that thin card, paper, foil and acetate can cause minor cuts; although minor, these cuts sting.

Instruct the children on the use of the bench hook, for lino cutting etc. Show them the way to hold lino tools, saws, craft knives.

All cutting knives should have the blades set so that only the tip of the blade protrudes from the handle – they make a shallower cut this way.

Dust

Dust can cause problems if children suffer from asthma.
• Fabrics can be dusty; foil with Cellophane backing can flake if crumpled, and the resultant dust contains harmful metals.
• Sawdust can irritate sensitive lungs.
• Dry clay should never be sandpapered to smooth it down as clay contains silicon.
• If kapok is used for stuffing soft toys, give the children a simple dust mask to wear.

Adhesives

All commercial adhesives, gums and pastes should be treated with care. Many are flammable, and some contain toxic ingredients. This is particularly true of spray adhesives, although the most recent products are non-toxic and environmentally friendly.

Paint

Most school paints are totally safe, but some watercolours contain undesirable elements. All household paints should be handled by the teacher, if the children are young.

Appendix 5
Photocopiable material

Pages 181 to 183 provide children with valuable experience in investigating texture and line. Page 184 comprises a basic assessment chart for Key Stage 1 which can be adapted for use with Key Stage 2 children.

Texture

Using paint, felt-tipped pen and coloured pencils, try to match the texture in the first square.

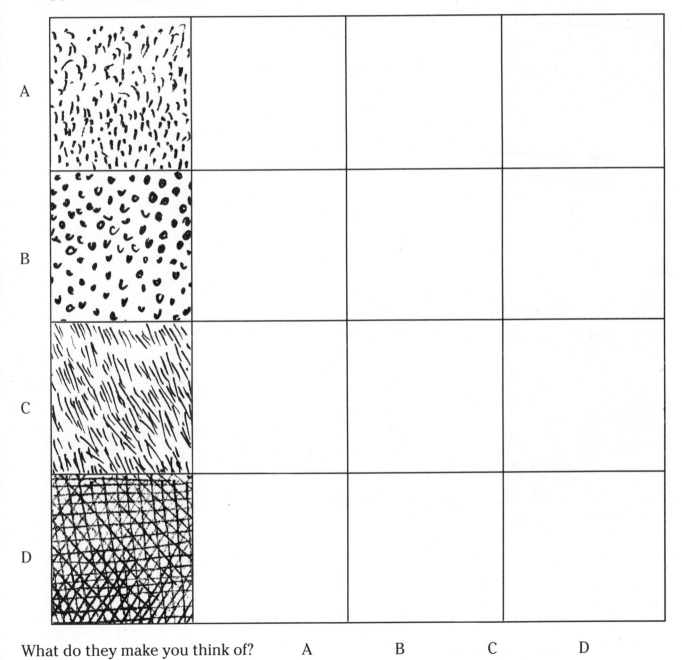

What do they make you think of?   A   B   C   D

Line

Using a pencil, a pen or a wax crayon, match the lines in the first square.

What changes can you see? What do they remind you of?			

Make some lines of your own.

Textures and lines

Use these as a basis for experiments with mark-making using a variety of tools (pencils, charcoal, felt-tipped pens, etc).

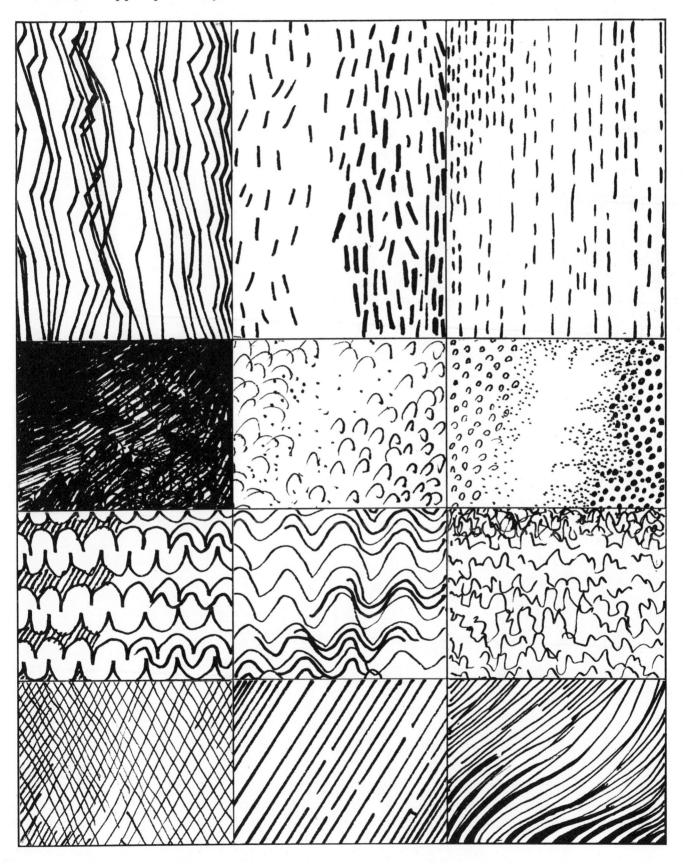

Assessment chart for use with children at KS1

This chart can be adapted for use with children at KS2. Tick off each category as appropriate.

Name _____ Age _____

KS1 AT1: Investigating and making

EKSSa Represent in observed form what is observed/remembered/imagined
- can draw accurately from observation
- can use memory in art work
- uses imagination in art work

EKSSb Select from a range of items collected and use them as source material
- contributes/originates collections
- can sort appropriately
- can arrange items in a collection
- can use collection items as source for art work

EKSSc Works practically/imaginatively with materials/methods, exploring the elements of art
- uses two-dimensional materials
- uses three-dimensional materials/makes three-dimensional forms
- uses: line
  tone
  pattern from: made forms
  natural forms
- can mix from primary colours
- explores the use of: space
  form
  shape

EKSSd Implement simple changes in their work in the light of progress made
- can discuss work
- changes work as needed
- can talk about how it was made

KS1 AT2 Knowledge and understanding

EKSSa Recognise different kinds of art
- identifies art   in school
  in the environment
- identifies past/present arts

EKSSb Identifies changes in art, past and present
- can look at, talk about art and artists
- recognises differences in cultures, chronology

EKSSc Makes connections between own work and that of others
- can translate   mood in work of art to own work
  theme in work of art to own work

Bibliography

The following list of books includes those mentioned in the text as well as books which would be of general use to the classroom teacher and of interest to children.

Teachers' books

General

Arneson, H H *A History of Modern Art* (Thames and Hudson)

Barnes, R *Art, Design and Topic Work 8-13* (Unwin Hyman)

Barnes, R *Teaching Art to Young Children 4-9* (Unwin-Hyman)

Belves, Peter and Mathey, Francis *Animals in Art* (Oldham Press)

ed. Bullen, J B *Post-Impressionists in England* (Routledge)

Chilvers, I et al *The Oxford Dictionary of Art* (OUP)

Clay, Jean *From Impressionism to Modern Art* (Chartwell Books)

Davies, Marian *Get the Picture: Developing Visual Literacy in the Classroom.* (Development Education Centre)

Gombrich, E H *The Story of Art* (Phaidon)

Greenstreet, Derek *Ways to Display* (Ward Lock)

Hadfield, John *Every Picture Tells a Story* (Herbert Press)

Hartharn, John *Books of Hours* (Thames and Hudson)

ed. Hudson, Kenneth and Nicholls, Ann *The Cambridge Guide to the Museums of Britain and Ireland,* (Cambridge)

Joicey, Bev *An Eye on the Environment (an Art and Education Project)* (Unwin and Hyman)

Lewis, John *The Twentieth Century Book (Its Illustration and Design* (Herbert Press)

Lister, Raymond *British Romantic Painting* (Cambridge)

Lommel, Andrew *Prehistoric and Primitive Man* (Hamlyn)

Lowenfeld, Victor and Brittain, Lambert *Creative and Mental Growth* (Collier Macmillan)

Morgan, Margaret *Art 4-11* (Simon and Schuster)

Murray, Peter and Linda *The Penguin Dictionary of Art and Artists* (Penguin)

Peake, Nigel *The Great Storm* (Portsmouth Books)

Read, Herbert *A Concise History of Modern Sculpture* (Thames and Hudson)

Reynolds, Graham *Victorian Painting* (Herbert Press)

Rosenblum *Modern Painting in the Northern Romantic Tradition* (Thames and Hudson)

Rowswell, Geoff *Teaching Art in Primary Schools* (Unwin and Hyman)

Tillyard, S K *The Impact of Modernism 1900-1920 (The Visual Arts in Edwardian England)* (Routledge)

Artists

Bernard, Bruce *Van Gogh* (Dorling Kindersley)

Boussel, Patrice *Leonardo da Vinci* (Tiger Books International)

Ernst, Max *Histoire Naturelle* (Arts Council)

Holbein's Portrait Drawings (Dover Press)

Howard, Michael *Gauguin* (Dorling Kindersley)

Jaffe, Hans L C *Picasso* (Thames and Hudson)

Rajnai, Miklos *John Sell Cotman 1782-1842* (Herbert Press)

Thomson, Richard *The Private Degas* (Herbert Press)

Welton, Jude *Monet* (Dorling Kindersley)

Techniques

Camp, Jeffery *Draw (How to Master the Art)* (Dorling Kindersley)

Cole, Alison *Perspective* (Dorling Kindersley)

Dubery, Fred and Willats, John *Perspective and Other Drawing Systems* (Herbert Press)

Fitzsimmons, Su *Start with Art* (Simon and Schuster)

Hodge, Anthony *Hands on Arts and Crafts series* (Franklin Watts)

ed. Johnson, Peter D *Clay Modelling for Everyone (Creative Pottery Without a Wheel)* (Search Press)

Lack, Mary *Bright Ideas: Art* (Scholastic Publications)

Simmons, Rosemary and Clemson, Katie *The Complete Manual of Relief Print-making* (Dorling Kindersley)
Smith, Ray *The Artist's Handbook* (Dorling Kindersley)
West, Keith *How to Draw Plants* (Herbert Press)

Children's books

Art and artists

Abrams Art Play series: individual artists Kadinsky, Picasso, etc. (Abrams)
Anderson, Lina *Linnea in Monet's Garden* (R & S Books)
Butler, Janie *Art Against Apartheid* (Oxfam)
Cummings, Robert *Just Look* (Viking Press)
Lambert, Rosemary *The Twentieth Century* (CUP)
Lucie-Smith, Edward *Art Today* (Phaidon)
McHugh, Christopher *Discovering Art: Water* (Wayland)
Merlion *People in Art* (Merlion Arts Library)
Merlion *Nature in Art* (Merlion Arts Library)
Merlion *Stories in Art* (Merlion Arts Library)
O'Keefe, Georgia *100 Flowers* (Phaidon)
Peppin, Anthea *National Gallery Children's Book* (National Gallery)
Powell, Jillian *The Arts: Painting and Sculpture* (Wayland)
A Renaissance Christmas (Bullfinch Press)
Rodari, Florian *A Weekend with Picasso* (Rizzoli NY Press)
Thompson, Dr. David *Visual Magic* (John Murray)
Venezia, Mike *Getting to Know the World's Great Artists* series (Children's Press)
Woolf, Felicity *Picture This* (Hodder and Stoughton)

Fiction

Ahlberg, Janet and Allan *Peepo!* (Picture Puffin)
Carroll, Lewis *Alice in Wonderland* (Armada Books)
Hughes, Ted *The Iron Man* (Faber)
McKee, David *Not Now, Bernard* (Andersen)
Norton, Mary *The Borrowers* (Puffin)
Sendak, Maurice *Where the Wild Things Are* (Bodley Head)
Swift, Jonathan *Gulliver's Travels* (Armada)

Poetry

Animals Matter (Puffin)
ed. Foster, John *A Second Poetry Book* (OUP)
McGough, Roger *After the Merrymaking* (Cape Poetry)

Techniques

Amery, H and Civardi, A *The Know How Book of Print and Paint* (Usborne)
Ames, Lee J *Draw 50* series (Kingfisher)
Biddle, Steve and Megumi *Make Your Own Greetings Cards* (Red Fox)
Lohf, Sabine *Things I Make...* series (Gollancz)
Kenneway, Eric *Paper Fun* (Red Fox)
Morris, Neil and Ting *Painting and Printing* (Firefly)
Motisi, Francesca *Patterns* (Wayland)
Philpott, V and McNeil, J *The Know How Book of Puppets* (Usborne)
Potter, T *Lettering and Typography (Including Calligraphy and Graphic Design)* (Usborne)
Potter, T *The Usborne Guide to Pottery from Start to Finish* (Usborne)
Potter, T and Peach, S *The Usborne Book of Graphic Design* (Usborne)
Valentine, M and Pace R *Recycled Paper* (Search Press Ltd.)

Museums and galleries

Some of the places on this list are mentioned in the text. Others are included as they contain specialist collections that could be useful to teachers. Many museums and galleries have trained education officers who may be able to put together a special programme to link up with themes or topics being investigated by your class. These museums and galleries are only a few of our great wealth of resources; do explore your local area – it's fun!

Miscellaneous

England

Abbots Bromley
The Puppet Theatre Museum, Edinburgh House, Bagot Street, Abbots Bromley, Staffordshire WS15 3DA (The history and techniques of puppet theatre)

Bradford
The Colour Museum, Perkin House, 82 Grattan Road, Bradford, West Yorkshire BD1 2JB (Exhibits about the science of colour, mixing colours, textile printing and dyeing)

Bath
Museum of Bookbinding, Manvers Street, Avon BA1 1JW (The history of hand bookbinding, with exhibits of marbled papers, endpapers and bookplates)

Gloucester
The Robert Opie Collection, Albert Warehouse, Gloucester Docks, Gloucester GL1 2EH (A collection of packaging, promotional items and advertising from the nineteenth and twentieth centuries)

Pocklington
Penny Arcadia, Ritz Cinema, Market Place, Pocklington, North Yorkshire YO4 2AR (Coin-operated amusement machines and exhibits about the cinema and records)

Upton
British Horological Institute Collection, Upton Hall, Upton, Newark, Nottinghamshire NG23 5TE (Historic clocks, watches and horological tools)

York
York Castle Museum, York YO1 1RY (A costume collection and a reconstruction of an old York street with genuine Victorian shop fronts)

Scotland

Duns
The Biscuit Tin Museum, Manderston, Duns, Berwickshire TD11 3PP (Over 200 biscuit tins made for Huntley and Palmer between 1873 and the present day)

Wales

Llangollen
Canal Museum, The Wharf, Llangollen, Clwyd LL20 8TA (The history of British canals and the living conditions of the people who worked them)

Pembroke
National Museum of Gypsy Caravans, Romany Crafts and Lore, Commons Road, Pembroke, Dyfed (A collection of caravans, tools and artefacts relating to Romany life)

Painting and sculpture

England

Birmingham
City Museum and Art Gallery, Chamberlain Square, Birmingham, West Midlands B3 3DH

Bristol
City of Bristol Museum and Art Gallery, Queens Road, Bristol, Avon BS8 1RL.

Cambridge
Cambridge and County Folk Museum, Castle Street, Cambridge CB3 0AQ
The Fitzwilliam Museum, Trumpington Street, Cambridge CB2 1RB

Chichester
Pallant House Gallery, 9 North Pallant, Chichester, West Sussex PO19 1TJ

Derby
Derby Museum and Art Gallery, The Strand, Derby DE1 1BS (Contains examples of the work of Joseph Wright of Derby)

Durham
Bowes Museum, Barnard Castle, Co
Durham DL12 8NP
Eastbourne
Towner Art Gallery and Eastbourne Local
History Museum, High Street/Manor
Gardens, Old Town, Eastbourne, East
Sussex BN20 8BB
Exeter
Royal Albert Memorial Museum, Queen
Street, Exeter, Devon EX4 3RX (The Fine Art
Gallery specialises in work by Devon
artists)
Ipswich
Christchurch Mansion, Christchurch Park,
Soane Street, Ipswich, Suffolk IP4 2BE
(Contains work by John Constable)
Leicester
Leicestershire Museum and Art Gallery,
New Walk, Leicester LE1 6TD
Liverpool
Sudley Art Gallery, Mossley Hill Road,
Liverpool, Merseyside L18 8BX
University of Liverpool Art Gallery, 3
Abercromby Square, Liverpool, Merseyside
L69 3BX
The Walker Art Gallery, William Brown
Street, Liverpool, Merseyside L3 8EL
London
The Courtauld Institute of Art, Somerset
House, The Strand, London WC2R 0RN
Dulwich College Picture Gallery, College
Road, London SE21 7AD (Contains an
extensive collection of Impressionist
paintings)
The Haywood Gallery, Southbank Centre,
Belvedere Road, London SE1 8XZ
The National Gallery, Trafalgar Square,
London WC2N 5DN
The National Portrait Gallery, 2 St. Martin's
Place, London WC2H 0HE
The Tate Gallery, Millbank, London
SW1P 4RG
The Wallace Collection, Hertford House,
Manchester Square, London W1M 6BN
Manchester
Manchester City Art Gallery, Mosley Street,
Manchester, Greater Manchester M2 3JL (A
good collection of early and later
Renaissance paintings)
Salford Museum and Art Gallery, Peel Park,

The Crescent, Salford, Greater Manchester
M5 4WU (Contains a number of paintings
by L S Lowry)
Whitworth Art Gallery, The University,
Oxford Road, Manchester M15 6ER
Newcastle-upon-Tyne
Laing Art Gallery, Higham Place, Newcastle-
upon-Tyne NE1 8AG
Oxford
Ashmolean Museum of Art and
Archaeology, Beaumont Street, Oxford
OX1 2PH
St Ives
Barbara Hepworth Museum and Sculpture
Garden, Trewyn Studio, Barnoon Hill, St
Ives, Cornwall TR26 1AD
Southampton
Southampton Art Gallery, Civic Centre,
Southampton SO9 4XF
Yorkshire
Yorkshire Sculpture Park, Bretton Hall
College of Higher Education, West Bretton,
Wakefield, West Yorkshire WF4 4LG

Northern Ireland
Church Hill
The Glebe Gallery (The Derek Hill
Collection), Church Hill, Letterkenny, Co.
Donegal, Ireland
Moneymore
Springhill, Moneymore, Magherafelt, Co.
Londonderry BT45 7NQ

Scotland
Aberdeen
Aberdeen Art Gallery, Schoolhill, Aberdeen
AB9 1FQ
Edinburgh
National Gallery of Scotland, The Mound,
Edinburgh EH2 2EL
Scottish National Gallery of Modern Art,
Belford Road, Edinburgh EH4 3DR
Glasgow
The Burrell Collection, Pollok Country Park,
2060 Pollokshaws Road, Glasgow G43 1AT
Glasgow Art Gallery and Museum,
Kelvingrove, Glasgow G3 8AG

Wales
Cardiff
The National Museum of Wales, Cathays

Park, Cardiff, South Glamorgan CF1 3NP

Haverfordwest
The Graham Sutherland Gallery, Picton Castle, The Rhos, Haverfordwest, Dyfed SA62 4AS (The largest public collection of the works of Graham Sutherland, many of them inspired by the surrounding countryside)

Welshpool
Powis Castle, Welshpool, Powys SY21 8RF (Works by Gainsborough, Romney and Reynolds)

Folk Art

England

Bath
The American Museum, Claverton Manor, Bath, Avon BA2 7BD (How American settlers lived from the seventeenth to nineteenth centuries, plus exhibits about American Indians and Spanish colonists of New Mexico)
Museum of English Naive Art, The Countess of Huntingdon Chapel, The Vineyards, Bath BA1 5NA

Cambridge
Cambridge and County Folk Museum, Castle Street, Cambridge CB3 0AQ

Ellesmere Port
The Boat Museum, Dockyard Road, Ellesmere Port, South Wirral L65 4EF

Glastonbury
Somerset Rural Life Museum, Abbey Farm, Chilkwell Street, Glastonbury, Somerset BA6 9DP

Stoke Bruerne
The Waterways Museum, Stoke Bruerne, Towcester, Northamptonshire NN12 7SE

Northern Ireland

Holywood
Ulster Folk and Transport Museum, Cultra Manor, Holywood, Co. Down BT18 0EU

Wales

Wolvesnewton
The Model Farm Folk Museum and Craft Centre, Wolvesnewton, Chepstow, Gwent NP6 6NZ

Photography/TV/Cinema

England

Bath
The Royal Photographic Society National Centre of Photography, The Octagon, Milsom Street, Bath BA1 1DN

Bradford
National Museum of Photography, Film and Television, Prince's View, Bradford, West Yorkshire BD5 0TR

Chippenham
Fox Talbot Museum of Photography, Lacock, nr Chippenham, Wiltshire SN15 2LG

London
Museum of the Moving Image, South Bank, Waterloo, London SE1 8XT
Science Museum, Exhibition Road, South Kensington, London SW7 2DD

Totnes
The British Photographic Museum, Bowden House, Totnes, South Devon TQ9 7PW

Wales

Swansea
Glynn Vivian Art Gallery and Museum, Alexandra Road, Swansea SA1 5DZ

Ethnic Art

England

Batley
Bagshaw Museum, Wilton Park, Batley, West Yorkshire WF17 0AS

Bournemouth
Russell-Cotes Art Gallery and Museum, East Cliff, Bournemouth, Dorset BH1 3AA

Canterbury
Ethnic Doll and Toy Museum, Cogan House, 53 St Peter Street, Canterbury, Kent CT1 2BE

Durham
Durham University Oriental Museum, Elvet Hill, Durham DH1 3TH

London
The Commonwealth Institute, Kensington High Street, London W8 6NQ
Horniman Museum, London Road, Forest Hill, London SE23 3PQ

Museum of Mankind, Ethnography Department of the British Museum, Burlington Gardens, London W1X 2EX
The Victoria and Albert Museum, Cromwell Road, South Kensington, London SW7 2RL
Norfolk
Sainsbury Centre for Visual Arts, University of East Anglia, Norwich NR4 7TJ (Includes an Amero-Indian Collection and a number of African artefacts)

Northern Ireland

Downpatrick
Down Museum, The Mall, Downpatrick, Co. Down, Northern Ireland

Childhood

England

Arundel
Arundel Toy Museum, 23 High Street, Arundel, West Sussex BN18 9AD
Bedford
Bedford Museum, Castle Lane, Bedford MK40 3XD (Punch and Judy)
Coventry
Coventry Toy Museum, Whitefriars Gate, Much Park Street, Coventry, West Midlands CV1 2LT
London
Bethnal Green Museum of Childhood, Cambridge Heath Road, London E2 9PA
Pollock's Toy Museum, 1 Scala Street, London W1P 1LT
Oxford
Rotunda Museum of Antique Dolls Houses, Grove House, 44 Iffley Turn, Oxford OX4 4DU
Stratford-upon-Avon
The Teddy Bear Museum, 19 Greenhill Street, Stratford-upon-Avon, Warwickshire CV37 0LF
Warwick
Warwick Dolls Museum, Oken's House, Castle Street, Warwick

Scotland

Edinburgh
Museum of Childhood, 42 High Street,

Royal Mile, Edinburgh EH1 1TG

Wales

Beaumaris
Museum of Childhood, 1 Castle Street, Beaumaris, Gwynedd LL58 8AP
Laugharne
Little Treasures Doll Museum, Ravenhall, Duncan Street, Laugharne, Dyfed SA33 4RY
Llandudno
Llandudno Doll Museum and Model Railway, Masonic Street, Llandudno, Gwynedd LL30 2DU

Embroidery/Tapestry/Textiles

England

Burnley
Gawthorpe Hall, Padiham, near Burnley, Lancashire BB12 8UA (The Rachel Kay Shuttleworth Textile Collections)
Chesterfield
Hardwick Hall, Doe Lea, Chesterfield, Derbyshire S44 5QJ (Embroideries by Bess of Hardwick Hall and Mary, Queen of Scots)
East Molesey
Embroiderers' Guild Collection, Apartment 41, Hampton Court Palace, East Molesey, Surrey KT8 9AU
Halifax
Bankfield Museum, Akroyd Road, Halifax West Yorkshire HX3 6HG (Costume displays and textiles from India, Burma, China, Africa and the Balkans)
Hatfield
Hatfield House, Hatfield Park, Hatfield, Hertfordshire AL9 5NQ (The four Sheldon tapestries of the seasons)
London
The William Morris Gallery, Water House, Lloyd Park, Forest Road, Walthamstow, London E17 4PP (Wallpapers, textiles, embroideries, carpets, stained glass and ceramics designed by Morris and his associates)
Nottingham
The Lace Centre, Severns Buildings, Castle Road, Nottingham NG1 6AA
Museum of Costume and Textiles, 51 Castle Gate, Nottingham NG1 6AF

Portsmouth
D-Day Museum, Clarence Esplanade, Southsea, Near Portsmouth, Hampshire PO5 3PA (The Overlord Embroidery)
Wolverhampton
Wightwick Manor, Wightwick, Wolverhampton, West Midlands WV6 8EE (Tapestries, tiles and other items influenced by William Morris and the Arts and Crafts Movement)

Scotland

Comrie
The Scottish Tartans Museum, Davidson House, Drummond Street, Comrie, Perthshire PH6 2DW (A history of tartans and Highland dress and a garden containing plants used for dyeing tartan cloth)
Perth
Scone Palace (Embroideries by Mary, Queen of Scots), Perth, Perthshire PH2 6BD
Renfrewshire
The Weaver's Cottage, The Cross, Kilbarchan, Renfrewshire PA10 2JG (A typical cottage of an eighteenth century Scottish handloom weaver where it is possible to see traditional weavings being made)

Northern Ireland

Cookstown
Wellbrook Beetling Mill, 20 Wellbrook Road, Corkhill, Cookstown, Co. Tyrone BT80 9RY

Wales

Llandysul
Maesllyn Woollen Mill Museum, Maesllyn, Llandysul, Dyfed SA44 5LO

Pottery

England

Manchester
Wythenshawe Park, Northernden, Manchester M23 0AB
Oxford
Blenheim Palace, Woodstock, Oxfordshire OX7 1PX
Poole
Poole Pottery Ltd, Poole, Dorset BH15 1RF
Stoke-on-Trent
Gladstone Pottery Museum, Uttoxeter Road, Longton, Stoke-on-Trent, Staffordshire ST3 1PQ

Wales

Cardiff
The Welsh Folk Museum, St. Fagans, Cardiff, South Glamorgan CF5 6XB (A number of potters and other craftspeople give demonstrations of their work. The museum also has an open-air section)

Resources

Materials and suppliers

Paper, paints and adhesives can be obtained through most educational suppliers, such as the ones listed below, as well as such diverse items as miniature skeletons, artsticks, pipe cleaners, sequins, glitter, feathers, offcuts of felt/leather/fur, marbling paint, holographic foil, card, pastels and charcoal.

Berol/Osmiroid Ltd, Oldmedow Road, King's Lynn, Norfolk PE30 4JR

CRAFTPACKS, 19 Brook Avenue, Warsash, Southampton, Hampshire SO3 9HP

Dryad, PO Box 38, Leicester LE1 9BU

Education Distribution Service, Unit 2 Drywall Industrial Estate, Castle Road, Murston, Sittingbourne, Kent ME10 3RL

Galt Educational, Brookfield Road, Cheadle, Cheshire SK3 2PN

Heron Educational Ltd, Carrwood House, Carrwood Road, Chesterfield, Derbyshire S41 9QB

Hope Education, Orb Mill, Huddersfield Road, Oldham, Lancashire OL4 2ST

LEGO UK Ltd, Ruthin Road, Wrexham, Clwyd LL13 7TQ

NES/Arnold, Ludlow Hill Road, West Bridgford, Nottingham NG2 6HD

Philip and Tacey, North Way, Andover, Hampshire S19 5BN

Philip Harris Ltd, Lynn Lane, Shenstone, Lichfield, Staffordshire WS14 0EE

Pictorial Charts Education Trust, (Photo pack on *Patterns in Nature*), 27 Kirchen Road, London W13 0UD

Technology Teaching Services, Unit 4 Holmewood Fields Business Park, Park Road, Holmewood, Chesterfield S42 5UY

Other useful addresses

British Wool Marketing Board, Oak Mills, Station Road, Clayton, Bradford BD14 6JD (Supplies fleeces and a sample pack of wools)

Confederation of British Wool Textiles Ltd, Merrydale House, Roydsdale Way, Bradford BD4 6SB (Supplies *Fabrics for fashion*, a free sample of nine different wool fabrics)

English Heritage Education Service, Keysign House, 429 Oxford Street, London W1R 2HD

Folklore Society, University College London, Gower Street, London WC1E 6BT

Friends of the Earth, 26-28 Underwood Street, London N1 7JQ (Has an education officer and a number of valuable packs for use with children)

Greenpeace, Canonbury Villas, London N1 2PN (A useful source for campaign material of an environmental nature)

National Trust, 36 Queen Anne's Gate, London SW1H 9AS

Scholastic Publications Ltd, Westfield Road, Southam, Leamington Spa, Warwickshire CV33 0JH (Topic pack *Patterns: Junior Education* and publishers of *Art and Craft* magazine)

Silk Education Service, Parkett Heyes House, Broken Cross, Macclesfield SK11 8TZ (Supplies a chart, silk cocoon and samples of silk yarn and fabric)

Tarquin Publications, Stradbroke, Diss, Norfolk IP21 5JP (Photocopiable pattern publication *Mathematical Patterns* by A. Wiltshire, 1988)